For Emplacemer

For Empl

Mario Blaser

acement

POLITICAL
ONTOLOGY
IN TWO ACTS

Duke University Press
Durham and London
2025

Project Editor: Michael Trudeau
Designed by David Rainey
Typeset in Garamond Premier Pro by Westchester Publishing Services

Library of Congress Cataloging-in-Publication Data
Names: Blaser, Mario, [date] author.
Title: For emplacement : political ontology in two acts / Mario Blaser.
Description: Durham: Duke University Press, 2025. | Includes
bibliographical references and index.
Identifiers: LCCN 2024017844 (print)
LCCN 2024017845 (ebook)
ISBN 9781478031291 (paperback)
ISBN 9781478028079 (hardcover)
ISBN 9781478060284 (ebook)
ISBN 9781478094166 (ebook other)
Subjects: LCSH: Human geography—Political aspects. |
Postcolonialism. | Globalization—Political aspects. | Emigration and
immigration—Political aspects. | Chamacoco Indians. | Innu Indians. |
Ethnology—Latin America. | Ethnology—Canada. | BISAC:
POLITICAL SCIENCE / Colonialism & Post-Colonialism |
POLITICAL SCIENCE / Globalization
Classification: LCC GF50 .B58 2025 (print) | LCC GF50 (ebook) |
DDC 304.2—DC23/ENG/20240808
LC record available at https://lccn.loc.gov/2024017844
LC ebook record available at https://lccn.loc.gov/2024017845

The open access edition of this work was made possible by generous
funding from the Social Sciences and Humanities Research Council
of Canada.

To El Calafate, the place I was with before the storm of which Walter Benjamin speaks blew us apart and made strangers of us.

CONTENTS

PREFACE

There, I've finished. Now, if you wish, it's your turn to present yourself, tell us a little about where you would like to land and with whom you agree to share a dwelling place.
—BRUNO LATOUR, *Down to Earth*, 2018

Growing up in Argentina, the dominant (and patrilineal) story I often heard about my family's origins centered on a Swiss great-grandfather who immigrated to the country at the turn of the twentieth century. He met and married my great-grandmother in Rio Gallegos, the southernmost city in continental Argentina, and they had three children in quick succession. My great-grandmother died after the birth of the third child, and soon after, my great-grandfather began a pattern that would last the rest of his life, migrating throughout the country in search of a better life. His descendants, including my grandfather and father, continued this transient pattern of moving between places within the country, although most returned to and then left my great-grandmother's hometown in the South. I have followed a similar migratory pattern, although my own search for a better life has taken me even further; my home for the past thirteen years is almost as close to the North Pole as my birthplace and my great-grandmother's hometown is to the South Pole.

With a family history that privileges four generations of migrations, and with more than two-thirds of my life spent hopping across the continent, I can say that the experience of very deep and intimate relationships with a place has been rather alien to my conception of the good life. Paradoxically, over the last thirty-odd years, I have become professionally and personally involved with communities commonly referred to as "Indigenous," in which many (but not all) people express that they are with their place—that is, their very way of being is emplaced. For these people, a good life is always with their place; so much so that to suggest that they could be extricated from the place they *are with* without terrible consequences sounds as nonsensical as saying that one can just move on after being dismembered. While I have worked with organizations of the Yshiro (Paraguay) and Innu (Labrador, Canada) communities in some of their struggles to prevent or mitigate processes that can be likened to dismemberment in the above sense, it never quite dawned on me the extent to which these struggles indexed the entanglements between our sharply contrasting experiences of place, at least not until I began to seriously question the practices and relationships that constitute "my place."

For a variety of personal reasons, which I will not bore you with, a few years ago I began to feel as a sore spot not having a strong connection and dense attachment to the place that I had begun to call home. Amid that feeling, and informed by my ethnographic experience, the naturalness of the kinds of relations to the places I had lived in came under question: What is it that makes it possible for me to *be* in these places in this way, without strong connections and dense attachments to them? I asked myself. Don't get me wrong—I have lived enough in some places (ranging from a megacity of over fifteen million to a small town of seven thousand inhabitants, and many others in between) to get to know them like the back of my hand and have developed attachments in each (to people, special corners, habits) that continue to be part of who I am, in spite of time and distance. However, when I compared my experience with the density of relationships that make up the places of some of my Yshiro and Innu acquaintances, I began to wonder if there was something other than my personal and family history behind the feeling that "my places" were constituted in such a way as to foster a certain readiness to move; a disposition according to which, when push comes to shove, displacement in search of better horizons might at worst be very painful but not the end of life, as dismemberment might imply.[1]

In that train of thought, I began to see that, at every jump, my displacements from a small town in Argentina's South all the way to a small city in the Canadian subarctic had been facilitated by a variety of infrastructures. The infrastructures I refer to include obvious things, like technologies and networks of transportation, systems of communications, and governments regulating migrations, but also less obvious things, such as ways of understanding and addressing, for example, problems of livelihood, changing notions of a better life, and what counts as worthy of consideration in the pursuit of what gets defined as "the good life." It may sound strange to speak of the latter kinds of things as "infrastructures" that enabled my displacement, but these are the things whose materiality we rarely pay attention to but which are crucial to our ability to act in certain ways and not in others. Now, while all these things, from communication networks to visions of the good life, could be seen as infrastructures that enable displacement, more generally, they can be conceived as what I call *grounding infrastructures*, that is, infrastructures that shape and give "our places" their character. I will expand on this soon; for the moment let me just offer a glimpse of how the kind of things I characterize as grounding infrastructures that enable displacement shape the character of my place, how that connects with the struggles of my Yshiro and Innu acquaintances to defend their *being with* place, and how all of this informs the purpose of this book.

A few years ago, I got a well-paying job (edging me closer to the "better life" I had been chasing) in the only university of the Canadian province of Newfoundland and Labrador when, riding on the expansion of extractive industries, financial resources were plentiful. The infrastructures associated with this expansion are largely the same that allowed me to hop across the continent—that is, infrastructures that in various ways propel and facilitate the smooth displacement of people, commodities, services, ideas, and what have you. These infrastructures have also made Newfoundland and Labrador a relatively welcoming place for "displaced people" like me. They make the place feel familiar, perhaps a bit like "home": I can talk to my family in Argentina through WhatsApp, hop on planes to visit old friends in previous homes, read news and support abortion rights campaigns in Latin America via internet, eat dulce de leche, and even get papayas in the middle of the Subarctic winter! At the same time, these infrastructures have reshaped the home Newfoundlanders and Labradorians knew before. For most of them, the "development" or "modernization" associated with the extractive boom was a welcome event; at long last the province's living standards began to catch up with those of wealthier provinces in Canada. And even when bust moments came, these same infrastructures made it possible for many people to move to other "welcoming places" in pursuit of better horizons—again, without implying dismemberment. And this is because the grounding infrastructures that make these displacements possible have become for many (long-established or newly arrived) Newfoundlanders and Labradorians constitutive of "our place." As long as these kinds of grounding infrastructures are present, we are relatively at home.

While I will not go into the details now, let me indicate that, for anyone paying attention to this Canadian province, it is plain to see that the expansion of these grounding infrastructures of displacement, if not directly overrunning them, is at least altering the grounding infrastructures that sustain the emplaced modes of existence of many Innu I became acquainted with as I came to the province. I met these Innu when they invited me to collaborate with them in their attempts to address some of the impacts that the expansion and intensification of extractivism have had on the grounding infrastructures that sustain their ways of being with place. These other grounding infrastructures (of emplacement) also include things that range from transportation technologies to visions of a good life but are not always congenial to what displacement requires, and thus conflicts often erupt when infrastructures with different orientations encounter each other. Some Innu staunchly resist having infrastructures that constitute them *with* their place interrupted or overrun by infrastructures agreeable to the needs of displacement—for example, a hydroelectric dam. In doing so, they often confront the governments and corporations that promote those infrastructures as vehicles to realize the "greater common good." But sometimes they must also confront some of their own peers who see these infrastructures as bringing a better life for their communities in the present circumstances. The point is not easy to refute, especially when it has become very difficult for many Innu to sustain practices that make them with their place without variously relying on those very same infrastructures of displacement they struggle to contain. For instance, the intimate relations with various nonhumans that hunting practices foster among Innu, and which contribute to constituting them with their places, can hardly be carried out nowadays without elements obtained from market-based supply chains. Not only does the purchase of these elements require cash (brought in by the extractive industries), but also the very supply chains that make them available can only function on the basis of the energy generated from, among other infrastructures, hydroelectric dams. In other words, the orientation toward emplacement in the grounding infrastructures that constitute some Innu *with* their places becomes slowly entangled with and subsumed under a dominant orientation toward displacement.

In the thirty-year span I have been working with the Yshiro communities in Paraguay, I have witnessed very similar processes whereby, in the wake of successive waves of modernization and extractivist expansion, the imperative of displacement slowly overruns what until then had been grounding infrastructures of emplacement. But, as it happens with the Innu, I have also witnessed how, even entangled and attenuated by the imperative of displacement as they might be, modes of being emplaced nevertheless endure. Thus, in these contexts, it is possible to perceive how grounding infrastructures of emplacement still give shape to places, in part because they continue to noticeably complicate the operations of infrastructures of displacement. This makes these places appear as "frontiers" where we can see with more clarity that in other places the procedures through which grounding infrastructures of displacement intensify their grip and expand beyond their present limits and with what consequences. And, precisely because of their heightened visibility, what happens in these places offers important clues to pondering, more generally, what might be done when grounding infrastructures of displacement end up appearing to constitute not just particular places but "the world" in which "we all live." This, in a nutshell, is the issue I engage with in this book.

I argue that grounding infrastructures driven by the imperative of displacement are constantly proliferating, weakening, and taking over grounding infrastructures more concerned with emplacement, to the point that for many it has become very difficult to realize visions of a good life premised on being emplaced, while for others imagining a good life in which infrastructures of displacement do not play a dominant role sounds utterly utopian, when not outrightly dystopian. This situation is central to, and with varying degrees of explicitness transpires in, contemporary debates about momentous challenges facing the world. We see these debates playing out daily in the news and in academic exchanges. They might take place under the banner of "climate change," "green deals," and "transitions" and in discussions of the role that technology might play in all of this. They may emerge in denunciations of further enclosures of the few remaining commons and the differential costs that humans and nonhumans will pay for staying the same or changing course. Or the debates may surface in calls and warnings of a world moving toward a "multipolar order" and "deglobalization" and in theorizations of exhausted liberalisms, emerging illiberalisms, neofascisms, and utopian alternatives. Polycrisis is the latest buzzword connecting all these topics of concern.[2]

Clearly, these are all issues that mobilize political imaginations—that is, the stories we tell and enact in response to the *fundamental political question of how to live together well*. My pitch in this book is that within debates about the momentous challenges we face are embedded responses to this question that naturalize and reenact the primacy of displacement in grounding infrastructures (ranging from technologies to visions of the good life and everything in between). The problem, I will argue, is that this primacy of displacement is itself constitutive of the momentous challenges. Thus, the question of how to live together well in the face of these challenges ends up being staged in ways that call forth more of what produces them, and the resulting dynamic begins to resemble a dog chasing its own tail with increasing fervor and without regard for the mess it leaves in its wake.

There are some voices, however, that in increasingly more articulated and audible ways, and from diverse positions outside and inside the academy, seek to intervene in these debates interrogating assumptions that are almost by default constitutive of the question of how to live together well and, hence, also of the kinds of answers that are advanced in the present conjuncture. Indeed, probing who the implied referent is, what is the kind of togetherness at stake, and what is the good being aspired to, these voices recast the fundamental political question as a cosmopolitical one—that is, as a question that (paraphrasing Isabelle Stengers) slows down the spurting of well-trodden answers so that a slightly different understanding of the problems they purport to address may emerge. In this sense, the purposely vague term *momentous challenges*, which I use throughout, signals a placeholder for a problem whose characterization is at the center of the discussions in which this book seeks to participate. Building on these cosmopolitical overtures, I propose a wager: that the dynamic between displacement and emplacement (skewed toward the former) offers a slightly different and potentially fruitful framework for grappling with what is at stake in momentous challenges. Such an approach underscores the importance of exploring what it might take to cultivate, in the face of those challenges, a political imagination that makes room for emplacement.

Though it was not purposefully conceived as such, this exploration has ended up responding to the invitation with which Bruno Latour closed his book *Down to Earth* and which I quoted in the epigraph above. In that work, Latour shared a set of coordinates that he found useful for orienting and positioning ourselves politically in the face of what he called the "new climate regime" (i.e., one way of defining what I call momentous challenges), and then invited his readers to make a similar gesture: to say who we are and how we see the problem that convokes us (i.e., how will we inhabit places in the face of momentous challenges?). In responding to this invitation/question, Latour has remained a constant presence and inspiration for my work, as you will soon see. So may this book be a show of gratitude and recognition of the enormous intellectual debt I owe to his work. That said, the place from which I see momentous challenges is certainly not the same as Latour's. For one thing, I am not in Europe, nor do I have a long family lineage that ties me to my place. Located in the continent that Europeans colonized and called America, and largely descended from generations of immigrants to the places where we have lived, my status as a "local," even in my birthplace, is complicated in ways that Latour's was not (which is not the same as saying that his was not complicated at all!). But this is just the surface of the complexities at stake in responding to Latour's invitation. Those familiar with his work will know that his invitation to introduce oneself is not about personal histories but rather about the most basic grounding assumptions, the ontologies, that we bring into play when we come to a matter of concern that we may (or may not fully) share with others. In this sense, the term *political ontology* in the title refers to the grounding assumptions and standpoint from which I conduct my explorations in the book. For now, it should suffice to describe political ontology as a militant intellectual "project" that, coalescing out of a loose network of scholars, analysts, commentators, and activists/researchers, implies a rejection of dominant modern ontological assumptions and associated knowledge practices. In line with this, I must emphasize that the book is above all an invitation to essay with and try out the political ontology presented here. Let's see where it takes us and whether it can indeed help us to understand the momentous challenges we seem to be facing in a slightly different and generative way.

The political ontology from which I seek to characterize this "problem" implies a reworking of usual conceptual grammars that may initially feel laborious to some readers. Aware of this, I have tried to use as simple a language as possible, gradually moving from relatively simplified to more dense examples and concepts. I expect the succession to work as steps on a staircase, to some extent in the same sense as Wittgenstein used the metaphor to say that his propositions were "elucidatory," and that once they had produced a certain understanding, they had to be overcome.[3] It is worth noting, however, that this staircase spirals; arguments, ideas, or concepts that are initially presented in a relatively simplified and/or perhaps unnervingly succinct manner are later revisited with greater conceptual density and with the subtlety that ethnographic materials allow. In short then, depending on your familiarity, or lack thereof, with some building blocks I use to assemble the conceptual grammar I mobilize here, I ask you to please be patient with or, alternatively, do not remain moored to the brief and simplified characterizations with which I start! Keep in mind that essaying an ontology in (writing) practice requires unfolding a necessarily circular argument, it implies an exercise in bootstrapping. Any beginning would thus feel insufficient, as little of what might initially be said will truly make sense until the full circle has been travelled. I hope, however, that with these few pages, I have offered you the tip of a thread enticing enough that you will come into the book to try out the political ontology I am proposing. If so, we will meet again at the end to revisit what the concerns I have sketched here look like from there.

INTRODUCTION

Political Ontology and the Problem
of Displacement/Emplacement

I am aware that arguing about the centrality that the unbalanced dynamics between displacement and emplacement has in momentous challenges is not a "problem" that everyone would quickly recognize, especially in the proposed terms. For the problem to be properly shared, I need to stage it carefully, and this includes making explicit the standpoint from where such dynamics can be conceived as problematic. Since political ontology, the militant intellectual project I previously mentioned, is this standpoint, I begin with a brief recount of its origins to then move on to unfold the conceptual armature that helps me stage the imbalance between displacement and emplacement as a concern.

For context, I want to recall two moments in the recent history of South America. The first was in 2001, when, amid economic collapse, demonstrators in Argentina chanted "Que se vayan todos" (they should all go) against the entire political class that, since the 1990s, had embraced the neoliberal mantra "There is no alternative." The second was in 2011, when, just before a violent police crackdown, Bolivian president Evo Morales accused Indigenous groups, who had been key allies in bringing him to power, of being manipulated by right-wing forces and by the US embassy because they protested against his government's intention to build a road across their territories.[1] The moments mark, on one end, the irruption of a wave of popular mobilizations and uprisings that threw wide open the issue of alternative political projects and, on the other end, the disavowal of the heterogeneity of projects that had propelled progressive administrations to power in Argentina, Bolivia, Brazil, Ecuador, Paraguay, Uruguay, and Venezuela. But, more importantly, such a disavowal was simply a consequence of the instauration of a new mantra adopted by governments in the region, regardless of their position on the political spectrum: "There is no alternative to extractivism."

Under the commodity consensus, as Maristella Svampa has called this coincidence between administrations of all political persuasions, governments in the region became engaged in an extractivist dynamic characterized by the pharaonic scale of projects in mining and hydrocarbons, agribusiness and biofuels, the integration of infrastructure to facilitate the extraction and export of raw materials, and the solidification of these countries' role as providers in (and thus dependent on) the international commodities markets.[2] For the case of progressive governments, Eduardo Gudynas baptized these dynamics as neo-extractivist and pointed out that one of its key differences from plain extractivism was that parts of the profits made from extractive activities were redirected to sustain expansive social programs that curtailed the potential spread of popular protest against the immediate and localized social and environmental effects of those activities.[3] But, by the same token, it also made the governability of those "progressive" countries dependent on a sustained flow of resources from the export of raw materials, thus generating a vicious circle fueling an ever-expanding extractive frontier.[4]

The expansive and intensifying dynamics of extractivism also expanded and intensified conflicts where governments and corporations stood on one side and communities and grassroots organizations that suffered and/or resented the consequences of particular extractive projects stood on the other.[5] Where progressive governments ruled, these conflicts increasingly involved groups who, in the struggle against neoliberalism, had formerly been allies of the party in government but did not see the neo-extractivism embraced by the latter as an alternative either. It was precisely in these contexts that the opening and (attempted) closing of alternative political projects became most evident. In effect, the popular mobilizations that self-defined progressive administrations rode to hold state power in various South American countries had been partly inspired and nurtured by grassroots projects that emerged or became particularly visible through the 1990s and early 2000s in response to the conditions created by neoliberal policies. Through those years, and having been made redundant to the market economy and to a state apparatus conceived as a mere scaffold for the former, increasingly larger segments of the population organized to protect and/or carve out spaces for their survival.[6] Within those spaces, but always under siege by the state and para-state forces, some grassroots organizations (of urban poor and unemployed workers, Indigenous and Afro communities, and landed and landless peasants) escaped the forms of subliving that neoliberalism offered them by nurturing their own, relatively autonomous, forms of living.[7] Of course, reacting to the exclusions generated by neoliberalism, an important (even majoritarian) component of social mobilizations of the period, articulated a political demand for social and economic inclusion (or re-inclusion), often interpreted as a generic demand for "development." But there was also an important undercurrent formed by autonomist and decolonial trends that were concerned not about the inclusion of communities or groups within the "system" but rather about the possibility of their existence in spite of it. Conversations among groups that shared these trends began to form a practical and analytical space centered on shared concerns about self-reliance, political autonomy, and, more generally, the pursuit of visions of a good life not tied to notions of development and their universalist underpinnings; inklings of what I will later characterize as *life projects*.

Although with variable presence in different countries, the movements, organizations, and groups furthering these visions of a good life were part of the wide alliances that, also including political parties, unions, and NGOs, lent support and propelled the establishment of progressive governments. Although the latter subsequently adopted what, except for an emphasis on redistributive policies, was the otherwise familiar developmentalist agenda—also promoted by neoliberal governments—based on the extraction and export of commodities. Thus, as the commodity consensus consolidated, governments of all ideological persuasions began to respond to movements opposed to extractivism in very similar ways. They were deemed to be manipulated by the right, according to progressive governments, or by the left, according to conservative governments; or they were variously labeled environmental fundamentalists, primitivists, romantics, and, ultimately, unrealistic. In short, according to both kinds of government, there was no realistic alternative to extractivism to achieve the greater common good; and yet, many grassroots movements kept refusing that claim! Public controversies and conflicts between governments and those movements, as well as discussions among analysts and commentators about these events, made evident that the very definition of "politics" was at stake in that conjuncture. If, as the famous aphorism goes, politics is the art of the possible, then what had become quite explicit at the end of the first decade of the second millennium in South America was how politics itself involves a struggle to define the possible and, by extension, "the real."[8] This is the milieu in which the version of political ontology I am presenting in this book took shape, a milieu marked by an increasingly obvious challenge to the hegemony of what I call *reasonable politics*.

Reasonable Politics under Question

It is true that when not attributing it to conspiracies of their ideological nemeses, Latin American governments often accuse opposition to extractivism of being "unrealistic" in terms of representing a dangerously naïve misreading of the geopolitical conjuncture and its realpolitik, but in the first decade of the 2000s, that was not all. According to governments, some opposition was even worse, for it represented mere beliefs that lacked any "factual" basis and conspired against the greater common good. This is what Alan Garcia (president of Peru from 2006 to 2011) had to say in 2011 about this kind of opposition:

> [What we need to do is to] defeat those absurd and pantheistic ideologies who believe the mountains are gods and the wind is god. [These beliefs] mean a return to those primitive forms of religiosity that say "do not touch that mountain because it is an Apu, because it is replete with millenarian spirit" ... and what have you.... Well, if that is where we are, then let's do nothing. Not even mining ... we return to primitive forms of animism. [To defeat that] we need more education.[9]

In other words, and to put it bluntly, opposing a mine to strengthen the position of ideological opponents (on the left or right) was execrable, and doing it in defense of local livelihoods or ecology could be naïve, but opposing it out of concerns for a "millenarian spirit" was utterly irrational.

The fact that presidents were forced, as Garcia was, to explicitly say something that just a few years before would likely have gone without saying was extremely interesting to me. Indeed, during my doctoral field research (1999–2000), on a European Union–funded development project targeting Indigenous peoples in the Paraguayan Chaco, one of the issues I problematized was precisely how stances such as these, deemed irrational and "primitive animism," were seen as "culture" and tolerated as long as they remained circumscribed to the "local communities." For instance, during that period I saw how Yshiro hunters translated the notion of sustainability, proposed by governmental agencies, into their own conceptions based on reciprocity with animal spirit owners. This "cultural understanding" did not generate controversies with wildlife managers until it became expressed in practices that the latter eventually came to consider unsustainable, at which point the managers began to call for police coercion to keep in check the irrationality of this cultural understanding (now relabeled "erroneous belief").[10]

I observed that policing kept disputes and conflicts over cultural beliefs at the local level, not very far from the communities. Thus, questions about the limits of multiculturalism remained in the shadows. In fact, rarely was anyone (even supporters of the Yshiro communities) in a political organization, NGO, or government office in the capital city of Asunción or in Brussels (where oversight of the project rested) confronted with the need to take a public stand on the rationality (or lack thereof) of the Yshiro "beliefs." That only a few years after my fieldwork this was no longer the case, that these cultural beliefs had to be refuted as unreasonable in public forums by presidents of nation-states, indicated that something had changed in the region. It signaled cracks in the hegemony of "politics as usual," as, with my cothinkers Marisol de la Cadena and Arturo Escobar, we began to call a politics that made sense only in terms of the long-standing left and right dichotomy, or the more recent tensions between "defenders of nature" (environmentalism) and (human-centered) "promoters of development" or, within the paradigm of human development, those that see identity politics as central to fighting inequalities and those that see the latter as distractions from what is truly important (i.e., economics).[11]

Given that politics as usual would explicitly or implicitly treat whatever slipped through those cracks as irrationalities, in contrast, it positioned itself as the rational, realistic, and/or (my preferred term) reasonable politics.[12] My use of the label is descriptive, not sarcastic; in other words, it tries to capture the specific assumptions and procedures through which this kind of politics, restrictive in scope, disavows anything that exceeds it. At the core of reasonable politics sits the modernist assumption of one world and multiple perspectives on it. Operationalizing this assumption, reasonable politics turns potentially contentious differences into the expression of different perspectives on the world. Differences turned into perspectives are amenable to be ranked according to putative degrees of equivalence between perspectival representations of the world and the "factual" world itself. This ordering, in turn, makes it possible to deem some perspectives spurious, erroneous, irrelevant, or dangerous and thus dismissible, as extractivist agendas do with whatever opposes them.

While the process of attributing factuality is extremely contested, the power of reasonable politics rests precisely in its capacity to set the terms of contestation (or disagreement) as a matter of perspectives competing for factuality. This very setup also gives primacy to an epistemology predicated on the notion that knowledge is a relationship between a real world "out there" and representations of it, which in turn positions what I call the *Reason Police* in the role of arbiter in the exercise of ranking the putative factuality of different perspectives. I use the label *Reason Police* to refer to a complex and always shifting tangle (often enshrined in the law) of modern knowledge practices (personified by Science, with a capital *S*) with accumulation practices (nowadays primarily personified by Capitalism) and control practices (personified by the State).[13] Although they are far from being coherent with each other, all of these practices find a point of connection and common justification in their avowed ultimate purpose of realizing the common good. The tangle between these practices is further strengthened by an often-implicit claim that technological prowess is a measure of the tangle's capacity to apprehend reality as it truly is. In blunt terms: "We [i.e., Reason Police] know that we know better how to achieve the common good, because we can send a man to the moon!" Faced with these claims, those who are not engaged in a contest over factuality in the terms set by "reasonable politics" (because they do not adhere to the ontoepistemic assumption of one factual world) have their claims automatically disqualified as being unreasonable or unrealistic.

The assumptions and procedures of reasonable politics are most evident in situations that resemble a typical ethnographic puzzle: how to gauge utterances of "others" that for the ethnographer appear to be manifestly counterfactual. One example would be that a rock is a powerful nonhuman person with will and intentions, when the researcher knows it is just a mineral formation. Usually, in classical ethnography, the resolution of these kinds of puzzles involves explaining to a public that shares the ethnographer's assumptions the logic whereby the culture of the locals begets such ideas. The resolution reflects the analyst's prior assumption that different cultural representations of "the rock" are at stake. Of course, smuggled into the "classic" form of addressing the puzzle is the implicit claim that the analysts get the world right because they can differentiate between the actual rock (i.e., a mineral formation) and cultural representations of it while the locals cannot. Now, while "counterfactual utterances" might be a trigger for edificant intellectual musings among ethnographers, in the wider realm of everyday lives, they can also trigger conflicts, in some of which matters of life and death are at stake. This is particularly the case when, as in many conflicts generated by extractivism, certain kinds of existence are deemed possible while others are not.

We saw these kinds of conflicts proliferate where, in the context of extractivism, defiant communities claimed that at stake were entities that were other-than-human persons with whom they had obligations while states, corporations, and even circumstantial allies could only "realistically" consider them as natural resources or components of ecosystems. What we were seeing in these cases was that the counterfactual claims of those communities were either outright dismissed or, in the best cases, treated in a similar fashion as (classic) ethnographers have done it: they were considered cultural perspectives requiring understanding or, what is usually the same, tolerance. But even tolerance can only go so far; at a certain point, when the greater common good is at stake, a reasonable politics cannot seriously entertain what ultimately amounts to unrealistic claims. And again, it was where progressive governments ruled that the limits of tolerance showed. Scorning as unrealistic (and violently repressing) the agendas of former allies did little to stitch back together a shared sense of the real subtending state-backed notions of the common good, but it did a lot to show the cracks in the hegemony of reasonable politics. Indeed, the proliferation of conflicts turned evident and intensified coercive practices which, often in the shadows, have always been required to sustain reasonable politics.[14] And to this one must add that the Reason Police's claims to authority (for example, to say that mining is safe, or that a certain species should not be hunted) began to ring hollow for many who would say, "You may be able to send a man to the moon, but you are wrecking the planet to do it. Why should we trust you?" The genie was out of the bottle, and there was no putting it back in.

For my cothinkers and I, these conflicts evidently posed a challenge that was simultaneously conceptual and political. In effect, those conflicts that involved entities that emerged as "natural" (resources or environments) through some practices but also as other-than-human persons through others exceeded the established conceptual repertoires of political economy, political ecology, and/or identity politics, which, sharing in the same ontoepistemic assumption as reasonable politics (i.e., one world and multiple perspectives on it), participated in and fed into its dynamics. The question for us was: How could analysis remain faithful to the politico-conceptual disruption that transpired in those conflicts that challenged reasonable politics, along with its associated critical repertoire? In exploring the question, we found in material-semiotics versions of science and technology studies (sts) and in strands of the ontological turn in anthropology some concepts useful to convey to audiences more attuned to that established critical repertoire, the insights that insinuated themselves to us through colaboring with our nonacademic cothinkers in the field.[15] Let's look to these concepts.

The Pluriverse and Cosmopolitics

A material-semiotics version of sts was the first body of scholarship I encountered that offered me a conceptual language to articulate, for audiences more attuned with a critical repertoire connected to reasonable politics, the radically different "realities" that I experienced in the field.[16] In effect, through its treatment of reality as the always emergent self-enactment of heterogeneous assemblages—a treatment that strongly resonated with the practices I encountered in my work with the Yshiro—material semiotics offers a way to gain distance from the basic assumption upon which reasonable politics pivots—namely, that the facts of reality are transcendent and that they supply a standard against which different human perspectives can be gauged.[17]

The conception of an always emergent reality has been greatly informed by what transpires in the sites where scholars study scientific practices. These are locations of initial ontological uncertainty, sites defined by concerns or issues that are contoured by the presence of actants—human and nonhuman agencies—which, if they are able to articulate successfully, might become a "fact." Bruno Latour provided a paradigmatic example of the emergent quality of facts in his study of Louis Pasteur's microbes. There, he showed that before everything articulated successfully into the fact "microbes," there was a "matter of concern," an issue, an undefined "thing," that convoked an assembly composed of Pasteur, his collaborators, the social hygienist movement and their detractors, and also of instruments, theories, yeast, and so on.[18] The trajectory of a "thing" from being a matter of concern to slowly emerging as a matter of fact (i.e., a stabilized and definite entity) is propelled through a process of mutual articulation or translation of the multiple (and potentially contentious) actants in the assembly.[19] To this, Annemarie Mol added a further crucial caveat by showing that reality is not only emergent but also multiple, always.[20] In effect, given that reality is done in practices and practices differ, there are always slightly different but coexistent versions of the reality/fact that get realized in practice at a given moment. This does not mean there are many discrete self-contained realities, for the point is that reality is *multiple*—more than one but less than many.

With these elements, material semiotics deactivates the basic premise of reasonable politics—a transcendent and already existing "factual world"—and its authority to adjudicate who and what can be part of engaging the fundamental political question of how we can live together well in terms of adherence to this particular version of factuality. Thus, in contrast to a mode of political critique that hinges upon what we could call "realist factuality" to adjudicate which facts are fabricated (and thus are untrue) and which ones are actually "true" (i.e., not "made"), the point of material-semiotics analyses showing how things are assembled or enacted is not to disavow their reality but rather to show (and participate in) how they become real (or can be *de*realized) through the layering and knotting of multiple concerns.[21] In short, where reasonable politics stands for a politics of hierarchically articulated perspectives on an already existing factual world, material semiotics enables a politics of worlding—that is, a politics concerned with the processes through which a world (multiple) is brought into existence. As Latour expresses it, no longer being about articulating different (human) perspectives on an already existing world, politics becomes "something entirely different . . . it is the building of the cosmos in which everyone lives, the progressive composition of the common world. . . . Hence the excellent name Isabelle Stengers has proposed to give to the whole enterprise, that of cosmopolitics."[22]

Although Isabelle Stengers had a very particular purpose when she coined it, "cosmopolitics" has become a widely used term—in no small measure through its popularization by Latour—to refer to a politics of worlding.[23] In this sense, cosmopolitics connects with the idea of the pluriverse—a sea of indiscernible multiplicity, a "chaosmos"—operating as the immanent substratum for politics.[24] Thus, politics, redefined as cosmopolitics, can be understood at its most basic level, and against this chaosmic background, as "group formation," to use Latour's terms—that is, as the processes by which existents are formed, made discernible, and take place through their intra-actions.[25]

Now, the very diversity of practices through which existents emerge implies the possibility that they might also group in clusters, forming diverse collectives—that is, self-differentiating associations of existents.[26] These collectives would each enact a different form of politics (understood as the arts of gathering and holding collectives together), expressing their own unique modes of existence, having their own spokespersons, and so on. In this respect, cosmopolitics (and the related idea of the pluriverse) resonates with recent efforts, often subsumed under the label of the "ontological turn in anthropology," to grapple with the ethnographic puzzle of counterfactual utterances without taking modern ontological assumptions for granted, as classical ethnographies did. The underlying premise in these efforts is that, far from signaling that the ethnographers and their interlocutors have different perspectives on a common world, the ethnographic puzzle makes evident that at stake in it are different ontologies or worlds.

Although authors put different emphases on them, a few important points follow from the premise of multiple ontologies. First, the pluriverse here is not just the immanent substratum on which politics operates to shape a cosmos, but a multiplicity that is also composed of self-actualizing collectives or worlds with their own cosmos. (Notice that the terms *worlds, ontologies, collectives,* and *cosmoses* begin to align as synonyms with slightly different descriptive emphases.) Second, in principle (albeit not in practice, as we will soon see), no collective (including the analyst's) has primacy qua frame of reference, for they are irreducible to one another. And third, the articulations between collectives are fraught with existential risks (i.e., they change them), which are unavoidable, for it is precisely through them that collectives (and the existents that compose them) emerge and take place as such.

For many commentators and critics, talk of the pluriverse, multiple ontologies, worlds, or collectives evokes the image of self-contained units that might be in contact with (or bounce against) each other like billiard balls but are not intrinsically entangled; and along with such an image come concerns about the crushing effect relativism has on critique.[27] However, this image is way off the mark concerning what the notion of pluriverse seeks to convey. With the appropriate caveats and a few jumps of the imagination, the well-known illustration in figure 1 provides a better approximation to begin grasping the shape this concept acquires when jointly inspired by the ideas discussed above.

FIGURE 1. The bird/rabbit illusion evokes the concept of equivocation. Unknown artist, "Kaninchen und Ente," from the October 23, 1892, issue of *Fliegende Blätter*.

Here we have a bird looking to the left and a rabbit looking to the right—more than one, but less than many. There is partial co-occurrence of the bird and the rabbit in their heads, but the difference is not canceled; the beak of the bird is the ears of the rabbit, the face of the rabbit is the back of the head of the bird, and we can imagine that the parts of their bodies not appearing in the picture do not coincide in time and space as the head(s) do(es). Let the rabbit and the bird stand for different collectives and the practices that world them. In part, they are in the same spatiotemporal location, and they share common traces in the drawing, but those very same traces also articulate them as divergent; they are not the same. And yet, they do not necessarily cancel each other.

Now, if we imagine a multiplication of figures that also partially co-occur with each other (perhaps with the head of one coinciding through similar articulations with the tail of another, which is the feet of yet another, and so on) we begin to get closer to the image of a pluriverse as a tangle of collectives (and existents). Of course, aside from delineating just two figures, another limitation here is that the picture is static. Collectives (as well as the existents that compose them) are dynamic and always emergent; their contours and articulations are always shifting, although partial and transitory stabilizations also occur. So, over the picture, we need to imaginatively overlay not only a more "multiple" multiplicity but also dynamism—and thus, at least mentally, convert into progressive-tense verbs (i.e., "ing") the nouns we use to describe those collectives. They are worlds insofar as they are constantly worlding themselves. We also need another, and quite crucial, imaginative jump: that we are not outside the figure looking in; rather, we are fully immersed in it. This jump not only removes the privilege of our frame of reference (an external view of the whole) but also situates our analytical practices right alongside all other practices—that is, as practices of worlding that configure and reconfigure the shape of this entanglement we are calling *pluriverse*.[28]

Having an initial image of the pluriverse at hand, we can now move on to look a little into its dynamics. I am interested in driving your attention toward the range of possible articulations one could expect between the bird and the rabbit, especially how certain asymmetries might play out in them and, more generally, in cosmopolitics. To address these issues, it is useful to turn to Eduardo Viveiros de Castro's concept of equivocation.

What Makes the Pluriverse Go Round

Equivocation refers to those situations where interlocutors fail to understand that while using the same term, they are referring to different things. Imagine we are discussing how well the drawing captures the character of the animal portrayed, but you mean the bird and I mean the rabbit, and we do not know we are not talking about the same thing. This is an equivocation. Now, against a background of multiple realities in the making, Viveiros de Castro's concept of equivocation describes the basic mode of articulation that constitutes existents and collectives and, by extension, the pluriverse.[29] In effect, far from being errors that need to be fixed, equivocations are constitutive of the pluriverse; they allow for the very possibility of multiplicity, for the possibility that the rabbit *be also* the bird. And given there is no common referent (a single world out there), different collectives/interlocutors are never referring to exactly the same thing. This does not imply the impossibility of communication. But instead of being understood as the less distorted possible transfer of stable meaning, communication must be understood as a *working* translation, a translation whose "veracity" is assessed in terms not of accuracy (i.e., a meaning remaining self-identical to its reference while moving) but of efficacy (i.e., it works for the articulated parties). We know that a translation is good only insofar as it works (as articulation).[30] This notion of translation as a working articulation is central to material semiotics' understanding of how realities realize themselves out of chaosmos and to political ontology's own conception of cosmopolitics.

In material semiotics, translations make possible the circulation of what, for lack of a better word, I will call the *vital energy* that moves through and articulates the multiplicities that compose collectives and existents, giving them, well, existence.[31] The working articulations/translations that enable circulation (keep this term in mind!) are what hold existents (and collectives) together as such. When the articulations fail or change, so do the circulations from which existents and collectives emerge, which is tantamount to saying that the existents and collectives also change, or disappear. From a political ontology that embraces the proposition of multiple realities as outlined here, whether different collectives can relate or communicate with each other is never in question—obviously, they can; their very existence attests to the fact that they are always already related and communicated. What is in question is the quality of their articulations as translations and what effects these have in their ways of being. Do these articulations work? How? To what extent? With what results? Are the bird and the rabbit still there as they translate each other? For these questions to remain at the forefront, one must never forget the lack of equivalence at stake in a translation, or, following Viveiros de Castro, one must control the equivocation inherent to translation.

Throughout the book, I will often reinvoke the image of the rabbit/bird to show how political ontology works through situations in which equivocations are at stake. But for this to work well, I need to come back to my point that the concept of equivocation allows us to get a sense of the various possible articulations between worldings and how certain asymmetries might play out in cosmopolitics. Let's begin by pointing out that sometimes (most times) equivocations go unnoticed; the bird and the rabbit might go on, blissfully unaware of each other. Sometimes, the equivocation is productive; the practices of one enhance the other and vice versa. It is when practices interrupt each other that attention to the equivocation becomes crucial, for how the interruption is addressed will yield a response that enhances the pluriverse or one that denies it, as reasonable politics does. Moreover, whether the interruption is even registered by one or more of the parties involved depends on the degree of asymmetry that the equivocation might harbor. Collective A might be more or less forcefully attuned to and aware of the presence of collective B, but not the other way around. For example, let's say that the rabbit is the "modern collective"—that is, a collective that emerges from, among other things, regularly enacting the modernist assumption that there is only one factual world and various more or less accurate perspectives on it. Now, the rabbit decides it can make better use of its ears and extracts them without even realizing that, at the same time, it is removing the bird's beak and probably killing it. Let's say the ears are mountains, or animals, or natural resources in the rabbit's world, but they are also ancestors or powerful and respected nonhuman persons in the bird's world—that is, they are existents without which it might be difficult, if not impossible, for that collective to live a livable life. The bird therefore tries to defend itself. The rabbit may hear the complaints of the bird but will dismiss them, for in the modern collective of reasonable politics, of one reality and one single world, ears are ears, they cannot also be beaks, and even less can there be bird where there is only rabbit. And while the rabbit might never fully evacuate from its constitution that which exceeds it (recall that multiplicity is inherent to all existents), it might indeed progressively render the bird (as well as other collectives) invisible, inviable, and practically inexistent, all of which implies that the pluriverse becomes a less plausible proposition.

Political ontology emerged as a militant project precisely at the historical moment when extractivism, through its effects, made it clear that the reasonable politics that sustains it is constantly at war against the plausibility of the pluriverse. It is true that even within the space of reasonable politics there are strong currents of opposition to extractivism, and these are very important, as they make possible alliances that, even if not intentionally, keep open some spaces for the multiplicity of the pluriverse to self-realize. Yet, these spaces are often like leftovers from the operations of reasonable politics; they are left to be as long as they do not interfere with what is important and urgent. In this context, and as I have put it with my colleague Marisol de la Cadena, political ontology wants to actively "enable political thought and practice beyond the onto-epistemic limits of modern politics and what its practice allows."[32] To do this, political ontology embraces the notion of cosmopolitics, along with its proposal of a pluriverse of divergent existents and collectives that are constantly worlding themselves (through negotiations, enmeshments, crossings, and interruptions) as part of the basic setup to conceive politics and its fundamental question of how to live together well.

As indicated before, from this standpoint, politics denotes the practices through which, with varying degrees of consistency and stability, existents and collectives gather and hold themselves together (or world themselves) as they intra-act with each other. Political ontology thus simultaneously stands for a reworking of what we imagine politics to entail, for a field of study and intervention (i.e., that power-charged terrain of entangled worldings and their dynamics), and for a modality of critical analysis that is permanently attentive to its own effects as a worlding practice. In this last sense, the use of the singular word *ontology* is not meant as a universalist claim but rather signals that the ontological assumption (i.e., a pluriverse of constantly emerging existents) that grounds this critical analytical practice is but one possibility. The word *political* then also advisedly signals a particular intention that guides the analysis as an intervention: to simultaneously open up spaces for the realization of the pluriverse and disrupt the processes through which reasonable politics closes them off. Thus, while critics and commentators usually situate it along a general theoretical turn to ontology in social sciences, political ontology is fundamentally a pragmatic proposition regarding how to go about disrupting reasonable politics' attempts to cancel expressions of the pluriversal.[33] In this way, the *political* doubles back on the *ontology*, for among other things, the analytical intervention seeks to enact its own ground. Of course, more could be said about the meaning of these two words and the work they can do together, but that is a task that transcends my intentions here.[34] For now, I think we have enough conceptual elements to move on to discuss how the political ontology I will try to articulate in this book comes to conceive the problematic that plays the role of guiding thread in it—that is, the dynamics between emplacement and displacement in grounding infrastructures.

Grounding Infrastructures

A central tenet of political ontology is that through their intrarelations, existents and collectives world themselves or, better, *take place*. Taking place means both that existents and collectives occur—*they are the practices that bring them into being*—and that such occurrences have spatial effects; they do themselves as places. I use the term *grounding* to direct attention to these spatial effects. I thus begin with the following proposition: all collectives are grounded, but they are not grounded in the same way. The words *displacement* and *emplacement* are precisely intended to distinguish between different ways of grounding (or of taking place). What I call *grounding infrastructures* are (so to speak) the empirical tip of the thread we can pull from to characterize those ways of grounding. Let's begin then with what I mean by infrastructures.

In the introduction to a volume dedicated to the topic, Kregg Hetherington reminds us that the term *infrastructure* always indexes an interpretive tactic, an analytic moment of figure and ground reversal, in which what initially appears as the background is brought to the foreground to show its importance (if not its necessity) to that which initially appeared as the important "action."[35] Let me emphasize what I suggested in my introductory remarks by using the term *infrastructures* to refer to such diverse things as technologies and visions of the good life; and this is that anything—a communication system, a hydroelectric dam, a development project, a microchip, a person, a story, a concept, a political imagination, an action—can be seen as an infrastructure for something else, for the key intent in using the term is to make evident the importance of the former for the latter. In this book, then, the phrase "infrastructures of" operates as an index to direct attention to the role that the "thing" treated as such plays in the "important action" that concerns me—that is, diverging forms of grounding. Depending on the context, though, and to keep with the flow of an idea, sometimes I use the term *practices* instead of *infrastructure* to alternatively stress the dynamism of the thing under analysis or remind readers that, despite their commonsensical association with an assumed immateriality, terms such as *political imaginations* or *visions of a good life* are thoroughly material references. Indeed, stressing the absolute continuity between what is commonsensically distinguished as material and immaterial is central to my use of the term *infrastructure*. One further point about this use: it involves, above anything else, *the analytical choice to foreground one*—and certainly not the most important or intended—*among the many possible affordances* a thing offers. This multiplicity of affordances, which is a feature of any existent qua infrastructure for other existents, has very important consequences to which I will return soon.

Since *emplacement* and *displacement* are the terms that I mobilize to differentiate grounding infrastructures, it is convenient to make explicit how I use a concept at the center of both, that is, *place*. I will not go over the very large body of literature that has critically discussed this concept's associations with modern binaries; rather, I put my use of the term in direct connection with the notion of a pluriverse of constantly self-realizing existents and collectives that I discussed in the previous section. In this vein, *place* primarily refers to the spatiotemporal point where the vital trajectories of a multiplicity of existents or, better, the relations that compose them, meet.[36]

The way I imagine this is as a particular spatiotemporal point of encounter of several threads in a textile. The spatiotemporal quality of place can be visualized by conceiving the threads that compose it as extending horizontally and vertically. Horizontally, the threads that meet in "this place" extend to and participate in configuring other places "somewhere else"; vertically, the threads extend to the somewhen else (previously existing or potentially future configurations) of the place in question. The play between both is unavoidable; new threads coming into the place must deal with, and will reconfigure, the already existing weft of the textile we call "this place."[37] And of course, what a "particular point of encounter" (or place) to which we are paying attention includes (or how far it extends) will vary depending on the scope of our focus. Our scope might delineate a particular existent or a collective of them, but in either case, they will be composed of the threads that (in meeting one another) compose both. The issue to keep in mind is that, regardless of the scope of our focus, while the threads composing a place might extend (spatiotemporally) beyond the one we are paying attention to, the specific quality of their knotting *in that particular spatiotemporal point* makes each place unique and unrepeatable.

With this notion of place in mind, I contend that the manner in which different collectives (and existents) grapple with the specific and unique multiplicity of the places they are worlding themselves as/in/through/with provides a benchmark to differentiate between ways of grounding or, what is the same, between ways of articulating the circulation of "vital energy" (which moves through the chaosmic multiplicities of the pluriverse) into existents, collectives, and/or places. In this context, *displacement* and *emplacement* designate contrasting forms that this circulation can adopt. When the specific multiplicities of a place appear as a problem that (*existents analytically treated as*) grounding infrastructures must overcome as expeditiously as possible, circulation manifests as what I call *displacement*; when those specificities appear as a condition that grounding infrastructures must carefully cultivate, circulation manifests as what I call *emplacement*.

Displacement and emplacement designate two maximally contrasting possibilities within a spectrum of ways of grounding that would not necessarily fully fall into either. It is worth stressing the point to make sure it is clear: I am not saying that the multiple ways in which existents and collectives ground themselves can be reduced to either displacement or emplacement. What I sustain is that ways of grounding can be *fruitfully characterized in relation to these contrasting points of reference*; and the contrast hinges on the orientation that grounding infrastructures show toward either overriding or cultivating the specificity of places. This is emphatically not a binary contrast where all grounding infrastructures are defined as either one or the other (o is defined as not 1 and vice versa). Assigning an orientation to grounding infrastructures *is never about absolutes or essences; it is always about contrasting degrees of inclination* within a whole spectrum of possibilities.[38] Thus, the labeling of displacement and emplacement is always relative within a comparison; to label a grounding infrastructure as *of displacement* is to say, "This infrastructure is more oriented toward displacement than these other infrastructures, which are (comparatively) more oriented toward emplacement."

These clarifications connect with an important point I promised to return to: that a multiplicity of affordances is a feature of any existent qua infrastructure for other existents. The implication is that, aside from other possible roles it may have, in its role as grounding infrastructure, a thing can be equivocal. In effect, as the bird/rabbit image, a grounding infrastructure might be both of displacement and of emplacement. Then, "if grounding infrastructures can both be of displacement and emplacement," you might be wondering, "how can one label some as either?" Or to put it in terms of my omnipresent example, How does contrast allow calling the equivocal drawing either rabbit or bird? I would say, you can't; the illustration is known as the rabbit-bird illusion precisely because of this. Indeed, in the drawing we have a good illustration of what we may call a balanced equivocation, but with the modification of some traces, and without completely eliminating the bird, we could make it more difficult to see it so that what systematically comes into view first would be the rabbit. Then, we could say that the drawing is oriented in that direction. The point I am trying to make is that, while in many cases a grounding infrastructure might approach the perfect equivocal balance of the drawing, in many other cases, the dominant orientation toward displacement or emplacement can be discerned if we pay attention to what kind of effort predominates in it. Let's explore the point through an example, simplified to its bare bones for heuristics purposes.

We can agree that a railway's intention, or, better yet, its imperative, is displacement—that is, the smooth and controlled circulation of "things." Certainly, the railway affords many other possibilities and might play the role of infrastructure for many other "actions." For instance, in a given place, the train station might become a refuge for squatters (perhaps themselves displaced from their homes to make way for the railway), kids from around might use the tracks to flatten coins when the locomotives pass over them, and termites might proliferate by burrowing in the wooden beams that support the tracks. But these possibilities will be allowed to unfold in practice only as long as they don't interfere with the functioning of the railway. Squatters will be chased, barriers to keep kids away will be erected, and beams will be fumigated as many times as needed to protect the railway's intention. It is precisely the effort put into controlling the potentially disruptive multiplicity constituting the places where the railway is grounded that gives away its orientation as grounding infrastructure. In this sense, I would consider as predominantly oriented to displacement an infrastructure that, in order to get on with the imperative of displacement, is grounded with *as little consideration as possible* for the specificity of a place and constantly seeks to contain expressions of the place's multiplicity that might disrupt displacement.

However, it is important to stress that the orientation of a grounding infrastructure is never completely *un*equivocal. Indeed, while in the case of the railway, the multiplicity of places may appear as a problem to be controlled, it cannot be completely disregarded. For example, train cars need to be properly fitted to the temperatures of the area they operate in or else they might not allow the "smooth displacement" of certain things. The bottom line is that regardless of the intensity of their orientation toward displacement, grounding infrastructures must always pay some form of attention to the specific multiplicity that constitutes a place, even if only to overcome it. But here comes the rub: this attention might become so intense that it starts turning into cultivation. Let's imagine for a moment that the needs and desires of the "locals" (i.e., the squatters, the playful kids, and the termites) become an important concern and actions are taken to adapt the infrastructure to somehow serve them too. In such a scenario the railway's imperative to displacement might become tempered, or, depending on the intensity of the "new concern," the imperative might even be so thoroughly thwarted that the (old) railway ceases to be an infrastructure of displacement to become one of emplacement. Thus, with the qualifier *of emplacement*, I am pointing to another imperative or intention that might orient, in variable degrees, a grounding infrastructure. Hence, I would see a given infrastructure as oriented to emplacement when it pays careful attention to and nurtures the complex array of existing relations that compose a place's multiplicity, to the point that it moves in the direction of overriding or at least containing the imperative of displacement.

There is one last point implied by our simplified example that needs to be emphasized. The equivocality of emplacement and displacement in grounding infrastructures is dynamic; the dominance of either orientation depends on a constant effort, and it can shift. With this, I close a first characterization of displacement and emplacement and their dynamics in grounding infrastructures, which, while admittedly schematic, I hope provides the minimal foundations to unfold the next proposition at the basis of the book's conceptual armature: that similar dynamics transpire within and between collectives in general.

Collectives as Infrastructures of Themselves

Moving from a particular infrastructure, like the railway, to "collectives in general" may sound as an unwarranted jump, unless we take into consideration that infrastructures form assemblages that are recursive and, thus, end up becoming infrastructures for the very worlds they are grounded in/through/as. Hetherington, in the work I mentioned before, leads us to this insight when he points out that the phenomena alluded to with the term *Anthropocene* have rendered obsolete the modern distinction between (natural) environment and (cultural) infrastructure because "it is our infrastructures of global transportation and consumption that produce the anthropocenic environment on which infrastructures are built. Following that logic, we would have to say that carbon is the infrastructure of the infrastructure of carbon."[39]

The takeaway is that if we are not beholden by the distinction between the natural and the cultural (and, I will add, the material and the immaterial), it is possible to see that infrastructures can, in assemblages, operate recursively to sustain the very collective arrangement that makes them what they are. The railway example is, again, illustrative in this regard. Once jumpstarted from previous (assemblages of) infrastructures, the railway enables the increasing extraction, circulation, and production of the very components (from iron to engineers) it requires to exist and expand into larger rounds of extraction, circulation, and production. Thus, even if not its only purpose, the railway becomes an infrastructure for itself and for other infrastructures that, in turn, further potentiate it. If we expand our focus and see the railway as one element in an assemblage of mutually reinforcing infrastructures (including visions of a good life, like those associated with extractivism, for instance), we get a glimpse of how an assemblage of grounding infrastructures can go on giving shape to a collective. Put in other words, since everything that composes a collective plays, in recursive loops, the role of infrastructure for everything else, collectives can be seen as infrastructures of themselves. I contend that as infrastructures of/for themselves, collectives can also be characterized, and compared, through their relative orientation toward one or another of the maximally contrasting poles of displacement and emplacement—that is, collectives might be (comparatively speaking) oriented more toward either displacement or emplacement.

You might object that, in contrast to the railway's imperative of displacement, which is somehow inscribed in its very design, collectives are not so clearly marked by a particular imperative that would incline them in one or another direction. To this I will say, true, collectives have no imperative in the sense that something purposely designed might have, but one can call "imperative," a pattern that regularly emerges from otherwise unique articulations between existents or infrastructures that have their own orientations and purposes. For example, by observing the frontiers of extractivism, where the modern collective most visibly manifests its expansionism, it is possible to discern how a variety of infrastructures (e.g., laws, enforcing agencies, communication networks, markets, and so on) work in concert, overrunning infrastructures of emplacement in ways that turn tangles of existents—that are only *with* each other—into displaceable commodities (more infrastructures).[40] These commodities can then be circulated to feed into the production of goods and services avowedly required to fulfill a specifically defined notion of the common good (another infrastructure). The latter, of course, implies a certain vision of the good life that requires, and justifies, further rounds of extraction, circulation, and expansion of the infrastructures that make it possible. As the articulations within and between infrastructures that make up the collective consistently privilege displacement, this becomes a regular and ever more entrenched pattern with a tendency to perpetuate the arrangement that produces it, both by becoming an obligatory point of passage and by precluding as best as possible alternative ones.[41] And as they continue to expand, these infrastructures go on constituting the modern collective in a way that is strongly oriented to displacement, not the least because interferences with that pattern/intention (from modes of being with place, for instance) are curtailed.

The modern collective's distinctive pattern of displacement is a familiar target of various critiques, albeit most commonly this is presented in terms of capitalism's voracity and expansionism through dispossession, which is of course part of what I am getting at. However, I want to also signal that this distinctive pattern of displacement produces an effect that is key to understanding what is gained from gauging the equivocal relations between collectives in terms of the dynamic between emplacement and displacement—namely, the universal effect, or what John Law calls the "one-world world."[42] The concept of a one-world world refers to the dominant understanding and experience that we live in one and only one world, reality, or universe. Endlessly being done and propped in "daily practices" that express the modernist metaphysical assumption of a transcendent world or reality out there and multiple perspectives on it, this understanding and experience is central to the distinctive character of the modern collective's pattern of displacement. In fact, for this metaphysics' claim to universality to be plausible and effective, its infrastructures of displacement must be constantly extended.[43]

As Latour famously argued, what moderns conceive of as universal can be seen (not by chance, I would say) as a railway, a network that is both global (because it extends beyond specific places) but also local (because the stations, the rails, and so on are at every step of the way grounded in specific places).[44] Like the railway, the universal might go far but is not actually everywhere; even a dense railway network leaves gaps between its track lines. Someone may object that there are some solidly established universals that, like gravitation, do not show such gaps; they are the same everywhere. Latour would retort that if, in material-semiotics fashion, we keep a focus on practices, even well-established universals such as "gravitation" can be equated to "frozen fish: the cold chain that keeps them fresh must not be interrupted however briefly." From such a stance, it becomes possible to see that

> the universal in networks produces the same effects as the absolute universal, but it no longer has the same fantastic [i.e., transcendent] causes. It is possible to *verify gravitation "everywhere," but at the price of the relative extension of the networks* for measuring and interpreting. . . . Try to verify the tiniest fact, the most trivial law, the humblest constant, without subscribing to the multiple metrological networks, to laboratories and instruments. The Pythagorean theorem and Planck's constant spread into schools and rockets, machines and instruments, but they do not exit from their worlds any more than the Achuar leave their villages.[45]

The emphasized segment in the quote is decisive. Barred fantastic causes, for a universal to be plausible as such, to appear as if it is everywhere, the infrastructures that ground it must be constantly extended. This means that the modern collective enacts a plausible universal effect or one-world world in a form analogous to the railway networks associated with extractivism, constantly displacing things in a way that further enhances its own capacity to expand the entire assemblage, over and over again. In this way, displacement becomes a defining imperative (or pattern) of the specificity or character of this collective. Thus, when I speak of displacement as the imperative that characterizes the modern collective qua infrastructure of itself, the term synthesizes the self-propelling circular relation between the generation, the accumulation, and the controlled circulation of displaceable things to feed endless rounds of extension. This is displacement at its most intense, where the various resonances of the word suitably describe a central feature of the way in which the modern collective grounds itself. In effect, the word *displacement* is associated with *deracination, dislodgment, supplantation,* and *disarticulation,* all terms that describe what happens to whatever comes in the way of this collective's form of grounding or taking place. Indeed, in the same fashion as the railway will try to capture, contain, and/or destroy those expressions of (pluriversal) multiplicity that, giving specificity to the places it is being grounded in or through, might directly challenge its purpose, so does the modern collective with whatever threatens to disrupt the dynamic that renders it universal-like—that is, whatever disrupts displacement. This constant work of suppressing and/or containing and controlling expressions of pluriversal multiplicity in a way that protects and props up displacement and its universal effect is coloniality in its most basic form.[46]

This mode of extending infrastructures of displacement has become exceedingly efficient at overrunning forms of emplacement or, in more general terms, the specificity of places. There are obvious consequences to this—namely, the cascading crises at the center of contemporary debates about "momentous challenges." But I am interested in another consequence, which, as I intend to show in the book, might appear tangential but is central to these challenges: it has become harder to clearly spot a significant orientation toward emplacement in grounding infrastructures anywhere. A quick example.

Hunting has always been a very important practice or infrastructure that constitutes the Yshiro with their place as a collective. Before the Chaco region (where their communities are located) was colonized by various agents of modernization, hunting as a livelihood was informed by standing technologies, knowledge of the entities being hunted, the role of their spirit owners, prescriptions about the proper treatment of remains, protocols for meat sharing, and so on. These were all infrastructures quite specific to that place—that is, they articulated the emplacement imperative that gave shape to the collective the Yshiro were with. In contrast, nowadays, hunting practices are strongly shaped by the imperative of displacement. For example, most hunting efforts are today directed mainly at species that, for reasons ranging from market demands to technologies of transportation, are profitable within a cash-generating circuit of commercialization. In these circuits, the Yshiro can sell the product of the hunt to acquire goods that, manufactured in faraway places, have become essential to sustain the collective they are with, which is now partially shaped by those very same infrastructures of commercialization and displacement! This does not mean that the imperative of emplacement plays no role in hunting, but clearly, it is no longer as discernible as such.[47] Of course, such imperative is even less discernible in an activity such as teaching in the school of the community, not to speak of the activities a migrant Yshiro to the capital city of Asunción does to sustain herself.

Let me stress again that I am not speaking of purity here but of intensity: the more intensely entangled with and inflected by the imperative of displacement that grounding infrastructures become, the less perceptible an orientation to emplacement turns out to be, and this is extensive to something I call *emplaced collectives*.

A Wager to Shift the Ground from Where We "See"
Momentous Challenges

The concept of emplaced collectives is the lynchpin of the empirically grounded wager I put forward in this book. I will devote the next chapter to explaining what this concept entails. For now, suffice it to simply say this: emplaced collectives are what emerge when the imperative of emplacement most intensely dominates in grounding infrastructures; in this sense, they offer the strongest possible contrast to the dominance of displacement and its empirical manifestation in the modern collective. I say that the concept of emplaced collectives is the lynchpin of a wager because it names a kind of collective that has become barely perceptible, and for many has even become implausible, due to the efficacy of the modern collective's universal effect. To unpack the point, I return to something I said before about the bird/rabbit image.

I pointed out that modifying a few traces in the drawing could make it harder to see the bird and at the same time make the rabbit what systematically appears first. Something of the sort happens as a consequence of the coloniality inherent to the modern collective's way of grounding. Its relentless domestication or suppression of that which, while being entangled with it, exceeds and potentially challenges it, makes it harder to see, hear, sense, or feel anything but its own infrastructures of displacement. For example, amid the destruction of forests brought about by the expansion of agribusiness in the Yshiro territory, the productivity of hunting (and fishing and gathering, for that matter) has declined enormously. As we will see later, this has led some Yshiro to see as a solution that their children be better schooled so that they can get jobs in agribusiness or the state apparatus or become professionals practicing in the capital city of Asunción. In other words, the infrastructures of displacement, which through their expansion challenge the Yshiro's way of being with place, appear for many as the primary resources to meet these challenges. And let us not lose sight of the fact that these infrastructures of displacement include not only technologies and visions of the good life but also supposedly universal categories such as "nature," "culture," "human," "nonhuman," and the like that are embedded in both and in many other infrastructures of displacement that appear as life jackets amid the present challenges. Infrastructures of infrastructures of infrastructures that become enrolled in that circular motion whereby the problems generated by the dominance of displacement in grounding infrastructures call forth more infrastructures of displacement, enhancing thus the efficacy of the universal effect.

While I agree with many analysts' insistence that we do not confuse the universal effect with plain universality, I would say it is also important not to confuse the word *effect* with artifice or illusion. The universal effect has indeed very practical consequences, and a significant one is that it limits what existents (and the collectives they constitute or might constitute) can do (and imagine) in terms of grounding themselves as (or taking) place in the face of momentous challenges. To put it in other words, one consequence of the universal effect is that political imaginations are pulled into becoming infrastructures of displacement as well. In this context, my wager is that tracing the contours of emplaced collectives' ways of being grounded against the grain of the universal effect— and its regime of (in)visibilities, (in)audibilities, and (im)perceptibilities— offers two kinds of payback. First, it offers a ground from which, in the face of momentous challenges, the fundamental political question can be staged in a way that makes room for emplacement. Second, it provides important clues about the trials that any attempt to cultivate and enact such a political imagination will have to go through. The wager and its potential payoff depend on turning the tension between the enormous efficacy of the universal effect and its nonuniversality into a productive gap from within which forms of grounding less intensely inflected by displacement might be imagined and enacted. To explain this, I need to return briefly to my discussion about changing the image so that the rabbit becomes what systematically comes into view first.

What comes first into view is, of course, a function not simply of what (supposedly) "is there" (in the drawing or else) but also of the relation between the "thing" and the standpoint doing the seeing. Let me put it this way: the rabbit world might make it very hard for many to see the bird's beak when looking at the picture, but it would take an enormous amount of colonizing work to make the bird not feel the beak any longer, and as long as the bird can feel it (and act in consequence), the possibility exists that others might come to sense it too, albeit not in exactly the same way as the bird does. This possibility is what gives political ontology a chance—first to perceive a tension, then to deny the "universal effect" as anything other than a pattern emerging from the dominance of infrastructures of displacement, and finally to begin to formulate the fundamental political question and the challenges it faces in the present from a different standpoint, one that is neither the bird's nor the rabbit's and yet is not external to them either. Indeed, while the possibility of "seeing" both the bird and the rabbit in the drawing (and imagining a possible dynamic between them) depends on there being a third term to this relation, the standpoint of the viewer, we must remember my proviso that this standpoint is inside the drawing, not outside it. This standpoint is clearly not one from which the whole is seen but rather one as situated, partial, entangled, *and interested* as those of the rabbit and the bird can be.

Although my political ontology is premised on an effort to refuse the invisibilities associated with the modern collective's universal effect, the standpoint it seeks to enact is emphatically not that of the emplaced collectives the figure of the bird stands for in my example. But then where is this standpoint grounded? Well, laying down these grounds is part of this book's experiment, and it begins with the effort to analytically extricate emplaced collectives from the invisibilities generated by the universal or one-world world effect with which they are entangled and in tension. This is what I mean by turning the tension between the universal effect and its nonuniversality into a productive gap. The idea is to analytically generate the maximum possible contrast between the poles of displacement and emplacement (each of which is associated with the universal effect and its nonuniversality, respectively) so that little considered or directly ignored political imaginations can enter the scene. The space created between the poles is also the ground from which I can then proceed to tease out clues about the trials that a politics oriented toward emplacement might have to face.

Let me resort again to the bird/rabbit image to trace in broad strokes what I intend to do, albeit with the caveat that, in principle, we do not even know what we are seeing in the drawing. In this sense, the image stands for the actual messiness of the way in which collectives (and existents) take place, thoroughly entangled with each other (and this includes us!). To get our bearings through this messiness, I will "stretch" the image in opposite directions so that two clearly distinguished figures become visible at the same time; something like this (see figure 2).

Obviously, I am manipulating the image, distorting it, perhaps even caricaturing it, to make patent the bird and the rabbit figures one could *possibly* see in it—and I stress "possibly" because if I were to distort the image in other directions perhaps other figures would appear, a point to which I will return soon. Now, imagine that you do not know what either a bird or a rabbit is. In that case, for my stretching to show you what I want you to see, I would first need to characterize them, on their own and/or through their intensified contrast,

FIGURE 2. Rendering visible, on their own, collectives that are always already entangled. Adapted from "Kaninchen und Ende."

even if actually in the image (i.e., the ethnographic situation), neither are ever on their own and easily distinguishable from one another! To some extent, I have begun doing this in this introduction by describing some features of the modern collective. I continue to do this in the next section of the book where I will characterize emplaced collectives so that you can spot their contours when we delve into the equivocality of ethnographic situations in which infrastructures of emplacement and displacement appear thoroughly entangled.

I stressed that the bird and the rabbit are one set of possible figures that can be made visible in the drawing and that stretching it in another direction could reveal other figures. This connects with my earlier comments about political ontology being more of a pragmatic proposition than anything else. With this, I was alluding not only to the usual definition of pragmatism as being concerned with the best way to address a task or a problem but also to a particular form of pragmatism that recognizes that problems are not given "out there" but instead are cut and staged out of situations, the complexities of which overflow any particular cutting or, to return to my analogy, any stretching. Other "cuts" or problematizations of a situation are always possible (i.e., the image could be stretched in three, four, or any number of ways, instead of two); but whether one or other cut/problematization holds well can only be determined ex post facto. This is because holding well depends on the problematization's capacity to make a difference in how a situation is "done" (conceived of, addressed, intervened on). Thus, my proposal of using the contrast between emplacement and displacement as coordinates to orient an exploration of momentous challenges is not advanced as a claim of "this cut is better than this other cut because *x*, *y*, and *z*." Rather, as I pointed out in the preface, its formulation is more experimental: "Let's see if, looking at these challenges in this way, we can grapple with them in a more capacious way." A more capacious way means one that contributes to enacting the pluriverse. Recall that, ultimately, political ontology seeks to enact its own grounding, which is no other than the pluriverse. I will flesh out more of this recursive pragmatism as I advance in the book. For now, let me close by bringing this already too abstract discussion down to the ground.

Refusing a Politics of Who

When I say that the political ontology that I essay here aims to explore the possibilities and challenges of cultivating a political imagination that makes room for emplacement and the pluriverse, I am referring to something as concrete as figuring out how to carry on with our mundane existences in our places without relying on the infrastructures of displacement that seem the only "realistically" available. Compared to the ways many of my long-standing Yshiro (and more recent Innu) friends and acquaintances inhabit the places they are with—and even considering the ravages that coloniality has already caused in them—it looks like I inhabit my place as a meeting point of various grounding infrastructures of displacement, a sort of transportation hub that enables as well as obliges its dwellers to be always ready to take off.

But I want to stress the point: grounding infrastructures (in general) are ambivalent; they simultaneously enable and oblige. Infrastructures bent toward displacement enable me to shrug off obligations to place—if I need to, I can move somewhere else relatively easily—but also oblige me to them; I only know how to be with them. Precisely because grounding infrastructures simultaneously oblige and enable, discussions about displacement and emplacement move into a troubling terrain where issues of choice and responsibility get muddled by the distributed quality of agency. This terrain is a barren one for unambiguous stances that would satisfy an appetite for easy condemnations and/or absolutions, but it is a fertile one for difficult yet relevant questions regarding the stories of "our" living together (well or badly)—that is, about political imagination. However, I surmise that for those questions to take shape, it is necessary to foreground a politics of *how* and, at least momentarily, background a politics of *who*.[48] This is especially important for this book, where given the materials used and my professional trajectory, too quick an association may be established between the identity politics of indigeneity and a politics oriented toward emplacement. Such an association, I argue, would throw the entire effort of opening up political imagination back into the confined terrain of reasonable politics that only offers more displacement. Thus, a brief but emphatic clarification is in order.

The issues that concern me in this book are, in general, the different ways in which collectives are grounded and what effects these have (i.e., a politics of how). In particular, I am interested in the kinds of grounding enabled by practices or infrastructures of emplacement and what they can offer to political imagination. I am not concerned with the identity label that may be (self-) ascribed to "human" practitioners associated with infrastructures of emplacement (i.e., a politics of who). Afro-descendants, seringueiros, non-ethnicized peasants in Latin America, and a variety of urban/rural communities of practice that, across the continent, do not fit into the Indigenous identity slot can be involved in practices that constitute, or might eventually constitute, emplaced collectives or collectives whose grounding infrastructures largely lean in that direction.[49] By the same token, and as I hinted at before, people and groups who do in various ways fit into the Indigenous identity slot might be engaged in practices that are antithetical to such infrastructures. However, it is also worth emphasizing that I am not in the business of adjudicating authentic (i.e., good) versus inauthentic (i.e., bad) indigeneity by way of someone's adherence to practices or infrastructures of emplacement or of ranking the relative authority of various identities to "own" or represent these practices.[50] This does not mean that issues of identity play no role in the dynamics of emplacement and displacement; in fact, identity is mobilized as leverage at particular junctures in these dynamics, as we will see in the coming chapters. Yet, the mobilization of identity says more about the purchase that certain categories have in the terrain of reasonable politics than about the practices associated with emplacement and displacement. Thus, although nowadays they are often entangled, I find it important to analytically distinguish the politics implicit in practices or infrastructures of emplacement from the identity politics component of indigeneity. The question of the relation between these kinds of politics is a legitimate and important one but it can only be meaningfully raised if the distinction between them is first established.

An important reason to draw this distinction is to refuse the minoritization of the politics associated with emplacement. The concept of minoritization, which I borrow from feminist scholar Rita Segato, directs attention to a public sphere that is patterned after a binary hierarchical structure where the universal political subject, the generalizable Human (the White, property-owning, heterosexual, patriarchal male) occupies the center while everyone else is minoritized.[51] Being minoritized means one is relegated to the realm of the particular (when not also rendered a lesser being). Thus, in contrast to the universal political subject whose issues and statements are considered of general interest, the issues and statements of those minoritized are treated as, well, minor, only concerning them and those who specialize in their "particular" issues.[52] In refusing minoritization, I seek to avoid having practices and infrastructures of emplacement treated as a minor issue. It is at this point where I ask you, my dear reader, to join me in the wager I am proposing in this book and exercise your imagination to transpose insights I have gathered from my own experiences in the "frontiers of displacement" to other settings, perhaps closer to your experiences and concerns as analyst and practitioner. This request is particularly pertinent if you conceive of your setting as urban (as opposed to rural) and non-Indigenous. Albeit the sharp distinctions these categories purport to describe are far from being stable and uncontested; they do index heterogeneities that cannot be brushed away easily. For instance, I am aware that these heterogeneities might raise two interconnected questions: whether the contrast between emplacement and displacement I work with in the book boils down to a contrast between the "Indigenous" and the "non-Indigenous," and whether the political ontology I propose has purchase outside "extractive frontiers" in "rural areas" and among "Indigenous communities." To the first question, I can advance a clear no: the contrast is not about Indigenous and non-Indigenous. Now, to the last question I will respond that the answer is largely up to you; however, there are a couple of things that I can emphasize so that political ontology can travel to your setting perhaps with more ease.

Political ontology emerged from what might loosely be described as "indigenous settings" because it was there that something that had always been obvious to our interlocutors in "the field" became visible to me (and my cothinkers): the ontoepistemic conflicts that reasonable politics denies but harbors at its core *whenever and wherever it operates and regardless of whether or not it involves what might be labeled "Indigenous peoples."*[53] For example, think how the Reason Police quickly shuts down questions about the "thing" at stake in a conflict through a derogatory remark such as "tree hugger" hurled at people chaining themselves to trees slated for removal by city authorities or, more prosaically, through the offhanded dismissal as "emotional" of a given person, family, or community's refusal to accept that some form of benefit or compensation (monetary or otherwise) will offset changes brought to their "way of life" by a policy or process that anyone in their "rational mind" should ultimately see as the greater good. In short, it is important to keep in mind that, as analytical practice, political ontology involves a particular way of interrogating conflicts so as to open up their ontoepistemic political potentials beyond the limits of modern or reasonable politics. Yet—and this is a crucial argument I am trying to make in this book—this opening up has to be done carefully. It cannot be done aimlessly or taken as a self-justified purpose—that is, it must address a problem that orients it; otherwise it turns into recklessness.[54] In this sense, it is the careful staging of the predominance of displacement in grounding infrastructures *as an orientating problem* that I work toward in the coming pages.

Enter the second point I want to emphasize. While present throughout my ethnographic materials, extractivism functions in the book as the archetypical figure of the modern collective qua infrastructure of displacement. Thus, its "frontiers/limits" are wherever the imperative of emplacement, timid as it might be, is pushing back on displacement—perhaps in the attempt to make a community garden in the city, perhaps in a cooperative's initiative to buy local, but also perhaps in the discussions of whether we should be eating papayas in the Arctic, or whether the destruction brought by sourcing lithium for a green transition is a necessary evil, or in debates about whether we should be supporting the export of "our" values somewhere else, and, if we think this is worth it, how far? Despite what? And at what cost? Of course, as I pointed out early on, limits and borders are much more perceptible and evident (for some of us) where infrastructures of displacement encounter comparatively more robust infrastructures of emplacement, and, for several reasons, this tends to be in areas that might be conceived of as rural. However, remember that the frontier/limit is fractal, internal to all grounding infrastructures, and inherent to their equivocality. This is crucially important, for the question of limits between emplacement and displacement—where one starts and the other finishes and, even more importantly, how these limits are traced, policed, and/or pushed in one or another direction—is at the center of my inquiry. In effect, as I have advanced previously, from a political ontology standpoint the problem that becomes foregrounded in the momentous challenges everyone speaks about is the pronounced imbalance that favors displacement over emplacement within grounding infrastructures, wherever the latter are.

Connecting both points brings us back to my refusal of having a politics oriented toward emplacement reduced to a minor issue and to my request that you exercise your imagination to help transpose to other settings some insights you may encounter as you read the book. In settings such as "urban" areas, where many, like myself and perhaps you, might feel that infrastructures of displacement are all there is, generating robust infrastructures of emplacement poses a challenge that is far from being minor. Indeed, this challenge is not about solidarity with a minority "over there" who is under threat by the advancing extractivist frontier. Rather, it is about imagining a good life "here" that is not premised on the infrastructures of displacement many of us depend on (and even love) so much. As I will argue, the challenge is embarking on a journey to cease being what we are.

Overview of the Book

Since I conceived this book as the essaying of a proposal, a tryout, I ended up visualizing it as the rehearsal of a theatrical play. Thus, following this introduction where I have laid out the "props" I will use, the curtains will open to a "play" in two acts punctuated by a prelude, an interlude, and a postlude. These three sections are extended "commentaries" that carry most of the weight of my wager about the fruitfulness of thinking about momentous challenges through the dynamics of displacement and emplacement. The two acts, in turn, delve more directly into ethnographic materials and are tasked with giving flesh to the commentaries that precede them and providing new elements to move my wager one step forward in the next commentary. This counterpoint between commentaries and acts will go slowly, tracing a circular movement that will eventually bring us back to my initial concerns, now better equipped for you to gauge whether the tryout has paid off.

In the prelude, while characterizing emplaced collectives (and their life projects) on their own, I address the question of how the limits or boundaries between collectives (and, by extension, between emplacement and displacement) can be traced analytically. Further, I argue that different ways of analytically conceiving and treating the boundaries between collectives suggest different kinds of political imaginations with diverging scalar orientations. In act 1, we leave the emplaced collectives "on their own" and plunge into the actual messiness of the "ethnographic situations," where we can only find them already equivocally entangled with the grounding infrastructures of displacement that are constantly extended and redeployed by the modern collective. Drawing on materials produced through my involvement with the Yshiro people's project to "recover the yrmo" (their traditional territory), I explore how, qua grounding infrastructures of displacement or of emplacement, divergent visions, and practices of the common good become fertile terrain for one another, generating impasses that underscore some of the trials that a politics oriented to emplacement must face. In the interlude, we emerge from the messiness of the ethnographic situation, carrying along some threads that allow me to discuss how the dominance of displacement is expressed nowadays in debates about momentous challenges. I argue that these debates also provide evidence that the distinctive coloniality of the modern collective is shifting in ways that are consistent with a postnatural formation of power. By analyzing a conflict that has pitted Innu hunters against wildlife managers, in act 2 we dive back into the messiness of the ethnographic situation to get a sense of how this postnatural formation of power might operate and what role science plays in it. I emerge from the ethnographic situation one last time in the postlude, where I weave together the various threads that I have been pulling throughout to present a succinct diagram of a political ontology in which a proposal for emplacement makes sense. On this basis, I then move on to make explicit and raise a series of questions about the challenges of enacting a cosmopolitics oriented toward emplacement that will have accrued throughout the counterpoints played between acts and my extended commentaries. By the end of the journey, I hope to have made a compelling case for the fruitfulness of this approach and to have provided a useful set of prompts for continuing a discussion on what it might take to address momentous challenges when these have been restaged as coextensive with the dominance of displacement in grounding infrastructures.

Small Stories

I first heard the term *life projects* in the early 1990s from a leader of the Yshiro people, Don Bruno Barras.[1] At the time, I was particularly interested in academic/activist debates about "modernization" and "development," terms often used as synonyms in Latin America and beyond. Those debates had emerged from critical studies that made evident that, at the bottom, the terms referenced a story about the "good life" that began to take its present shape in the sixteenth century and became (and has remained) dominant for the last three hundred years.[2] In its bare bones, this story could be sketched as follows. Given that nature or reality is external and transcendent (i.e., universal), the attainment of a kind of paradise is possible by following two parallel paths: on the one hand, by discovering the laws of nature through Reason, humans can control them for their own benefit; on the other hand, once all humans are educated to recognize the sovereignty of Reason as nature' spokesperson, the disputes generated by the parochialism of their traditions will end and a truly cosmopolitan society will emerge. In this story, the good life became associated with the presumed primacy of "man," the consequent right to control nature for "his" benefit, and the universal validity of such an understanding. By the twentieth century, all of this would transmute into a commonsensical assumption (especially in governmental circles) according to which endless economic growth and unrestrained technological innovation, which underpin the relentless extractivist drive, are inherently reasonable.

This has been a "big story," as it refers to a universal community of humans (though who has counted as fully human has varied through time) in pursuit of the common good life on a planetary scale, the global common good. This story, the promise of modernization, has been a crucial infrastructure through which the modern collective has grounded itself as it expanded. Of course, a good deal of the momentous challenges being widely discussed today are related to the negative legacy of that promise, a legacy that some saw coming and tried to prevent. The modernization/development debates that interested me in the 1990s were an expression, within a longer history, of these attempts. At the time, I felt that when it came to so-called Indigenous peoples, these debates were overtaken by a creeping Manichaeanism: Do they want the change brought by development and modernization or do they reject it? Don Barras's concept of "life projects" was attractive to me because it seemed to cut through a shared essentialism that surfaced in both positions. In effect, he used the term "life projects" to draw a contrast between the modern story of a good life being furthered through "development projects" and the story his people lived by. But rather than being about whether a good life was associated to remaining "traditional" (i.e., the same) or "modernizing" (i.e., changing), as was implicit in the standing debates, the distinction he drew was about the grounding and orientation of the respective stories. According to Don Bruno, the story of the good life that oriented development projects emerged from other places and experiences and disregarded the reality the Yshiro lived in. For this reason, he thought, development projects continuously failed in their purpose of bringing the good life to the Yshiro. He argued that Yshiro life projects, in contrast, emerged from and responded to the specificities of the place where they lived.

The concept of life projects made evident to me that Yshiro stories about the good life, rather than being reactive to (in favor or against) development, were emergent—they had their own roots in the specificity of a particular mode of existence.[3] Of course, after decades of colonialism, developmentalism and its effects were part of that specificity, but only a part. In this sense, the concept of life projects also alluded to the many ways in which the grounding infrastructures associated with the agenda of modernization could become part of other collectives without overdetermining their unfolding stories and visions of a good life. This allowed me to introduce a useful distinction to sort between practices and infrastructures that are often as thoroughly entangled as the bird/rabbit image we have seen in the introduction, a distinction that hinged upon the different orientations of practices of a good life. For the agencies promoting it, the story of the good life embodied by the notion of modernization does not emerge from a particular place and set of experiences; rather, when all is said and done, it is universal. Against this background, I began to use the term "life projects" as a conceptual placeholder for political imaginations (stories and practices of a good life together) that are bound to be different among themselves precisely because, in contrast to the (purported) universalism of modernization, they share a primary orientation toward the specificity of place. Because of this orientation, I have come to see life projects as a potentially powerful political imagination that embodies "small stories" about the good life, stories that rather than assuming (or even aspiring to) the status of universal are fundamentally concerned with enhancing their own plausibility amid and alongside other ongoing stories about the good life that might constitute a place.

As will become evident later in the book, life projects in general are central to my overall wager for emplacement. However, in this prelude, I am specifically interested in the life projects associated with what I call *emplaced collectives*. In the introduction, I provisionally defined emplacement as a particularly intense form of the attention that, in general, grounding infrastructures must pay to the specific multiplicity that constitutes a place. I pointed out that what characterizes this particular mode of attention is that it goes beyond attending to that multiplicity and moves toward cultivating and nurturing it. Sometimes, this "going beyond" ends up overriding, even if only a little, the imperative of displacement in a given infrastructure, thus making it what I would call *an infrastructure of emplacement*. In that sense, and to the extent that they are strongly oriented toward the specificity of place, life projects can be generally considered infrastructures of emplacement. However, given that their concern with the specificity of place can have variable intensity, *not all life projects end up generating emplaced collectives*. And here comes a further layer of complexity associated with the word *emplaced* as a qualifier of the word *collective*. In this particular case, I use the word to single out a very specific form of groundedness. To do this, I am borrowing from geology one of the connotations of the word *emplacement*. In geology, this word describes the process by which igneous rock (i.e., lava) oozes into older rock in such a way that only through intensive chemical and mechanical processes (like mining) can the formation be decomposed into "components."[4] It is this intensity of attachment and entanglement, resistant to partition, that I want to capture when I position the qualifier *emplaced* in front of the word *collective*. Those cases where "human" spokespersons express that being disentangled from the landscapes they *are with* will result in their undoing is the most succinct image I can summon to convey what is at stake in this particular form of groundedness.

Emplaced collectives are not the only materialization of the life projects' orientation to the specificity of place, but they are the most intense. It is for this reason that I am interested in their life projects here: they offer the empirical elements to draw the strongest contrast with the modern collective qua infrastructure of displacement, and to explore the dynamics between emplacement and displacement when it comes to the relations between entangled yet divergent collectives. As I advanced earlier in the introduction, to begin drawing this contrast I need to characterize emplaced collectives on their own through selected (and purposely intensified) contrasts with the modern collective. I start this task with a discussion of some of the elements that, under the rubric of principles, make the life projects of emplaced collectives (and these collectives themselves) an especially intense version of infrastructures of emplacement. In the second section, I discuss the spatiality of collectives in general, and of emplaced collectives in particular, in order to make evident important analytical consequences of taking "limits" or "boundaries" (that define existents and collectives) as the sites where the fundamental political question of how to live together well gets its traction. In the third and final section, I discuss the (atypical) way in which emplaced collectives engage this question. I argue that in contrast to the usual concern with overcoming heterogeneities, which is often the unstated concern lodged in the "how" of the fundamental political question, emplaced collectives are concerned with cultivating them. This ends up orienting life projects toward what I call *the small.*

The Practical Principles of Emplacement

For the purpose of characterizing the life projects of emplaced collectives, I propose to begin from a series of very general assumptions or principles that intellectuals familiar with, or embedded in, these collectives often glean from the practices that bring them into being.[5] Notice that the presumption here is that practices, the way things are done, precede their stabilization as principles. Thus, while the latter might be more or less explicitly inscribed in a variety of forms, including but not restricted to origin stories, they can only be singled out through careful observation, selection, and distillation of certain patterns in ongoing and historically situated (i.e., changing) practices. But, true to their role as infrastructures, these practical principles of emplacement most often go largely without saying.

RELATIONALITY, SYMMETRY, AND INAPPREHENSIBILITY

The first or most fundamental principle to consider is that of relationality, the idea that everything that exists is in-relation. One could argue that the orientation to the specificity of place—that is, the uniqueness of the knot that a particular set of threads of relations form in a given location—encourages keen attention to, and an intimate experience of, the codependence and coemergence implied by relationality. It is important to stress that relationality is not simply the idea that there are relations between discrete existents but rather that those relations precede and shore up the formation of the existents that compose a given emplaced collective. Relationality as a fundamental principle implies that there is no absolute outside, and hence, binarism is not possible. This does not mean that distinctions cannot be made; however, these are grounded in location and orientation. The fact that this notion, taken for granted within emplaced collectives, has become the "theoretical novelty" laboriously brought about by discussions of ontology in the social sciences is indicative of how entrenched its denial within the modern collective has been.[6]

In emplaced collectives, relationality in this strong sense works as the default interpretive key to understand phenomena and constitutes the foundation of practices from which other principles can be gleaned.[7] Daniel Wildcat stresses that this understanding, based on "experience and empirical trial and error," begets a series of premises crucial to politics and ethics:

> First, public policy issues in Native worldviews involve consideration for the rights or we might say more accurately, following Deloria, the "personalities" of plants, animals, and the physical features of the natural world—for example, land, air, and water as well as our relationships among our humankind. . . . Second, the goals of this indigenous theory are practical and utilitarian in a sense akin to Aristotle's *summum bonum*; however, as emphasized above, the framework for the measurement of the *summum bonum*, or the "greatest good," is not human society but the ecosystem or natural environment that forms one's political and ethical community in the broadest sense. In short, the Native view advocates an understanding of the public sphere, which includes many persons, including many other-than-human persons. . . . Third, and contrary to many misinterpretations of Native worldviews, nearly all indigenous North American worldviews that I am familiar with consider the world as dynamic, not static. These views acknowledge the biological and physical principles of emergence—especially in their accounts of creation.[8]

While the last premise discussed in the quote expresses the general principle of relationality, the other two express what I will call *the principle of symmetry of value*. The latter refers to the idea that everything and everyone in the collective is valuable because everything plays the role of, to use my term, an infrastructure for the collective. Everything plays a part in making the collective continually emerge and hold together as such, and therefore it is not politically or ethically acceptable to systematically privilege some of its "members" over others.[9] Consequently, the valorization associated with the distinction between human and nonhuman does not apply in the same way as it does in the modern collective. So as Ailton Krenak points out, a point of divergence with the modern collective is made evident in the latter's conception of nonhumans as resources: "The Doce River, which we, the Krenak, call Watu, our grandfather, is a person, not a resource, as economists say. He is not something that someone can take ownership of; it is a part of our construction as a collective who inhabits a specific place, where we were gradually confined by the government, so that we can live and reproduce our forms of organization (with all that external pressure)."[10]

A somewhat extended parenthesis is in order here. It is important, first, not to confuse the attribution of personhood with the attribution of humanity and, second, not to assume that the concept of "human" applies across the board. Thus, the tendency, in emplaced collectives, to generalize the attribution of personhood to most (if not all) existents is not an extension of "humanity" to all existents. It is precisely for this reason that, in the context of discussing emplaced collectives, I use quotation marks for the word "human." The marks (which I will henceforth use sparingly to contextually stress the nonuniversality of the term) signal the ahuman status of these collectives. By this I simply mean that the category human, and the set of attributes (which are always a system of relations) that characterize it, arises in the particular milieu of the modern collective. Thus, when it is used to designate existents emerging in other collectives, an equivocation occurs, for as much as the term might capture attributes that are relevant from the perspective of the modern collective, it misses a whole other set of attributes that might be crucial to the composition of those other existents.[11] A quick example to convey the point. As is often the case with ethnonyms, the term *Yshiro* is usually translated as "human beings"; however, when one delves more deeply, it becomes evident that this translation misses quite a lot. A contemporary, mostly monolingual yshir-au-oso speaker would understand but find a bit forced the grouping of maro (Paraguayan mestizos), dihip'kunaho (Whites), and yshiro together as humans in contrast to another group formed by ylipiot (jaguar), peikara (maracas), and ologolak (capivara) as nonhumans. Forming these two domains (of humans and nonhumans) would imply missing fundamental attributes that make the differences between maro, dihip'kunaho, and yshiro as relevant as those between the latter and ologolak, peikara, and ylipiot. Hence, I subsequently capitalize the word *yshir* (plural *yshiro*) selectively to signal when I am using it as a marker of ethnic identity rather than to refer to a specific existent that is not simply human.

Now, notwithstanding the implied equivocation, it is difficult to disregard that the imposition of a humanist matrix of value through colonialism and modernization has made the category "human" pervasive and difficult to dispense with. In this matrix, whatever is not human is variably expendable in the pursuit of human purposes. Thus, who would not want to be counted among the humans? The insistent demand of subordinated groups to be recognized as "humans" involves countering the negative consequences that automatically come with not being such. And yet, although it carries some analytical complications I will discuss soon, the pervasiveness of the category "human" can serve as a relatively stable frame, or communicational shortcut, to refer to existents pertaining to diverse modes of existence—as long as the equivocation it implies remains "controlled," meaning we always remember that the word *human* refers to existents that are not exactly the same within different collectives.[12] Having made this clarification, let's return to the principle of symmetry of value.

This principle informs Richard Atleo's interpretation of how the story about the Son of Raven and the quest for light supports what he calls Haḥuułism, an "emergent form of contemporary constitutionalism":

> The quest for this light, made allegorically manifest in the story of Son of Raven, provided the ancient Nuu-chah-nulth with an appropriate way to negotiate reality. They found that this light enabled and illuminated as many lifeways and points of view as there are life forms without their society dissolving into innumerable fragments. Thus, the Salmon people, the Bear people, the Eagle people, the Wolf people, the Cedar people, the Nuu-chah-nulth peoples, the Salish peoples, the Haida peoples, the European peoples, the African peoples, and the Asian peoples all have their own ways of life, their own points of view, their own written or unwritten constitutions.[13]

This enumeration that puts Salmon, Bear, Eagle, Wolf, Cedar, Nuu-chah-nulth, Salish, Haida, European, African, and Asian standing *as equals* in an "emergent constitutionalism" clearly reflects the principle of symmetry. The list is also reminiscent of that famous list that Jorge Luis Borges attributed to an apocryphal Chinese encyclopedia and which Michel Foucault felt shattered "all the familiar landmarks of my thought—our thought that bears the stamp of our age and our geography—breaking up all the ordered surfaces and all the planes with which we are accustomed to tame the wild profusion of existing things."[14] In effect, what appears lined up symmetrically in Atleo's list are not only particular entities but entire categories which, for a modern human-centered notion of politics, are utterly asymmetrical, even if their relative rankings might be a matter of dispute.

Another important principle, closely connected with the symmetry that Atleo attributes to different "ways of life," is the inapprehensibility of existence writ large. Here is how Atleo expresses the point:

> To the traditionally oriented Nuu-chah-nulth, different perspectives on creation are not a source of disagreement, confusion, or conflict; rather, they are a source of enrichment. Faced with an incomprehensible and mysterious creation, the ancient Nuu-chah-nulth came to believe that their ability to comprehend it, both ontologically and epistemologically, was so comparatively insignificant as to make hegemony a concept with no basis in reality. Who could begin to pretend to know and understand creation? Even the most powerful, the most gifted were perceived within a context that assumed their insignificance. One of many consequences of this ancient view of reality is that each person and each family were free to experience for themselves the nature of creation without being subjected to hegemonic coercion.[15]

The inapprehensibility of existence writ large has often been described by spokespersons of emplaced collectives as the unfolding and always changing story of a creative force or principle that manifests through dynamic and perceptible relations but is ungraspable in its full magnitude and complexity.[16] This calls for a certain humility or cautiousness regarding the scope of one's own desire to know and about what is supposedly "known," and this, in turn, grounds a particular form of pragmatism. It is this kind of pragmatism, rather than the strands usually invoked in academic philosophy, that informs political ontology.[17]

THE PRAGMATICS OF CAREFULNESS

As Brian Burkhart explains, where relationality in the strong sense is the default assumption, the search for ultimate causes is utterly futile, as it leads into unending recursion—any "ground" claimed as foundational would just be a field of relations that remits to another "ground," which is a field of relations, that remits to another, and so on.[18] To illustrate this, Burkhart brings up the well-known story of the elder who, after telling how the world is set on the back of a turtle who is, in turn, set on the back of another, keeps being pestered by an interlocutor with the question, "What is below the last turtle?" To which the elder answers: "It is turtles all the way down." The story underscores that in a context of strong relationality, knowledge is more concerned with how to do something effectively than with pursuing the final answer to an abstract question; it is eminently practical rather than propositional. In this sense, instead of seeking the ultimate causes for a given state of affairs to, once and for all, orient action, the path followed by this pragmatism involves a relentless experience of trial and error. Adam Arola points out that in this framework "something is believed to be true if it is verified *by experience* to have sufficient explanatory power to enable a person to accomplish tasks."[19] Thus, even if a certain way of doing things is "known" by experience to work—and since experience cannot but be partial and (spatiotemporally) situated—nobody can claim to "really know" the unending recursive relations that bring about an existent, event, or situation that one has to deal with. In other words, one should not assume to know beyond the limits of one's own situated experience and needs. This does not mean that emplaced collectives have no tested "truths" gained through experience, but these are revisable, for any account of truth qua function can be communicated as the *best* thing to believe, the *best* way to accomplish a task, that we know so far. But openness, to the possibility that experience may show us superior ways to accomplish a task, indicates that this conception of truth is always understood to be flexible and at the mercy of what is shown in experience.[20]

Accordingly, when the principles of symmetry of value and of the inapprehensibility of existence are operative against a largely taken-for-granted background of relationality in the strong sense, we obtain an ethos, a way of moving through life, that assumes that all beings—even if we do not know exactly how—cocontribute through their living (i.e., their specific configurations, vital trajectories, and reciprocal relations) to the unfolding of the story of life. In this context, the greatest practical task existents face during their life cycle involves the question of how to live well—that is, in a way that contributes to the unfolding story of life. Deborah McGregor puts it thus:

> Creation is regarded as a gift. To be sustainable means to take responsibility and be spiritually connected to all of Creation, all of the time. Everyone and everything carry this responsibility and has duties to perform. All

things contribute to the sustainability of Creation. It is not a responsibility carried only by people. All of Creation contributes, and this includes everything from the tiniest animals to the powerful sun. It includes the land, the weather, the spirits—all of it. An important principle that emerges from the Creation stories is that we cannot interfere with the ability of these elements or beings of Creation to perform their duties. When we interfere, then the sustainability of Creation is threatened (as we now see).[21]

It is telling that in the stories of some emplaced collectives, the existents that we are calling "humans" are portrayed as pitiful creatures when compared with others, precisely because they seem to be the most clueless about how to go along with the dynamic flow of the story of life. But as Vine Deloria points out, these creatures are not without resources:

> The wise person will realize his or her own limitations and act with some degree of humility until he or she has sufficient knowledge to act with confidence. Every bit of information must be related to the general framework of moral interpretation [i.e., participating in the unfolding of the story of life] as it is personal to them and their community. No body of knowledge exists for its own sake outside the moral framework of under-standing. We are, in the truest sense possible, creators or co-creators with the higher powers, and what we do has immediate importance for the rest of the universe. This attitude extends to data and experiences far beyond the immediate physical environment, including the stars, other worlds and galaxies, the other higher and lower planes of existence, and the places of higher and lower spiritual activities. . . . In the moral universe all activities, events, and entities are related, and consequently it does not matter what kind of existence an entity enjoys, for the responsibility is always there for it to participate in the continuing creation of reality.[22]

Given that no existent is exactly the same as any other, that "the world is constantly creating itself because everything is alive and making choices that determine the future," and that there are no detailed "maps" established once and for all for us to participate appropriately in the continuing creation of reality, Deloria signals that a certain attitude or disposition involving both humility and responsibility is key.[23] I want to propose that such an attitude or disposition expresses another principle, the characteristics of which are well captured by the concept of *carefulness*. This is similar to but strikes a slightly different note than *care*, which feminists have fruitfully pushed into scholarly and activist thinking. To me, the term *carefulness* not only better captures the complexities that María Puig de la Bellacasa has helped to foreground in the term *care*; it also makes it possible to stress the hard-nosed pragmatism informing practices that beget emplaced collectives.[24] Let's see how this is so. Puig de la Bellacasa starts from a generic definition of care that includes "everything that we do to maintain, continue and repair 'our world' so that we can live in it as well as possible," but she then pushes us to avoid "the tendencies to smooth out [the concept's] asperities—whether by idealizing or denigrating it."[25] To put it somewhat simplistically and in plain words, care might involve affection and willful self-sacrifice, but it also might imply burdensome yet unavoidable obligation that is differentially taken up or distributed. This is very important to bring into the picture inequalities and hierarchies that the "nice" connotation of the word *care* might erase. But there is a further dimension that becomes visible when we add the suffix *ful* to *care*; now the word also connotes dread, and even avoidance, as when a dangerous situation or existent requires careful handling, sometimes to the point that the best course of action is to stay away from it or repel it by force.

As a pragmatics, carefulness cannot be further from a general "goodness toward others" or from the image of collectives as harmonic assemblages free from conflicts. Rather, carefulness signals the arduous work of achieving livable stabilities amid the perils implicit in a state of affairs in which divergent existents are utterly dependent on each other to bring themselves into being, precisely as divergent existents! Moreover, the term *carefulness* pays better heed to the caveat implicit in Deloria's description of the proper way to navigate this state of affairs: not all existents are wise enough to perceive the requirement to be careful, and some might be reckless; this is also an unavoidable feature of the terrain that needs to be navigated. It is with this complex and demanding terrain in mind that we need to understand how a pragmatics of carefulness works in the context of emplaced collectives' stories of a good life, or life projects.

The story of life, or mode of existence, of any given emplaced collective emerges out of the mysterious dynamism inherent to the emergent relations that beget and are begotten by divergent but equally crucial vital trajectories. Again, the word *mysterious* simply stresses the degree to which the dynamics of relationality, with its unending recursions, is inapprehensible beyond experiences that are always necessarily situated and, thus, partial. In this context, acting carefully becomes paramount because in the story of life, divergence and heterogeneity do not constitute a problem to be overcome but a condition that demands simultaneously to be dealt with and nurtured. This is because relations are always consequential, and it is always in and through these relations that existents, and the emplaced collectives they form, come into being. In this way, within the story of life, carefulness orients pragmatic responses to the challenge of remaining dynamically entangled in a web of relations in such a way that divergence between relatively symmetrical existents continues to be generated. And what goes for an existent also goes for emplaced collectives and the relationships between them. For the principles of emplacement operate fractally and across any particular scale one may draw. Thus, when the trajectory and uniqueness of the existent one encounters (including those collectives of existents I call *emplaced collectives*) are engaged carefully, the story of life is more likely to unfold properly—that is, generating a pluriverse of divergent modes of existence.

Oriented by the general responsibility and overarching task of carefully rebirthing a pluriverse, the pragmatism that emerges from emplaced collectives (and informs my political ontology) has a particular performative bent. Indeed, this pragmatism seeks to perform the pluriverse that grounds and justifies it. Vine Deloria's interpretation of an interaction between the Oglala Sioux medicine man Black Elk and poet John Neihard evokes for me how this works. Deloria explains that, after telling Neihard the story of how the Sioux received the sacred White Buffalo Calf Pipe, Black Elk paused and then said: "This they tell, and whether it happened so or not, I do not know; but if you think about it, you can see that it is true." Deloria goes on to explain how this reflects a "principle of epistemological method": the truth of the story is demonstrated by the positive effect experienced when living by it.[26] And here we come back full circle to the centrality of experience. Indeed, what provides the ultimate, if ever revisable, justification of the entire disposition is the accumulated experience that, as infrastructures, these practical principles of emplacement generate worlds or collectives that are good to live in.

The Limits of Collectives (Emplaced and Not)

A DIZZYING SPATIALITY

When introducing the concepts of "life projects" and "emplaced collectives," I said the latter are the most intense expression of the former. This means that while all life projects share an orientation to the specificity of place, their actual practices might engender variable intensities of attachment and entanglement among the existents that compose a given collective. In effect, even if what I call *life projects* participate in its constitution, sometimes the qualifier *emplaced* might not do justice to the kind of attachments and entanglements that hold a collective together. In part, this variability echoes fluctuating degrees of coherence with which necessarily heterogeneous experiences of place (and related practices) bundle together as a collective. As its etymology indicates, the word *coherence* simply means "sticking together" and has no necessary connotations as to the "how"; consequently, when it holds, this sticking together might be very tight (like a rock) or very loose (like a ball of yarn), and this, in turn, depends on how diverse agencies become entangled, flow along, and enhance, redirect, or even interrupt each other. The holding together of emplaced collectives tends to be on the tighter end of the spectrum. In effect, while the infrastructures of emplacement that beget emplaced collectives respond to the general require-ment of attending to the specificity of place, their intention is also intensely shaped by the concern with carefully rebirthing relatively symmetrical entan-glements among the existents that compose them. This has an impact on how these collectives "stick together." For their practices and infrastructures foster particularly dense arrays of attachments and entanglements among existents, including (crucially) the less mobile ones, which either present themselves as "landscape features" or dwell in specific sites. Then, one of the qualities that distinguishes them from other collectives (including but not restricted to the modern one) is that emplaced collectives blend with specific "geographical lo-cations," even if also exceeding them. This might lead one to assume that an emplaced collective is the same as "the territory" *of* "a community." Let me present an anecdote to illustrate why this is not exactly the case.

Yshir au oso speakers refer to the place they live as *yrmo*, which is a polysemic and expansive term. The word might be used as a descriptor of the landscape (e.g., the bush when compared to the river), it might refer to the entire area of land the Yshiro used to be familiar with (closest to the concept of "tradi-tional territory" that most Yshiro speakers nowadays foreground and outsiders assume), or it might refer to the known world or reality. In this last sense, yrmo can be aptly described as an emplaced collective insofar as it is unique, com-posed of entities and dynamics that are specific to it, and, in many cases, re-main anchored to specific landscape features. Nowadays, however, not all these meanings are equally significant for yshir au oso speakers, and this reflects the specific kind of heterogeneity of experiences and ways of living that the expansion of infrastructures of displacement has made possible in their com-munities. This was made evident to me by a conversation I had with the elder Doña Anita Martinez in 2010, after a meeting organized by the Yshiro leaders' federation, Unión de las Comunidades Indígenas de la Nación Yshir (UCINY), to discuss a strategy to "recover the yrmo" (understood as the "traditional ter-ritory"). I observed that Doña Anita remained silent throughout the meeting and walked away grumbling when it finished. Later on, during a visit to her house, I asked what she thought about what had been said in the school, where the meeting had taken place. Gesticulating in its direction she said,

> Those teachers [who called the meeting with UCINY's leadership] say this meeting is important for all the Yshiro, that UCINY will recover the yrmo. But they don't care for the yrmo, they just want land [nimich]. Look at that leader who keeps talking about scholarships for students; the owner of Puerto Leda [ranch] gave him money already so that he does not tell [the authorities] how he [the rancher] is clear-cutting there, chasing all the doshipo [land "animals"] away. They say this idea is for the good of the Yshiro, but they are not yshiro; they don't care for the yrmo.

In her remarks, Doña Anita explicitly distinguished the emplaced collective yrmo from simply *land*, but she inadvertently also gave us a way to trace another subtle distinction (which I emphasize with my selective use of capitalization), between different connotations of the term *yshiro*: on the one hand, as an ethnic identity marker associated with land that is mobilized by the Yshiro federation in its negotiations with the state and other external agencies, and on the other hand, as a descriptive category referring to an existent that only obtains in relation with yrmo as it is also understood, and stressed, by many (but not all) Yshiro. A Yshiro person would remain such even if they moved permanently to Paraguay's capital, Asunción City, and cut all relations with the place. In contrast, maintaining the condition of yshiro would depend on sustaining such relations. This is why I have insisted on using the construction "the emplaced collective yshiro *are with*" when referring to the yrmo. But the distinction I hear in Doña Anita's words also signals that the spatiality of the yrmo (with all its constituents, including yshiro) transcends conventional notions of territory as a perimeter of land that might be agreed upon by humans against a background of Euclidian space. In effect, while the question "Where is your territory, and how far does it go?" makes total sense in terms of Euclidian space and a modernist frame of reference, when asked in reference to collectives, it is like asking someone, "Where is your reality, and how far does it go?"

Of course, such a question makes no sense from a modernist standpoint, for reality is everywhere and includes everything. However, from a standpoint that assumes that, rather than being *in a place* in the world, collectives *take place* or *occur* as worlds, it is possible to answer this question with: "My collective/reality/world is where the practices and relations that constitute it are, and it goes as far as to the point where those practices and relations encounter a stoppage or interruption—that is, a limit." Such an answer implies that the spatiality, and therefore the limits, of collectives in general is better conceived in topological terms.[27] And since limits and borders imply inclusions and exclusions—that is, what is set together and what is set apart—the whole point has a bearing on how politics is conceived, as we will soon see. But let's first take a look at the implications of conceiving the spatiality of collectives in topological terms.

As a first approximation, we can visualize this spatiality as being like a subway system map that, when we stand in a particular station, shows us our location within a system of relations punctuated by other stations. Now, since the topological spatiality of collectives is not that of a transcendent reality, it is better to think of it in terms of the intensity with which the existents that constitute those collectives both manifest themselves and are experienced from particular standpoints. I am restaging here in terms of "experience" the same point I raised in the introduction when I argued that the "visibility" of the figures in the rabbit/bird illusion depends not only on how traces are arranged in the drawing but also on the viewer's standpoint. Thus, in experiential terms, the presence of existents at stake in a situation might be tenuous or self-imposing, but also, from particular standpoints, they might be more or less perceptible, or even not at all. So, we do not have a map of a set of transcendent relations between preexisting existents (or stations, in the subway system analogy), which a tenacious observer is bound to eventually "discover." Rather, what we have in the case of collectives is an ongoing process of simultaneously attuning to other existents, making relations, and mapping (so to speak) from the particular standpoint of a given existent (or observer/participant). It is critical, however, not to associate *standpoint* with the notion of individuality. While *standpoint* and *individuality* share a connotation of uniqueness and unrepeatability, the former can never constitute a self-contained unit, for it is always an emergent knot generated by the encounter of traces, trajectories, and relations that transcend it. This implies that the frames of reference are always relative and can never be fully stabilized, making the conceptualization of collectives' spatiality quite a dizzying exercise. A set of unpolished examples should, however, be enough to convey the analytical consequences of all this as concisely as possible.

Let's assume we adopt the standpoint of the existent *yshir*. From this standpoint, the yrmo (as reality, what there is) *is* everywhere and includes existents such as ylipiot (jaguar), ologolak (capivara), bahlut (spirit owner), dihip'kunaho (White people), and maro (Paraguayans-mestizo), as well as everything else known or yet to be known. Based on experience, *for* the yshir, each of those existents figures in the yrmo in a particular way in relation to the self and in relation to each other. This constellation of relations—seen from the self, between the self and the others, and among the others—shapes the yshir sense of self, which is also the standpoint called *yrmo*; for, strictly speaking, each existent is a collective in itself, as each is always the uniquely localized expression and account of relationality's unending recursion.[28]

Now, from the standpoint of what yshir call "dihip'kunaha," those existents—including yshir and dihip'kunaha themselves—figure quite differently, as "humans" (Yshiro and Whites, respectively), "animals," and "cultural beliefs," forming a constellation of relations that shape the human sense of self, which (to give it a label) is the standpoint we can call *the (modern) world*. And the same happens as we shift from one existent's standpoint to another, regardless of the frame of reference we want to begin from (e.g., the yrmo of the yshir; the world of the human; the roar of the jaguar; or the grrum-grrum of the ylipiot!).

I playfully use the onomatopoeic words that (English-speaking) humans attribute to jaguars and yshiro attribute to ylipiot, to signal that those entities (which are not the same) also have their own standpoints, and thus to bring us back, with a more robust feeling of it, to the initial point that in this play of mutually facing mirrors, each existent/emplaced collective has its own account of itself and of other existents' standpoints, which are, of course, not the same account that those existents/collectives have of themselves and of the existent/collective of reference.[29] And yet, this does not mean there is no anchoring in this dizzying spatiality. From any standpoint of reference, and as long as existents behave within the range of established experience and relations remain relatively stable, the accounts generated by experience about our collective of reference can be taken to be reliable because they work in practice. It is precisely when accounts do not quite work that a sense of the limit of the collective manifests. So, we are getting now closer to the issue of limits, but before fully getting into it, I first need to clear away potential objections and misunderstandings.

HOW FAR DOES THE HUMAN GO?

I have used the pairs yshir/dihip'kunaha and Yshiro (human)/White (human) to illustrate how the standpoints associated with each pair express different frames of reference or collectives (for ease of presentation, I will keep referring to these as *yrmo* and *the world*, respectively). This might raise two related objections. The first could be that in *the world*, only humans have a standpoint proper; what can we possibly know of the standpoint of nonhumans, especially inert ones, if they have none? The second objection would go something like this: "The difference between standpoints that you are foregrounding is elicited from your particular standpoint, which is as human as theirs!"

To the first objection I would say that if one establishes an equivalence between the words *standpoint* and *disposition* (*nature* being the first synonym in my thesaurus for the latter word!), it quickly becomes evident that "humans" do get to know a good deal about the *standpoint* of nonhumans, and this without stretching too far the premises about agency that dominate in *the world*. Indeed, "humans" have protocols to elicit these standpoints (even if they are not conceived as such), the reliability of which, without being fail proof, are considered good enough according to the regime of veridiction that applies in *the world*. Well, the same goes for yshiro in relation to other existents that populate the yrmo (which are *not* nonhumans but rather other-than-yshiro); they have reliable protocols to elicit those standpoints and relate to them accordingly. The (far from minor) difference between "humans" and "yshiro," in this particular regard, is the kind of agencies (or lack thereof) that their "others" display.[30]

About the second objection, that my description of standpoints is itself made from a human standpoint, I have two things to say: First, that the objection reveals a misunderstanding about what I am referring to when speaking of a standpoint, and second, that such misunderstanding is grounded on the assumption that the category "human" is a universal. This has expansive analytical consequences. Let us begin with the misunderstanding, which stems from overlooking that political ontology seeks to craft a standpoint that refuses "the world" associated with "the human" as a universal standpoint, and that crucial to this is remaining attentive to the limits of our categories, or better, the limits of the collective we are enacting through those categories. This not only means making evident the limits I see in the assumptions of the world of the human when I compare it with the yrmo of the yshiro; it also means not losing sight that the way I am tracing a difference through this comparison is not the same as the way each of those existents would trace their mutual differences themselves. To put it in other words, neither the "humans with their world" nor the "yshiro with their yrmo" see and account for themselves as I do it here—that is, as existents in different collectives.[31] However, that our ways of accounting for ourselves and our worlds do not coincide does not automatically invalidate any of them. What it does is raise the question of the kinds of relations these accounts might sustain with each other. Yet, if we lose sight that our categories (our worlds of reference) are not that of others, that question cannot be truly posed with all its depth, which is precisely what happens when we assume that the "human" is universal. And here we get to the second point about the expansive analytical consequences of such assumption.

Even amid the conceptual decentering of the category "human," associated to academic buzzwords such as posthumanism, multispecies, vital material-ism, and agential realism, among others, its universality resurfaces in a concern shared by many (but certainly not all) working within these lines of inquiry: How can we take into account nonhumans without reducing them to human ideas?[32] This concern assumes the possibility that in one way or another, nonhumans might speak by themselves and therefore that it is important to somehow circumvent the humans that profess to speak on their behalf. How-ever, such an assumption misses a fundamental lesson of material-semiotics science and technology studies (STS). In effect, while STS showed that there is a substantial amount of "human labor" invested in the setup through which sciences, for example, make us "hear" nonhumans speaking, it also showed that this does not mean that humans alone are speaking. The fundamental, yet often downplayed, lesson drawn from this was that it is always an entire as-semblage that speaks, regardless of the kind of existent we, as audience, most immediately hear.

It is paradoxical that the figure of the spokesperson, which assisted in grasping the idea of speaking assemblages (or collectives), seems to have also contributed to the subtle reaffirmation of the universal applicability of the category "human" via a concern with who "really speaks." In part, I think this is because the assumption is that "spokesperson" equals "human." But accord-ing to material-semiotics, all existents in an assemblage are spokespersons that function as relays in a chain of communication (understood in the wider sense of circulation). What needs to be kept in sight is that agency does not reside only in the one we hear but in the entire assemblage of relations. This implies taking into consideration that the one doing the "hearing" must be reliably equipped to elicit the standpoint of its immediate interlocutors, otherwise there is a communication breakdown, and things do not work. To offer a crude example: I look at a graph from an electrocardiogram and cannot "hear" what my veins spoke to it, which is part of what my heart spoke to my veins—and one could keep tracing back the chain as long as one wishes and/or needs. But here comes my doctor who plays the role of the last relay/spokesperson I need to hear what my heart is saying through the veins and the electrocardiogram. I have the basic capacities and reliable protocols to "hear" my doctor but not, di-rectly, the electrocardiogram that heard my veins who heard my heart—or not without training myself in the art of hearing these specific nonhuman spokes-persons in a form that "the world" considers reliable, which most assuredly im-plies bringing into relation a whole other set of spokespersons/relays (theories, universities, and so on) that are part of "the world."

Given that under proper conditions, the existents that "the world" labels "humans" seem to have a more widely and evenly distributed capacity to "hear" each other than to hear those labeled "nonhumans," it is not surprising that the existents that could fall within the former category are, for each other, the usual last relay/spokesperson for the speaking assemblage. And, incidentally, given this, it is not surprising either that the specific practices through which these existents perform the role of the assemblage's spokesperson for each other would tend to form clusters, which in "the world" are labeled "cultures."[33] However, the preponderance that these existents (here equivocally labeled "humans") have vis-à-vis each other as the spokespersons for a given assemblage should not lead us to think that they are the ones who speak. Whether these spokespersons are faithful to their particular assemblage, or whether the way in which they relay the standpoints of their "others" actually works, is quite another matter, one that can only be dealt with according to criteria appropriate to that assemblage.

Thus, particularly in cases that involve different assemblages or collectives, the desire to account for nonhumans in their own terms is even more problematic. Trying to subtract (or improve on) the spokespersons of these assemblages and, assuming we are all "human," put ourselves in their place (or above them) does not give us any deeper insight into the standpoint or disposition of their "others." It only gives us insight into the "nonhumans" of "the world." For example, as a social scientist, I might learn from natural scientists the biology and ethology of the jaguar—that is, I might learn the protocols that, in "the world," are appropriate to relay the dispositions of this "nonhuman," but this would not quite teach me what I would need to hear and relay the standpoint of the ylipiot in the yrmo. Of course, I can also try to learn the necessary protocols with an yshir teacher, and then, perhaps, my experience of the ylipiot's standpoint will echo that of my yshir teacher (as my experience of the jaguar's disposition might echo that of the natural scientist). But in neither case would this learning get me closer to the unmediated roar of the jaguar or the grrum-grrum of the ylipiot.[34] Instead, if the inevitability of mediations is not kept in mind, what might happen is that those practices that are assumed to be based on a "less mediated understanding" of the existent in question end up being imposed over those practices that are deemed somehow more mediated (and distorted). For example, the practices of care associated with the jaguar (such as environmental regulations) might clash with and be imposed upon the practices of carefulness associated with the ylipiot (such as killing it on the spot). In this way, the yrmo and the world might end up encountering each other in the equivocal jaguar/ylipiot as interference, but with the added problem that "the world" is totally oblivious to that.

We will see a very detailed example of these kinds of encounters in act 2, but with this sketch of the problem we finally arrive at the issue of how a sense of limits of the collectives arise, for these interferences constitute a sort of stoppage, a relative limit that one *might feel*, and that marks where one's accounts/practices (of the world or the yrmo) cease to work smoothly. I stress *might feel* to foreground again that the presence of another collective (or, what is the same, the limits of our own) also depends on our capacity to perceive it; we must be able to attune ourselves to the manifestations of the limit. But besides our attunement to it, the experience of the divergence raises the question of how the respective collectives are going to deal with each other and their mutual asymmetries; whether, and how, they can go on together; and with what results. In short, the encounter poses the fundamental question of politics; and, as we will see next, emplaced collectives have a particular way of engaging it.

The (Cosmo)politics of Emplaced Collectives

THE CIRCLE AND THE EIGHT

Many spokespersons for, or intellectuals familiar with, emplaced collectives often use specific words to refer to the ways in which those collectives gather and hold themselves together. For example, Richard Atleo uses the term "Haḥuułism" (an emergent form of constitutionalism); Leanne Simpson uses the term "Nishnaabewin" (Nishnaabeg-grounded normativity); Hector Na-huelpan refers to the concept of "itro fill mongen" (inherent interdependence) as that which gives shape to the emplaced collective the Mapuche call mapu.[35] I could go on with examples from every corner of the continent, but the point I want to argue is that, with or without a specific terminology, and beyond the specific ways in which they are operationalized, these political practices share a similar challenge, since they have to ensure that the existents they hold together can unfold their unique vital trajectories, thereby contributing to the unfolding story of life of the entire collective. In this context, what makes existents unique and different from each other is not a problem to be overcome but a condition to be nurtured along the unfolding of one's vital trajectory. It is precisely here that the challenge of politics lies for emplaced collectives, a challenge that, paraphrasing the evocative formulation of Hellen Verran, I summarize as: How can we go on together in divergence?[36]

To exemplify what this challenge entails, Verran has offered a contrast between Latour's idea that politics traces the figure of a circle, and the one she learned from Yolngu teachers, according to which the movement that politics traces resembles a figure eight.[37] Latour proposed that the figure of the circle epitomizes the movement politics traces when it forms (human) groups. In the interlude I will return to how Latour extends this notion of the political circle beyond human politics; for now, it will suffice to indicate that this circle "is [a]bout transforming the several into one . . . and subsequently, through a process of retransformation, of the one into several."[38]

The movement traced by Latour's political circle (see figure 3) gathers what is heterogeneous and dispersed (the Several) through a process of delegating representation, thus forming "a group" (the One) that through persuasion and/or coercion retains the "obedience" of the many (back to the Several). The "group" is sustained as an autonomous entity only by the continuous circling back between the One and the Several, with the challenge and goal of politics always being to successfully regather the Several into the One, a movement that I will call *commoning*. The term comes from discussions on "the commons," where it has a particular meaning to which I will return in the interlude. Here I mobilize it primarily as a generic concept to refer to practices that, by grouping divergent existents together, bring to fruition a common, a collective. Commoning responds to a challenge that can be captured with a question that seems almost connatural to politics: How can a "we" (undefined as this might be) be articulated in spite of differences? How can this be done properly so that this "we" can live together well? I sustain that what the politics of emplaced collectives show us is that commoning does not exhaust what politics, as the arts of gathering and holding together collectives, involves.

In effect, as I understand it, the politics of emplaced collectives conceived as the tracing of a figure eight is not only concerned with commoning, with gathering a group into existence (i.e., becoming the One); it is also concerned with uncommoning, with ensuring that the Several remain Several after going through the One, repeatedly. In the figure of the "eight-like politics," the Several converge together (the One), redoing and re-sorting their mutual differences in order to then move on in divergence (the Several). The terms of the divergence will be reiteratively *and carefully* reworked as conditions change, so as to enhance the entire collective's possibilities of existence, which, as I have been discussing, depends on the continuous rebirthing of heterogeneous and unique vital trajectories. Insofar as it is oriented to rebirthing the Several, as a grounding infrastructure, carefulness can thus be seen as doing the opposite work of coloniality, which entails, as may be recalled from the introduction, the constant suppression and/or containment of those expressions of pluriversal multiplicity (i.e., the Several) that might disrupt displacement. In general,

Latour's Political Circle

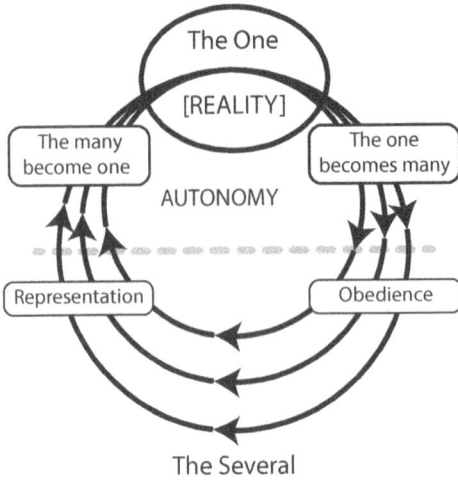

The Eight-like Politics of Emplaced Collectives

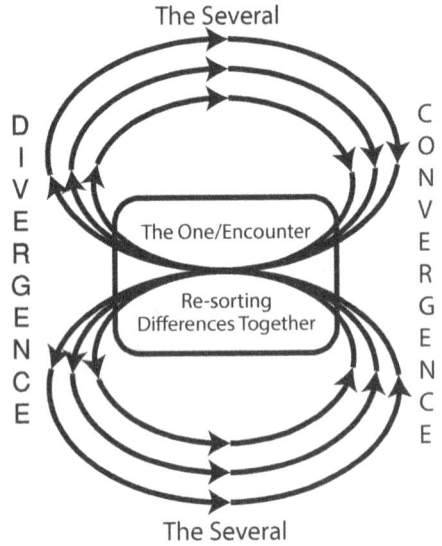

FIGURE 3. Different figurations of politics. Reasonable politics always turns around the constitution of the One. The politics of emplaced collectives remains concerned with cultivating the Several. Drawing by Steve Chapman.

what the eight-like movement of politics reflects is a process whereby the very being of the diverging existents that come to form an emplaced collective can no longer be disentangled from the relations/encounters from which they originated; like the bird/rabbit, they are or become part of each other without becoming one. For example, under the rubric of nishnaabeg internationalism, Simpson describes how stories, ceremonies, political practices, intellectual endeavors, and technologies of the Rotinonhseshá:ka (Haudenosaunee) and the Michi Saagiig Nishnaabeg are profoundly imprinted and shaped by their mutual friendship, collaboration, and reciprocity and yet are not the same.[39] A similar mutual entanglement happens with the "Deer Nation" and other (other-than-nishnaabeg) nations that, in addition to constituting collectives on their own, are also part of the emplaced collective nishnaabeg are with. I will venture that the stronger the relations of friendship, collaboration, and reciprocity between and among existents are, and the more the diverging existents become vital parts of each other, the more closely the tightness of the collective will resemble that of a rock.

And yet, we must not forget that relations of indifference, avoidance, and enmity are also ways in which divergences manifest. For example, the divergence between yshiro and ylipiot (jaguar) is tinged by mutual avoidance and deep enmity, as the elder Don Veneto Vera told me once, "Ylipiot and yshiro don't want to see each other; they were same before but those boys [the primordial jaguars] killed their parents and became our enemies; if we meet, one or the other is going to die." The ylipiot is enemy, and yshiro must be careful with it, not only because it is dangerous but also because it is part of the emplaced collective yshiro are with. Thus, it is true that emplaced collectives are not free from conflict and violence; however, the pragmatics of carefulness operate both as a warning signal in the face of danger and as a brake so that conflict does not become a drive toward extermination. Even our enemies, through their relations with other existents, play a role in sustaining the emplaced collective we are with![40]

POLITICS AS AN EXPERIMENTAL QUESTION

The more life projects (qua grounding infrastructures) enact the principles of emplacement, the more the two sides of the eight figure will tend to be symmetrical, thus reflecting that rather than being reduced in the encounter, the overarching concern of rebirthing relatively symmetrical divergences has been properly taken care of. But what happens when life projects encounter infrastructures of displacement, those that enact a one-world world, for instance? A story told in 1911 by Santee Dakota writer Ojaiesa (Charles Eastman) will help me illustrate this to further underscore how the forms of politics associated with the circle and the eight figure diverge from each other, in practice:

> I am reminded of a time when a missionary undertook to instruct a group of our people in the truths of his holy religion. He told them of the creation of the earth in six days, and of the fall of our first parents by eating an apple. My people were courteous and listened attentively, and after thanking the missionary, one man related in his own turn a very ancient tradition concerning the origin of the maize. But the missionary plainly showed his disgust and disbelief, indignantly saying: "What I delivered to you were sacred truths, but this that you tell me is mere fabulation and falsehood!" "My brother," gravely replied the offended Indian, "it seems that you have not been well grounded in the rules of civility. You saw that we, who practice these rules, believed your stories; why, then, do you refuse to credit ours?"[41]

The first elements of contrast in the story are the missionary's and his interlocutors' respective dispositions to the otherwise—dispositions that I correlate to the circular and the eight-like figures of the political. The reaction of the missionary to the courteous listening of his interlocutors perfectly describes the regime of reasonable politics. In effect, albeit anchored in "sacred truths," we see in the missionary the ranking of factualities typical of this politics. This politics, fundamentally concerned with (to use the Foucauldian expression) taming the wild profusion of existing things, would result in conquest and in the children of those courteous interlocutors being kidnapped into boarding schools to make them conform to the One (in the nineteenth century, still Christendom under God). Later, when straightforward coercion proved ineffective in achieving the goal, the political circle would turn once more, attempting to bring these divergent beings into the One (which by the twentieth century had become "reality" or "nature") through the persuasion of multiculturalism and identity politics, with police operations always ready to intervene when unreasonable "cultural beliefs" resurfaced. In act 2, we will see the shape that the mix of "persuasion and coercion" is taking now, as the modern categorical division between nature and culture seems to be supplanted by notions of lively assemblages. But I am jumping ahead of myself. My point is that through the ranking of factualities that justifies the imposition of the One, when the eight-like politics meets the circular politics, the process of re-birthing the Several is forcefully truncated. In part this is because the ranking of factualities of reasonable politics is itself tied to the concern of bringing the otherwise (the Several) into the fold of an existent/collective taken to be a transcendent truth, a reality that, whether it is called God, nature, or lively assemblage, cannot be questioned; even if this implies that the task of policing must always resume again and again because "obedience" to this "reality" is never perfectly achieved.

All of this implies that, when addressing the question of how to live together, reasonable politics operates in a semi-rhetorical register. Indeed, in the face of the otherwise, when reasonable politics must translate what is not already within its domain, its translations are haunted by anxiety over equivalence. This anxiety is, at the bottom, fueled by the need to preserve the self-identity of a presumed transcendent reality, or what is the same, the universal effect generated by infrastructures of displacement. Material-semiotics would put what I call *anxiety* in a less "personalized" manner and would simply speak of a sort of conservative economics at play: for those obliged to them, transforming established networks/reals is extremely costly, so it is more economical to go along with them.[42] In either case, reasonable politics' disavowal of the multiplicity of reals, and of the equivocations that make multiplicity possible, is part of this self-preserving or conservative move. Via effectively treating divergences as rankable perspectives, it goes on thickening the one-world world effect. It is in this sense that, for reasonable politics, the fundamental question of politics is to some extent rhetorical; the "how" is already largely sorted out: exclude the unreal and the erroneous and the results are guaranteed by the transcendent reality that is being continuously reinforced in that very process of exclusion.

Now, unlike the missionary, the "offended Indian" does not assume that different stories must compete to see which is true or who can explain away the other (as an error), but instead assumes that all stories have validity. Again, recall Atleo's point regarding the presumption within his emplaced collective that nobody can claim to "know and understand creation." By believing the missionary's "truths," the Indians in the story accept the claims as what they seem to be—claims about a collective/world in which there is a single creator, God. Crediting the truth of the missionary's story doesn't diminish in the least the truth of their own stories; after all, grounded experience tells them that the emplaced collective that emerged from the living of those stories has been a good enough one to live in. But the experiential trust in their lived stories in no way precludes their change and adaptation, for they always have to be retold along the changing flow of other stories, both known and yet to be known; and Ojaiesa's people were indeed facing a story they did not know of! Hence, the "civil" attitude toward the story of the missionary is nothing like liberal tolerance. As I pointed out before, it involves serious consideration of the consequences of this encounter with the otherwise, with the limits of one's own accounts. What does this world we did not know of before imply for our world? What will be required of our worlds so that they can, from now on, flow in relation to each other and along the story of life? As we can see, the moment of movement toward the One (i.e., the encounter) also poses for emplaced collectives (and existents) the fundamental question of politics of how to live together well, but rather than in a semi-rhetorical register, as is the case with reasonable politics, the question here is posed as a thoroughly experimental one: a "how" must be invented at each step, and the results of these inventions are uncertain! This is in very close step with the notion of cosmopolitics that I presented in the introduction, which also raises the fundamental political question without the guarantee of a transcendental reality. However, aside from being cosmopolitics avant la lettre, the politics of emplaced collectives comes with a key extra condiment that is largely missing in the most recent cosmopolitics—that is, what before I referred to as *uncommoning*, the purposeful cultivation of the multiplicity of place. I will expand on the significance of this added ingredient later when I can present in more detail the "more recent" versions of cosmopolitics with which my own project is also in conversation. For now, I would like to conclude my discussion of the cosmopolitics of emplaced collectives by linking the importance they assign to uncommoning with a "pragmatics of scale" that will become increasingly important in my subsequent discussions.

I borrow the concept from E. Summerson Carr and Michael Lempert for whom a "pragmatics of scale" assumes that "scale is always a matter (and materialization) of a carefully fashioned perspective that orients actors in particular ways."[43] I contend that a concern for cultivating the multiplicity of place (or uncommoning) orients the cosmopolitics of emplaced collectives toward the *small*. The term does not imply a ready-made calculus of size; rather, in tandem with its counterpart, the *big*, it designates one of the directions in which, due to the way in which their infrastructures ground them, collectives might scale themselves. The modern collective, for example, embodies and performs a "big story" about the good life (i.e., modernization) whose assumed universality only gains plausibility insofar as, buttressed by extractivism, the grounding infrastructures of displacement it rests on can expand, overrunning the specificity of places. In effect, instead of simply excluding the otherwise that it encounters, the modern collective is compelled to tame or eliminate it (recall the contrasting dispositions of the missionary and Ojaiesa's people). Thus, the horizon of its commoning (that circular movement that brings the Several into the One) is expansive; to keep being what it is, the modern collective can only go "big(ger)." In contrast to this expansive orientation, I propose that emplaced collectives, with their concern for uncommoning, for cultivating the specificity of places, are oriented to the "small." In addition to not being a necessity for emplaced collectives to be what they are, expansion itself might conspire against the performance of that which makes them what they are; in effect, it might hamper the intensity of attention to the specificity of place that careful cultivation requires.[44] As Leanne Simpson puts it, "The alternative to extractivism is deep reciprocity. It's respect, it's relationship, it's responsibility, *and it's local*."[45] And yet, in a context where they expand everywhere, the specificity of "the local" is often brimming with infrastructures of displacement (including in the form of stories of a good life)! Let's now begin to explore some of the most salient challenges that such a terrain imposes on those who might want to journey toward emplacement and the small.

ACT I

Uncommoning the Territory of the
Common Good (On Being Faithful to
the Pluriverse)

Acknowledging that *climate change is a common concern of humankind*, Parties should, when taking action to address climate change, respect, promote and consider their respective *obligations on human rights*, the right to health, the rights of indigenous peoples, local communities, migrants, children, persons with disabilities and people in vulnerable situations and *the right to development* as well as gender equality, empowerment of women and intergenerational equity.—UNITED NATIONS, *Report of the Conference of the Parties* (a.k.a. the Paris agreement), 2015

As a story about the good life, which had a "universe" as its grounding assumption, modernization has always aimed big, but we can take 1949 as the moment in which this orientation explicitly turned into a pursuit for the "global common good." In that year, US president Harry Truman launched the era of development, promising to modernize the world and bring prosperity to all of humanity through a "more vigorous application of modern scientific and technical knowledge."[1] It is not without irony that Earth System scientists signal this moment in time as the point at which every indicator of the impact of human activity on the Earth's life systems began to undergo a sharp rate increase.[2] This infamous "great acceleration" is key to the "momentous challenges" at the center of our attention and traces an evident connection between them and modernization. In effect, many of the phenomena that compose these challenges can be seen as the side effects of pursuing this vision of a good life, which, in a twisted paradox, erodes its possibilities of realization. Thus, stories told about momentous challenges can be seen as successors of this vision of a global common good: they inherit the "promising" story of modernization as a problematic to which they must respond, whether it be by fixing, reclaiming, or rejecting it.[3]

Nowadays, modernization and its successor stories encounter and mingle with each other, and with what I call *life projects*, in the practical and conceptual site of "territory." The concept is implicit in the term *parties* in the epigraph to this chapter, as well as in the references to "their respective obligations" and to "the right to development." In effect, the excerpt from the Paris Agreement remits both to a geography of nation-states (i.e., the parties) with their respective territorial jurisdictions and to the challenges that tackling a concern made commensurable with all of humanity might pose for those jurisdictions. Central among these challenges is the possibility that addressing the "common concern of humankind" might preempt the right to development that every party has—that is, the right to partake in the global common good promised by modernization. The way the agreement describes it gives away that the problem is not climate change per se but rather how to continue in the pursuit of modernization's promises to all of humanity (represented by nation-states) without the unwanted environmental side effects that have become evident. In other words, in the way that this momentous challenge (climate change) is storied, the problem appears as the negative proxy of a developmentalist vision of the global common good. But this can be fixed; and then we could have something called *modernization fixed*. Although some politicians and analysts might open it up to questions of whether capitalism or other societal forms are best suited to tackle it, this way of conceiving the problem (and the vision of the global common good lodged in it) dominates in governmental circles and associated epistemic communities.

Given its avowed inclusion of the command to "respect, promote and consider" all the obligations the parties must observe in addressing climate change, land use planning (*ordenamiento territorial*, in Spanish) stands out among the interventions that translate this conception of the problem into governmental practice. In effect, presented as a relatively consensual procedure aimed at rationally balancing the needs of the environment and the human right to development of different groups, land use planning exercises proliferate, particularly in sites where the expansion of various forms of extractivism generates conflicts. In land use planning, territories (conceived as differentiated domains within nation-states) appear as the privileged locus to ground a developmentalist notion of the global common good, refurbished to take into account the environment. However, grassroots movements across the continent also frame their confrontations with state-sanctioned developmentalist designs in terms of territory—more specifically, in terms of its defense.[4] For many of them, territory designates the locus of heterogeneous life projects, with their own definitions of common good.

Paying attention to how the concept of territory is mobilized in contested practices, analysts in the last decade have produced a rich corpus of research and critique that has expanded the concept beyond describing areas of control drawable as polygons on topographic maps to designating the complex and entangled spatial projections and materializations of diverse political imaginations.[5] Without losing sight of the equivocality of the term, I build on these insights to argue that territory can be conceived as "the how" and "the where" diverse assemblages of existents ground themselves and take place as collectives, always complexly entangled with each other. In their becoming through relations (their "how"), existents and collectives do territories (their "where") in which and through which other existents and collectives weave their own modes of existence. Based on this understanding, I probe in this chapter how divergent visions of the common good meet in territory, become equivocally entangled with each other, and through these dynamics redo territory. I argue that these enacted visions of the common good engender, in practice, collectives that while thoroughly entangled have divergent orientations, precisely because of the differential prominence that emplacement or displacement has in them. Here, I return to the situation of equivocality in grounding infrastructures that I evoked with the image of the bird/rabbit. In that sense, I am particularly interested in exploring how, in their role as infrastructures of displacement or emplacement, respectively, divergent visions and practices of the common good become the ground for each other in asymmetrical ways and what consequences we can derive from this with regards to a cosmopolitics oriented to emplacement and the small.

With governmental action increasingly justified in terms of addressing momentous challenges, it has become easier to discern visions of the common good through what I described previously as negative proxies. Today it is easier to catch a glimpse of these visions not so much by their positive affirmation but by the ways in which concerns or challenges to be faced cut them out as a backdrop. Hence I follow a strategy of getting at visions of the common good primarily by looking at concerns with what challenges them. In this vein, I begin exploring a set of challenges Yshiro life projects face to be realized amid ongoing attempts at fixing the "environmental" consequences of previous rounds of extension of the modern vision of the common good.[6] In the second section, I show how Yshiro attempts at realizing their life projects become an opportunity for new or reshaped infrastructures of displacement (such as emerging visions of a more "environmentally friendly" common good) to be extended, always with the aid of coloniality. In the third section, I discuss how an emplaced collective can be unworkable for practices of displacement, but also how coloniality skirts this unworkability by trying to simultaneously uncommon the small common good associated with such a collective and common it into the (big) global common good. However, the story does not end here, for life projects are persistent and constantly seek to reweave themselves as (small) visions of the common good, even if only in the gaps produced by the mutual interruptions between different practices or infrastructures of displacement. I close with a reflection on why faithfulness to the pluriverse is required to grasp that, by persevering in the gaps left by infrastructures of displacement, life projects trace a strategy (of sorts) to move beyond perseverance.

The Yshiro Territorial Concern

At least until the late 1920s, the ancestors of the contemporary Yshiro people sustained their existence by moving through, sharing, and disputing with other groups an area the size of Belgium in what is known today as the Chaco region. When, in the 1980s, the Yshiro began to seek state recognition of their relation with the place, most of the land had been sold by successive governments to private investors.[7] The Yshiro's efforts yielded legal recognition of only fifty-five thousand hectares composed of various noncontiguous tracts of land, ranging in size from a few thousand to a dozen hectares—veritable "Indigenous (is) lands" amid an ocean of privatized lands (see map 1).

For a time, the lack of contiguity between the lands legally held by the communities did not pose a major problem. Except for a few ranches along the Paraguay River, the privatized lands were largely held for real estate speculation, and the Yshiro were free to transit, hunt, fish, gather materials, and visit across the entire area, regardless of who held the legal titles to the lands. But from the late 1990s onward, things started to change dramatically when, in a new wave of modernization, mechanized cattle-ranching enterprises (mostly coming from Brazil), followed by soy plantations, began to clear-cut the forests and build

THE YSHIRO COMMUNITIES

According to a self-administered census, the Yshiro communities in the Chaco region are composed of about two thousand people. They are connected to the rest of the country by a dirt road that cannot be used during rains (a third of the year, at least), by a weekly flight from the capital Asunción City to the neighboring Paraguayan towns of Fuerte Olimpo and Bahia Negra—but the landing strip in the latter is inoperable when it rains, and flying is prohibitively expensive for most Yshiro—and by a weekly boat along the Paraguay River. Each community regularly elects three leaders to run the affairs of the communities and to interact with the state and other institutions. In 1999, the Yshiro leaders formed a federation, Unión de las Comunidades Indígenas de la Nación Yshir (UCINY), to deal more effectively with external agencies. The federation operates as an assembly, where leaders make decisions by consensus, and actions are executed under the leadership of a general coordinator and a secretary, who are appointed by the leaders' assembly.

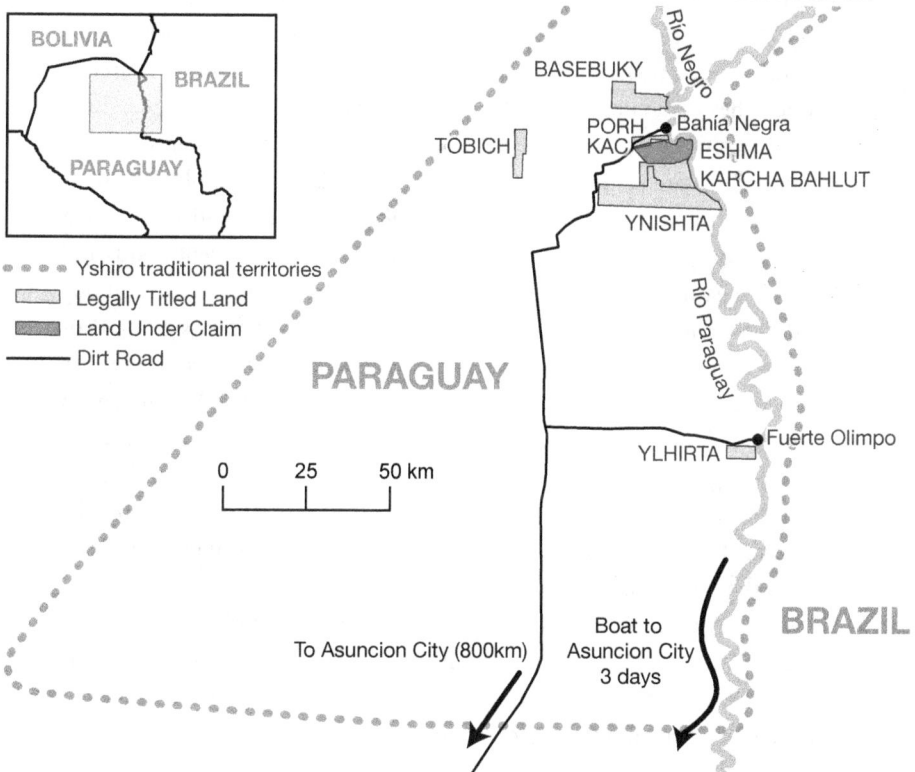

MAP 1. The Yshiro communities today. Notice the scale of territorial loss by comparing the boundaries of the traditional territories and the current land holdings.
Map by Steve Chapman.

fences parceling up the land. The change has been swift, positioning the region among the top in the world's ranking of forest loss.[8] Not surprisingly, a range of public and private initiatives—such as the creation of natural reserves and national parks—aimed at curbing deforestation and the loss of biodiversity associated with these processes followed.[9]

Having started to visit the Yshiro communities in 1991, I witnessed how this process slowly ramped up year after year until, after a hiatus of two years in my visits, I returned in 2003 to see it proceeding at a frenzied speed. Since then, complaints about the combined effects of deforestation and the establishment of protected areas have become a permanent feature of my conversations with friends and acquaintances. By 2005, Yshiro leaders began to promote discussions in their communities about how people were experiencing these processes in their lives and what they thought their federation, UCINY, should do about them. The majority of people who depend on the land complained that not only were they prevented by ranchers and park wardens from moving through the area in pursuit of their regular activities (from gathering materials and food to rituals with other-than-yshiro beings), but also whatever source of livelihood they could obtain within community lands was not enough. Albeit more indirectly, the people who had temporary or permanent waged jobs in agribusiness or state institutions were also impacted. They complained about the pressures from extended families and neighbors who demanded their help amid an almost permanent state of crisis, exacerbated by recurrent floods and droughts. Regardless of whether the impact was direct or indirect, everybody seemed in agreement about the source of the malaise, as UCINY's general coordinator Cesar Barboza put it to me in a conversation: "Our people are very concerned about the yrmo; it is all being destroyed. And the Yshiro can no longer go to all the places we used to go, our *traditional territory*. How are our children going to live here in the future? UCINY will need to recover that." In short, according to Cesar, what they had heard from their people implied a mandate for UCINY: ensure access to the yrmo, the "traditional territory." But what was the traditional territory?

I would say that the late 1920s was when the groundwork for the notion of an Yshir "traditional territory" began to enter the scene, although not exactly as such. As tensions with Bolivia about the disputed possession of the Chaco region were mounting, the Paraguayan government commissioned General Juan Belaieff to survey and draw a map that included the area where the predecessors of the contemporary Yshiro (then called by the government "Chamacoco"—Ebidoso, Tomarha, and Horio) lived. After the war with Bolivia (1932–35), what the general recorded in his map was published as an

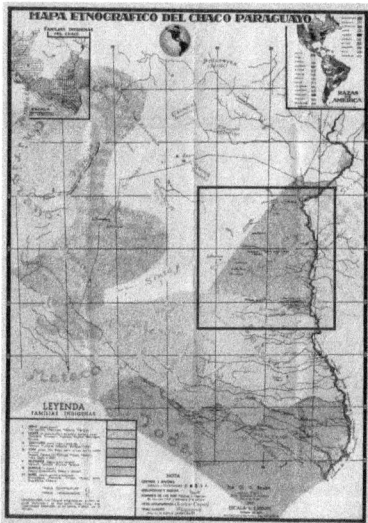

FIGURE 4. The Yshiro's traditional territory around 1930, as reported by General Juan Belaieff. From Juan Belaieff, *Mapa etnográfico del Chaco paraguayo*, Sociedad Científica del Paraguay, Asunción, 1941.

"ethnographic map of the Paraguayan Chaco" (see figure 4), marking the geographical areas "corresponding" to different Indigenous peoples.[10]

The Yshiro use this map nowadays to establish a historical baseline, both to gauge (in its topographical dimension) the dispossession of the yrmo that followed after Belaieff's explorations and to claim restitution for that loss. This use neatly captures the dynamics that ensue from the entanglement between practices of displacement and emplacement under the shadow of coloniality. Belaieff's mapping exercise was meant to realize a nation-state's territory, with all this entailed in terms of establishing the infrastructures (such as national borders, claims of ownership, and so on) through which modernity was grounding itself at the time. On the brink of a war that was to take place in an area famous for its arid terrain, securing water sources for the troops that would help to realize this territory was key. To locate these places, Belaieff resorted to the assistance of "Chamacoco scouts"—that is, he relied on yshiro intimacy with the yrmo. (Notice my selective use of capitalization to stress the term *yshir/o* designating an identity or a particular existent within the emplaced collective yrmo.) As it might be appreciated from the expansion of Belaieff's map, besides the denominations of the "ethnic groups" (in bold italics), the most important features on the map are lakes, lagoons, and rivers that are associated with toponyms in Yshir au oso (indicated in plain fonts). These toponyms appear in stories of how the yrmo, as an emplaced collective, has come to be as it is. For example, Lake Pitiantuta (the useless anteater), river amormichit (the armadillo's ghost), and lagoon hipurit (reddened soil) all designate events that, condensed in the oral tradition, narrate the establishment of certain kinds of relations between existents and lay down ways of doing things appropriately in the yrmo so that yshiro can have a good life, including access to water! Now, fast-forward to the present when to claim their "traditional territory" the Yshiro use a map originally produced to secure Paraguay's control of the "national territory"; folded together, these two moments emerge as a perfect example of a process of deep entanglement. In effect, we see how the modern collective grounds itself (takes place) by latching onto and becoming entangled with the yrmo's infrastructures of emplacement (for example, the oral tradition and the practices associated with it) to expand, and, conversely, how the yrmo subsequently sustains itself by latching onto the modern collective infrastructures of displacement (such as its notions and practices of territory), even if, as we will see later, they go against the grain of those infrastructures' intention.

This mutual latching presents a situation reminiscent of my ubiquitous bird/rabbit illusion: in many cases, it does take an active beholder to distinguish between practices of emplacement and practices of displacement because, as their entanglement intensifies, they begin to appear indistinguishable. This is indeed what progressively happened with the yrmo as waves of modernization incessantly arrived through the twentieth century. Without going into its details, I want to highlight, though, that through what elsewhere I have called *pedagogical and piecemeal violence*, this process of mutual entanglement between practices of emplacement and displacement progressively became asymmetrical, to the point that more than entanglement, perhaps one should speak of entrapment.[11] Thus, infrastructures of displacement have gradually engulfed ever more of the practices through which the emplaced collective yrmo holds together, to the point that for many (including many Yshiro), the yrmo has become to some extent unexperienceable as an emplaced collective; even for some components of the bird, only the rabbit seems to be perceptible!

One of the effects of the asymmetrical entanglement of emplacement and displacement in grounding infrastructures has been an intense diversification of experiences and ways of living in the yrmo. Although given their location and relatively small population, the Yshiro communities are very closely knit; they are also very heterogeneous. In the same community, one might find a few people with college degrees, people who are semi-literate, and people who are only fluent in the Yshir au oso language; people whose livelihood depends on wages from state institutions (e.g., municipality, regional government, school system, and so on) or nearby ranches, people who manage family-scale operations of cattle ranching, and people who mostly depend on commercial fishing, supplemented by hunting and gathering for consumption. And there are also Baptists, Pentecostals, Catholics, and *tobich oso* (members of the tobich).[12] The latter often present themselves to outsiders as *cultureros*, or those who follow *la cultura*—meaning that they live by the word of Eshnwherta, which for ease of presentation, I will simply describe as a moral code given to the original yshiro by the mythical *anabsero* beings.

One way of sorting out this heterogeneity in line with my argument is through the positions to which different clusters of families might be assigned within a continuum that stretches between practices that more clearly instantiate infrastructures of emplacement and practices that do the same with infrastructures of displacement. Practices of emplacement are often glossed (for outsiders) as cultura (hence, their practitioners' self-denomination as cultureros) and imply the involvement in all aspects of the tobich oso's lives of powerful other-than-yshiro existents that can be described as animal and place owners called *bahluts*. For various reasons, including the fraught relations that their families historically had with missionaries and other modernizing agents, tobich oso are more likely to be little enthusiastic about sending their children to school, consequently know little Spanish, and tend to rely heavily on the forest and the river for subsistence, which in turn means that they sustain a more intimate relationship with the other-than-yshiro existents that compose the yrmo. On the other end of the spectrum of practices, we can find families who historically managed to sustain closer and less antagonistic relations with missionaries and other modernizing agents. These families have their children attending school more consistently; tend to be fluent in Spanish; are most likely to hold permanent, waged jobs; have little interest in or taste for moving through the forest; tend to live in one of the two Yshiro communities that are near Paraguayan towns; assist regularly at a Christian church; and are likely to reject anything associated with cultura because they consider it "backward superstition" or devilish.

These contrasting sets of practices are often associated with varying understandings of what the term *yrmo* implies, as I already hinted at in the prelude. For tobich oso, yrmo implies what I have described as a unique emplaced collective (i.e., composed of entities and dynamics that are specific to it, incommensurable with those composing other collectives, and irreplaceable). For those who experience the yrmo in this way, sustaining the practices that bring it into being is central to their vision of a good life. In contrast, for Yshiro families whose practices can be located toward the other end of the spectrum from those of the tobich oso, yrmo implies either simply the "bush" (as landscape descriptor) or, when connected with the idea of territory, no more than the land on which the Yshiro communities are (or could be) settled. Their vision of a good life resonates with modernization, as a universal horizon of the common good, and its associated disregard for the specificity and irreplaceability of place. In fact, as we will soon find out, some of these families see their children moving to the capital city in pursuit of professional careers as the epitome of a good life. This is, however, a relatively reduced group, as the practices of most families imply stronger connections to the yrmo. In effect, even for those who conceive it mainly as an area with resources for the sustenance of the present and future generations of Yshiro, the yrmo is also a place in which their personal and family history is inscribed and where they strongly wish their children to stay. Although with varying intensities, their visions and practices of a good life remain oriented to the specificity of the yrmo.

It is important to stress that the opposing extremes in the continuum stand for a very strong correlation of practices within each set that I mentioned, which is rare. In effect, while the correlations are indeed verifiable, they are weaker as we move our focus toward the center, which is where most Yshiro families could be located. Thus, for example, some families whose members are tobich oso do make significant efforts to send their children to school. Likewise, many individuals working permanently in the cattle-ranching industry would not fail to enroll the help and mediation of tobich oso in order to appease bahluts and ensure that a trip through the forest goes well. Tobich oso often rely on the better-off families that, having steady salaries as teachers and state employees, operate as intermediaries, buying from them forest products and handicrafts that are later sold in urban centers. In a similar fashion, some of these families rely on tobich oso to protect their cattle when the animals are roaming far from the settlements. And perceived differences in terms of availability of resources are closely matched by intense pressures and feelings of obligation to share and help extended family and neighbors, regardless of where they may stand on my spectrum. And last, but not least, there is the constant work of commoning done by the collective to hold together as such, and this includes the work of UCINY, whose creation was coterminous with the coming into being of the Yshir Nation in 1999 out of a set of previously not very well articulated Yshiro au oso–speaking groups.[13]

What I want to stress with all this is that when the Yshiro territorial concern was taking shape, the multiplicity of the yrmo (as landscape descriptor, traditional territory, and/or emplaced collective) was holding together as a collective life project, expressed in the form of a common concern that was not exactly the same for everyone. In this life project, practices of emplacement and practices of displacement had found temporary (albeit uneven) balances and stabilizations. In this sense, these divergent practices were (and remain) so thoroughly imbricated with each other that it might seem unwarranted to make a distinction between them. And yet, the distinction is warranted insofar as the divergent orientations of these practices (and the "kinds" of yrmo they sustain) could become active and undo the relative stabilizations of "the common good/concern" achieved by the collective at earlier times. And indeed, this is what happened as the Yshiro territorial concern became entangled with the concerns of other non-Yshiro actors.

Humanitas and Natura: Grounding the Global
Common Good

Seeking to address its territorial concern, UCINY reached out to two networks, each formed by a mix of nongovernmental and governmental organizations, agencies of the United Nations and the Inter-American System, and a host of international cooperation agencies from various countries. Although some institutions—and individuals who compose them—move back and forth between them, I label these networks with the fictitious names of Humanitas and Natura for two reasons. First, it allows me to foreground their main mandates and concerns with human rights and the environment, respectively, and second, it enables me to single out these concerns as interscalar vehicles through which the vision of developmentalist common good, championed by modernization and some of its successors, gets grounded, extended, and done as global. I will explain.

I use the figure of an interscalar vehicle, which I borrow (with some tweaking) from Gabrielle Hetch, to analytically hold in sight the continuities of the "global common good" as it morphs, traveling and being extended through variable topologies.[14] The term *interscalar vehicle* does not refer to a particular kind of thing but to the role different things might play in delineating various scalable dimensions (be they spatial, temporal, moral, political, and/or affective, to name some possibilities). I find this figure useful because it chimes well with the figure of the railway that I used to convey the idea that the universal (effect) of the modern collective gets realized as such by grounding through infrastructures of displacement. I imagine these vehicles as wagons that are themselves (or carry) materials and artifacts adaptable for building and extending in particular terrains the "railway" infrastructure through which they travel. Facing a river, a boat unloaded from (or made with elements of) a wagon becomes the carrying vehicle that both moves other wagons across that particular feature of the terrain and offers a platform for building a bridge (perhaps with components of the wagons), which subsequently will extend displacement and make its control smoother. In other words, interscalar vehicles enable each other to move and create articulations (as well as interruptions) that delineate variable scales and topologies. Continuing with this metaphor, the focus of my subsequent discussion is on how Humanitas and Natura's concerns, even if sometimes at odds with each other, become vehicles for each other, and both for a vision of the common good assumed to be universal, the global common good that can only be extended and get bigger.

The relation of UCINY with Humanitas goes back to the 1990s, when the Yshiro federation was formed, although specific communities and leaders had had connections with this network since the mid-1970s.[15] The focus of Humanitas is the promotion and defense of human rights in all their dimensions. In the last decade, the environment has also come within its purview in the form of concerns with environmental justice and equity. The network had its heyday in the 1990s, when it played a crucial role in the drafting of a new constitution and several laws that enshrined Indigenous rights. Nowadays, it continues defending and expanding those rights. Besides working through the judiciary, the network operates through social mobilization, public campaigning, and political lobbying. Members of the network are not shy about their "political" stance, which could be described as located in a broadly defined left. Indeed, many individuals and institutions have strong connections with left-leaning political parties, peasant unions, and grassroots organizations long engaged in confronting Paraguay's extremely unequal access to land.

The network plays an important role in offering legal and logistical support to UCINY (as well as other Indigenous organizations) to confront a mostly indolent, if not hostile, state in order to defend their legal rights. For members of the network, the way in which UCINY framed the communities' concerns about the processes taking place in the area promised to break new ground in Paraguay. To put it briefly, although the law is not exhaustive on this point, in practice, the Paraguayan state recognizes Indigenous rights just to tracts of land necessary to sustain, by means of agriculture, the livelihood of a certain number of families forming a community; it does not recognize the right of an Indigenous people to a territory. In this sense, and despite it being a signatory to the International Labor Organization's Convention 169 and the UN Declaration on the Rights of Indigenous Peoples, which explicitly recognize Indigenous rights to a territory, Paraguay lags behind regional trends. UCINY's concern about recovering territory appeared to Humanitas as an opportunity to expand on Paraguayan ground, a globally recognized set of human rights that touches upon the unequal land-tenure system.

UCINY's connection with Natura developed more recently, from the first actions that the federation undertook in the mid-2000s to have its concerns about what was going on in the area attended to by the Paraguayan government. Natura gained prominence in the country along with increasing anxieties about, and international funding for, biodiversity loss and climate change. Lacking the resources to address these problems, the Paraguayan government largely depends on international funding and the nonstate agencies within the network to design and execute most environmental initiatives that take place in the area where the Yshiro communities are located.[16] These agencies, in turn, gain the acquiescence of the state and channel international funding, by framing their interventions as "technical" and carefully skirting issues considered "political," particularly Paraguay's position among the top in the world ranking of unequal access to land.[17]

It would be fair to say that Natura perfectly embodies those successor stories of modernization that present fixes to "environmental problems" as the proxy (in negative) of a developmentalist vision of the common good. This is evident in the mission statement of the Paraguayan organizations that compose the network, wherein the environment constitutes a concern insofar as it is a resource needed to fulfill the human right to "sustainable development" and "better quality of life." Not surprisingly, some of the most ambitious interventions promoted by the network involve land use planning, which, as stated in the most recent iteration of one of these processes in the Yshiro area, "must be the result of a consensual and yet ambitious vision of the district's future. The challenge consists in articulating and finding equilibrium between different development goals: at the same time that agricultural production and other economic activities are promoted, a balanced environment must be protected in order to set the basis to improve the quality of life of the population."[18] In other words, these processes profess to articulate the interests or concerns of different stakeholders in pursuit of a developmentalist vision of the common good that is not up for discussion. In order to achieve this, the (at least formal) participation of everyone who has stakes in the resources being considered is required. Thus, when UCINY started to raise concerns about what was happening in the yrmo, Natura saw it as an opportunity to include a very iconic "stakeholder" in its planning process.

As we will see, when UCINY began reaching out to these networks, the equivocal commonality of the Yshiro life project (expressed as a territorial concern) became more complex and less stable. In effect, in addition to the divergences that were articulated under the banner of a common concern for the traditional territory, Humanitas and Natura brought to bear their own visions of the common good (also expressed as concerns, albeit to some extent competing ones) to the making of the territory. For Humanitas, the territorial concern of the Yshiro was a vehicle to realize and expand the legal framework of universal human rights (and through it contest the unequal land tenure system). For Natura, it was a vehicle to realize and expand its version of an environment in balance with development. These vehicles are far from always compatible, a point made patent by the way both networks criticize each other. A couple of examples of these mutual critiques will help paint the general context in which their engagement with UCINY has unfolded.

In a conversation, an acquaintance summarized how many members of Humanitas see Natura's work: "By not pushing the state to address the thefts of these lands from their original owners, they [Natura] naturalize the status quo." This is not always seen as innocent; indeed, she continued: "Look, they use the global warming produced by the North to advance the neoliberal agenda in our country." Pushed to consider the possible relation between deforestation in the Yshiro area and "global warming," she commented: "Climate change has another name: capitalism. This is what needs to be tackled first, right here, in this country, and in each country. In Paraguay you do that by attacking the present land ownership system." When I presented this critique to a member of Natura who fashions himself as "moderate" in the political spectrum, he retorted: "That is the old story of the primitive left to all problems: revolution!! Change the system!! But you know what? Climate change will not wait for its Lenin; the world must deal with it with what it has at hand now, and that is a globalized world of international institutions, national governments, corporations, and communities that, like it or not, dance to the tune of the market economy. Our projects are providing benefits to every stakeholder and actually doing something about climate change." The comments are remarkable because, even though Natura's and Humanitas's visions of the "common good" expressed in their contrasting positions are far from being coherent with each other, the vehicles through which they advance them work in tandem to make an overarching developmentalist vision of the common good to travel and ground itself in multiple sites.

Interscalar Vehicles' Scaling Work

After several unsuccessful attempts to be received by the governmental institution responsible for establishing protected areas and controlling deforestation (the Secretariat of the Environment), in 2007, and advised by Humanitas, the Yshiro leaders sent a letter to its head indicating that according to the International Labour Organization (ILO) Indigenous and Tribal Peoples Convention, to which Paraguay had subscribed, the unilateral establishment of conservation areas violated their human rights.[19] The letter concluded by saying that if they were not received in a meeting, they would denounce the violations to the international donors that funded the secretariat's programs and required their grantees to abide by international legal frameworks and best practices for human rights. A few weeks later, UCINY received an invitation to discuss their concerns with secretariat's officers in the capital city of Asunción.

I was able to accompany the leaders, who explained to their governmental interlocutors that the loss and destruction of territory had left their communities in peril. Confined within relatively small tracts of lands, surrounded by deforested private ranches and forested conservation areas where they could not enter, "our way of life is threatened," the leaders said. They further explained that the majority of the Yshiro depended on "the forest" for their livelihood: "This is our natural supermarket," one of the leaders said, "and now we cannot even go there; our children go hungry, we cannot build our houses!" The officials responded that the scarcity of land the Yshiro communities suffered was a "large problem beyond the purview of the Secretariat" and noted that conservation was "absolutely necessary on the face of environmental problems that affect us all." However, they recognized that not enough had been done to involve the Yshiro in conservation planning and promised to make changes, so that instead of being detrimental, such actions "could be also of benefit for the communities." Concretely, the Yshiro would be involved by Natura in land use planning, with the purpose of "harmonizing their development needs" with conservation plans underway.

Natura initiated its activities with a "participatory workshop" organized in one of the largest Yshiro communities. I was present. The workshop began with the facilitator pinning a large sheet of paper on the board, with the words "Desired Scenarios" written in red, and inviting participants to think how the community could be "satisfied and happy." Given the discussions that had already been taking place in the communities, I was not surprised when people responded with a rather consistent message: with access and free movement within the territory they had always used. The facilitator wrote on the sheet of paper "General Goal = Recovery of Territory" and started another exercise based on the question, "Why is territory important?" At the end of that exercise, the facilitator had listed three reasons ("economic," "cultural," and "environmental"), with several activities exemplifying them. Through subsequent exercises, these labels were used as domains containing "specific problems," and their potential solutions were expressed as goals; the goals, in turn, were further subdivided into smaller objectives to be achieved through specific tasks. In this way, the workshop moved sequentially from establishing a set of "desired scenarios" to drafting a plan with a roadmap of actions (including the distribution of individual or institutional tasks and responsibilities).[20]

At first sight, this process appears to be simply scaling down the general vision of a good life to the size of specific and manageable problems that could be solved to achieve that vision. However, the "scaling operations" at stake were more complex. With each new exercise, the Yshiro territorial concern was reframed and guided in directions that simultaneously would deactivate it as a potential challenge to the vision of a global common good and turn it into something this particular infrastructure of displacement could latch onto to ground itself. To appreciate the point, let's take stock of the whole sequence so far.

The Yshiro concern about what was happening in the yrmo was grasped in all its heterogeneity by the leaders' phrase, "Our way of life is threatened." Advised by Humanitas, the Yshiro made "this concern" to travel into the government in the vehicle of human rights. Once there, the Secretariat officers "loaded" the (now) human rights concern into the vehicle of development, which, in the case of Natura, travels in the vehicle of environmental concerns. (Recall that the problem for Natura is to sustain a developmentalist vision of the common good by fixing its environmental side effects.) The problem here was that, simultaneously problematizing the side effect (deforestation) and its "fix" (conservation areas), the Yshiro territorial concern was recentering this vision of the global common good as "the problem." Furthermore, the solution sought by the Yshiro (recovering access and freedom of movement in an extended area) almost automatically appeared as unworkable in relation to a political economy that, based on expanding agribusiness and concurrent governmental schemes for conservation, sustains in Paraguay the developmentalist version of the common good. As we soon will see, this "political economy" is, from Natura's standpoint, too big (i.e., too entrenched and too costly) to go against when seeking to realize its own environmental fixes.

The successive nesting of interscalar vehicles reframed the Yshiro territorial concern as obstacles the Yshiro faced in fulfilling their human right to development (i.e., the common good). For Natura, the obstacles were their own environmental fixes (conservation areas), which took away resources the Yshiro had so far used for their "development needs" but were nevertheless now essential for the larger common good of environmental conservation. Thus, the solution was to find alternative paths to satisfy the development needs of the Yshiro. "Alternative" meant not requiring access to an extended territory, which was what the "solutions" arrived at in the workshop had to (and did) boil down to. In this regard, it is not surprising that as soon as there was any sign that other definitions of "the problem" (and its solutions) were being brought to the fore by participants in the workshop, the facilitator would attribute to them a scale that turned their discussion in the workshop "unrealistic." For example, when some Yshiro participants started to vent their frustration that the Secretariat was creating protected areas instead of protecting their rights, enshrined in Convention 169, by stopping cattle ranchers from clearcutting the forest the Yshiro have depended on since before the creation of the Paraguayan state, the facilitator pulled the discussion back on track: "Guys, guys, let's keep on topic. Yes, it is true the ranchers keep cutting down trees, but we cannot do anything about this here in this workshop. You have to petition the government and speak with the *diputados* [parliamentary representatives] to modify the laws. In the meantime, we have to be realistic and work with what we have."

The facilitator's call to remain realistic reflects two aspects of the scaling work that can be done with vehicles of the global common good. The first is that scalar comparison can be used to shield the definition of a problem. In this case, the comparison was between the "smallness" of the workshop and the "bigness" of the problem that some Yshiro participants wanted to push into it—that is, the political economy that makes agribusiness and environmental conservation two sides of the same global common good. The difference of scale foregrounded by the facilitator implied that the "small workshop" had to treat the "big problem" as a given and focus on the feasible—that is, alternative development projects. In this way, development was reaffirmed as the only effective ("realistic") vehicle through which the Yshiro territorial concern (transformed into the human right to development) could travel and be realized. However—and here comes the second aspect of the scaling work—a key element for development to appear as the only effective vehicle is that any alternative to it must appear impossible. This is precisely the situation Natura puts in front of its interlocutors (including the Yshiro) when sometimes naively buying into its own pretendedly neutral realism, and sometimes with clear consciousness it counts on the colonial violence that has cemented as a normal state of affairs to confidently advance its "solutions" as a take-it-or-leave-it offer. Let's take a look at this.

Aside from directly occupying lands or disregarding the limits of private properties—both of which, in Paraguay, private owners routinely respond to with state-condoned violence—the only other way that UCINY has for moving Yshiro territorial concerns in the direction of recovering access and freedom of movement in an extended area is through proceedings in the judiciary. With the support of Humanitas, UCINY started these proceedings at almost the same time as it began to work with Natura. However, because they potentially involve expropriations, not only do these judiciary proceedings take decades to gain some traction in the courts, but also, when they do, the implementation of the resolutions is intentionally delayed or diverted by the legislative and executive branches of the government.[21] In the meantime, the combined effects of deforestation and conservation relentlessly eat away at the very conditions of possibility for a livable existence, let alone one that expresses the principles of emplacement! This state of affairs constitutes an infrastructure of colonial violence that, central to the operations of the Reason Police in this setting, is activated simply by the possibility that Natura could walk away and do nothing if the Yshiro refuse to be "realistic."[22] Thus, whether its spokespersons agree with the situation or not, Natura's alternative development solutions seem to be the only "workable" ones, in part, at least, because coloniality makes it thus.

Summing up, then, with the backing of the infrastructural colonial violence that sustains the present state of affairs, the Yshiro territorial concern was confronted with the infernal alternative of becoming part (by traveling in the interscalar vehicle "development") of the global common good or languishing unattended. In this attempt at limiting and containing the excess implicit in the Yshiro territorial concern within the vehicle of development, we see coloniality at work, suppressing and/or containing and controlling expressions of pluriversal multiplicity in a way that simultaneously grounds and extends (i.e., renders global) the modern collective. As we will see next, this had an impact on the balance between practices of displacement and emplacement through which the yrmo had so far held together as a common, yet multiple, concern.

The Unworkable Excess of an Emplaced Collective

Before UCINY took any action, there seemed to be a consensus in the communities that what needed tackling was the recovery of access to, if not control of, the yrmo. Yet, when Natura intervened, the problem was reframed as a matter of "development needs." From the very beginning, this framing began to work as a catalyst that intensified and turned conflictive the divergent versions of the yrmo of which I spoke before. An incident during the workshop is illustrative. As I mentioned, after establishing that the general goal was the recovery of territory, the facilitator moved on to determine why territory was important. Matching a person who could not write with one who could, the facilitator invited participants to write on a card the answer to the question. As the group discussed the cards, the facilitator went on writing labels on a pinned-up sheet of paper. For example, after reading a card that referred to gathering food as an important reason to have territory, the facilitator wrote the label "Economic Reasons" and subsequently added all similar activities under that label. At one point, he began to read the card of a pair formed by a tobich oso elder and a young man: "Cannot sing; *el monte* (the bush) is being destroyed; cannot hunt, no food." The pair was invited to explain. The young man said he could not explain. He had just jotted down a translation of what the elder had said, but he did not understand what he meant very well. The elder, Don Ramon Zeballos Bibi, started to speak, and the young fellow translated into Spanish:

> I am a *konsaho* [shaman]. All those animals that are there are my children. I am their child as well. If I sing, those animals come out [come into being]. If I do not sing, there are no animals. When I was a child, I ate *pitino* [anteater]. I was not supposed to eat it. Prohibited!! But I ate anyway. I was hard-headed. Then I got sick. And that guy came. The *pitin'bahlut* [the young man translated into Spanish, *dueño del oso hormiguero* (the owner of the anteater)]. "You are very hard-headed; you will not withstand my power. You will die now." But I spoke to him. That guy has a daughter, she was fat, beautiful girl. I spoke to that guy to let me marry his daughter. Then I married her.

At this point, one of the leaders interjected in Yshir au oso, not in Spanish: "This is not the place for *monexne* [traditional stories]." Don Ramon gave him a mean look as he continued:

> Then, that pitin'bahlut let me go. Now he is my father-in-law. He gives me his song, to bring about the pitino. If I don't sing, there are no more [anteaters]. Nobody will eat pitino. Nobody will be able to hunt it. Then that bahlut gets mad. There, around *nepurich* [the name of a place where the soil is red] I have to go. But now there is a *patrón* [cattle rancher] that does not allow anyone to pass [through his property]. He is destroying the yrmo [the word was translated into Spanish as *monte* (bush) by the young fellow]. I have nothing for [i.e., materials to make] *peyta* [maracas]. How can I sing? All those animals are not coming out anymore; they no longer have their house, because nobody takes care of the yrmo [again, the young man translated as *monte*].

For a brief moment after the elder finished, the facilitator looked disconcerted, glancing at his Yshiro assistant as if expecting an explanation. But none was forthcoming. After a long pause, he said: "So, what Don Ramon is reminding us is how important the cultural traditions of the Yshiro are, and how this will get lost if the forest is destroyed. So, it is not only the food that gets lost," he said as he underlined the words "Economic Reasons" that had been written before on the pinned-up sheet, "but also the culture," and beside the previous label, he wrote, "Cultural Reasons." He turned around, smiling, and called for the next pair of participants to present their card.

Before offering my reading of what transpired in these interactions, it is worth listening more attentively to what Don Ramon said. He first speaks of a relation with a bahlut that carries with it obligations (to sing) so that pitino come into being and people can eat them. Then he says that he can no longer go to a specific place where he can get the materials to make maracas to play along with his singing because the patrón (cattle rancher) doesn't let him pass by. So, he cannot sing any longer, and the animals are not coming out. And it is precisely because the cattle rancher is interrupting these yrmo-making practices, these infrastructures of emplacement, that he is destroying it. There is no need for an extended argument to signal how the emplaced collective, to which Don Ramon alluded in his reference to the yrmo, was lost in translating this word into *monte* (bush).

The facilitator's translation of Don Ramon's intervention into "Territory is important for cultural reasons" followed a beaten conceptual track: the mention of the animal owner and singing obviously referred to culture, the destruction of yrmo, translated as *monte*, to nature—hence, monte destroyed, culture lost. But the translation also obeyed the workshop's requirement to make the Yshiro territorial concern realistic and manageable, and concerns for an emplaced collective are even less workable than concerns for territory understood as a potential dispute for resources, which Natura recognized as present but ultimately hoped could be addressed by way of "alternative development." Concerns for an emplaced collective offered no easy equivalence to Natura, to the extent that they could not even register. I believe it is the profound unworkability of concerns for an emplaced collective that the facilitator's initial disconcertment reflected.

For different reasons, the unworkability of concerns for an emplaced collective was also reflected in the leader's interruption of Don Ramon. I saw similar reactions in subsequent meetings where "development agents" came into contact with community members. As soon as someone started to make references to the yrmo in ways that for some Yshiro individuals clearly indicated it was something else than "the bush" or the traditional territory (in the sense of a polygon in a map), they would become very impatient. In this case, the leader was particularly rude, but the feeling expressed was shared among those Yshiro for whom stories of modernization as the good life resonate the most. This is how Calixto (pseudonym) expressed the point to me once:

> Many of our people are ignorant; they are backward and do not understand how things work. They don't understand that *now things are different*, that you need to have a job, send your children to school so that they can tomorrow have a good salary. *They do not think of the future, they have no foresight; they only want to eat now.* Those tobich oso of yours are the worst. I know they are your friends and I also like their dance [the main ceremony], but they don't think well. They are not well organized so they can really make a profit from that. Why don't they prepare a project with [Natura] so that they can get money from tourists? Instead, when the NGOs come to do the participation, they don't understand anything and confuse everyone with their stories. At the end, we don't come to any conclusion, and the only thing they get is having the NGO staff buying their handicrafts and paying them to take their pictures while singing. Look at me; I always pay attention to what the NGOs are saying, and this is how I get benefit from them. Look at my house. I have many nice things, TV, motorcycle . . . I bought some cows, and all my children, except the youngest, went to university and are now professionals living in Asunción.[23]

Calixto is part of one of the extended families whose members are largely literate. The majority are Christians, and several are relatively well off, many of them being teachers or, as he is, state employees with steady salaries. Through numerous conversations, Calixto has expressed a "developmentalist" vision of the good life that is well reflected in the passage above. I italicized the temporal references in it because I want to pay them closer attention. When Calixto says that things are different now and that one needs to have foresight, he is indirectly referring to the processes the Yshiro are experiencing, which make increasingly unlikely a mode of existence that makes the yrmo an emplaced collective. In our conversations, Calixto has been ambivalent in his appreciation of these processes, sometimes speaking of them as injustice done against the Yshiro, sometimes as an unavoidable consequence of *el progreso*. In either case, these processes generate anxiety and concerns for the future as well as a constant search for ways to ride them. I surmise that, given the tenuous role practices of emplacement play in their everyday experiences, Calixto and other people like him are more readily convinced that further attaching themselves to the infrastructures of displacement associated with development is the most sensible alternative to the challenges of the present. Thus, when Natura made "development" available as an interscalar vehicle to mobilize Yshiro territorial concerns—a vehicle that was not necessarily present in the early discussions within the communities—the offer resonated very well with the stance and experiences of those peoples. At the same time, this resonance intensified and turned conflictive the divergences that had been previously articulated as a common (if multiple) Yshiro territorial concern.

Conflictive Divergences

For the NGOs that are part of Natura, the logistics involved in conducting activities in "remote" Yshiro communities are quite complex and require an average of four days for travel alone. Thus, their activities are typically rushed over two or three days, which means that time is of the essence when attempting to arrive at some actionable conclusions. In this context, people like Calixto or the leader who interrupted Don Ramon, who could quickly "understand" what "the participation" was about and could profit from it, began to resent the interventions of tobich oso. From their perspective, people like Don Ramon conspired against a "profitable" result by producing "noise" with their stories that "confuse everyone." Of course, as I hinted at before, worries about the confusion that tobich oso could sow in workshops also indexed the colonial violence that could be triggered by the assumed unworkability of the tobich oso's concerns. Natura could make this violence effective by giving up and doing nothing about a situation that affected all the Yshiro, albeit in different ways. However, if at the beginning it might have seemed like a matter of expediency that began to drive a wedge between people like Calixto and people like Don Ramon regarding their territorial concerns, it increasingly became evident that actually, the suitability or not of development as a vehicle to carry all those concerns was doing it.

Several tobich oso, like Don Ramon, had felt quite mobilized by the discussions about what was happening in the yrmo and eagerly participated in the first and subsequent workshops organized by Natura. It is very common that from the perspective of non-Indigenous visitors, a "traditionalist" elder appears to be the epitome of cultural difference. Thus, every time one of these elders intervened, the staff from the NGOs took notes and filmed, following the translations as if they had received ultimate words of wisdom, even if, as was the case with Don Ramon's intervention, they could make little sense of what was being said! That Natura's interlocutors could not understand them was not lost on most tobich oso, and some found engaging in these activities a futile if not potentially negative endeavor. For instance, the late Don Veneto Vera, another respected shaman and a good friend of mine, was very direct when explaining to me why he never took part in these kinds of activities: "These people [the NGOs organizing workshops in the communities] cannot know the yrmo. You tell them about the tobich, but they do not change, and then they fuck up everything. They are different. Their work is different. It's better to stay here in the tobich working with the weterak [initiated youth], and they stay there in the school, working with the teachers on their project."

The commentary is thick with implications that, at the cost of substantial simplification, I can only skim over, starting with the reference to the weterak. These are young males who are initiated into the tobich. Among other things, the initiation involves instructions conveyed through stories not very different from the kind Don Ramon shared in the workshop. It is expected that the initiation and the instruction will produce a transformation of the initiates into yshiro proper. The transformation involves developing a fine-tuned capacity to discern what needs to be done in particular circumstances (*eiwo*), which is itself very important for the sustenance of the yrmo, as the latter's status partly depends on how yshiro conduct themselves.

According to Don Veneto, an illustration that NGO staff could not know the yrmo and then would "fuck it up" was Natura's naming "tobich" the tract of land bought in conjunction with UCINY for a carbon credit project. In 2009,

Natura invited UCINY to join it in a project within the Reducing Emissions from Deforestation and Forest Degradation (REDD) program. The project consisted of purchasing a privately owned tract of land that Natura had already selected in the Yshiro traditional territory. The land's green cover would be kept untouched for twenty years as a carbon sink, thus generating carbon credits that an offshore oil corporation had committed to buy. The involvement of local communities, especially Indigenous peoples, is often a litmus test for these projects to be certified by the REDD program. Hence, Natura foregrounded the participation of UCINY in all project documents, but above all else, it showcased its multicultural credentials by underscoring that the land selected—without consulting the Yshiro in advance, it must be said—was a "sacred site," a "place of cultural encounter." Obliquely referencing the male initiation ritual, it stressed that the "Yshir can use Tobich [the land bought] for traditional uses, for example, cultural ceremonies." However, this naming disregarded that as a locative reference, the term *tobich* designates a secluded site on the outskirts of a settlement, where the tobich oso meet to instruct the younger initiates and to prepare *debylylta* (an annual ritual). It also disregarded that while there is a geographical locale where the original tobich of mythical times was situated, taking as a parameter the daily trajectory of the sun (as it should), the recently bought land was positioned exactly opposite to where the original tobich was and to where any contemporary tobich should be located in relation to settlements! When I mentioned this to a member of Natura, my concern was first brushed off with an attitude of "no big deal," and when I insisted, I was told they had asked some leaders for a name that would have strong cultural significance, and "tobich" was what they got. Be that as it may, Don Veneto's concern was that Natura's project was meddling with the way in which the yrmo is done, which includes being careful with how things (including places) are named.

Don Veneto's response to the carelessness of Natura was to leave them alone to do their "project" with the Yshiro who understood them (to whom he alluded as "the teachers") and keep them from meddling with that which they could not know (i.e., the yrmo). For people like Don Veneto, fitting concerns for the yrmo into the vehicle of development posed an unacceptable risk for the emplaced collective, so they decided to ignore invitations to do it; they kept "playing their own game," one whose exact rules and stakes noninitiates do not know—and, as I have learned, should not know but should nevertheless respect by not meddling with them. In short, they felt not only that the yrmo would not be properly done by getting it entangled in the projects promoted by

Natura but also that the latter could interfere negatively with what needed to be done to sustain the yrmo as an emplaced collective.

In contrast to Don Veneto, for others of my Yshiro friends and acquaintances (including other tobich oso), interference by projects like Natura's is, at least in the present circumstances, unavoidable, and what needs to be done is to deal with them carefully. Thus, Natura's carelessness did not deter other tobich oso from engaging in the activities promoted by the network. Calixto's reference to the staff from NGOs buying handicrafts and paying to take pictures of tobich oso "singing" signals the shape that this engagement acquired as successive workshops and activities followed. In effect, as it became evident that Natura was more interested in their displays of "cultural difference"—especially in the context of the carbon credit project—than in investing time to learn what being careful in the yrmo required, some tobich oso began to request from network members financial contributions for their participation in activities, which increasingly involved groups of male and females "singing" while donning various "ritual" paraphernalia.

I surmise that we have here another instance of latching but in the reverse direction: the yrmo as an emplaced collective latching onto an infrastructure of displacement (i.e., "multiculturalism") through which Natura grounds modernity in the "Yshiro territory." In effect, there was more in the singing than simply obtaining a little payment for a display of ethnic exoticism, as Calixto implied. The singing is just the most public expression of protocols through which tobich oso try to enroll bahluts and other powerful other-than-yshiro into their pursuits. In this case, the tobich oso understood that they were participating in tackling the negative processes underway in the yrmo in the way they knew how. "We all came to help the leaders; we will sing so that they have *fuerza* [potency] to defend the yrmo," Ñeka told me when, in 2011, I expressed my surprise at seeing many tobich oso showing up at a meeting UCINY had with Natura in Asunción. How singing might give fuerza to the leaders is something I am not authorized to explain in detail. However, and as reported by other colleagues working in the Chaco region about similar "ritual" interventions in the interactions between Indigenous organizations and agents of the state, in general, they seek to mobilize powerful existents, which, in turn, act upon the will and dispositions of those participating in the meetings, directing their actions in the ways desired.[24] Of course, the success of these interventions is never guaranteed, as they are dependent on many variables. Yet, as we will see next, it is my impression that the interventions of the tobich oso that I witnessed were at least partially successful.

Reiterating the Yrmo as a "Small Common": A (Fragile)
Controlled Equivocation

As Natura's activities increasingly turned divergent versions of the yrmo conflictive, the leaders began to realize that a very thorough process of community
discussions was needed, not simply to gain an understanding of how people
experienced the processes taking place in the yrmo (as the earlier informal
consultations had done) but mainly to publicly and clearly display and work
with the diverse visions of a good life that informed those experiences and the
responses that community members expected from UCINY. Insofar as the federation had to grapple with the different "kinds of heterogeneities" at play in
each of their communities, obtaining support that would lend stability to a
long-term strategy posed a veritable challenge for UCINY.[25]

The entire process of discussions took more than a year (2010–12), as much
attention was paid to involving a variety of groups selected on the basis of criteria relevant to the specificity of each Yshiro community—such as social age,
self-identification as tobich oso, degree of literacy, reliance on wages versus
direct access to the forest for livelihood, and so on.[26] Diverse expectations that
people had about how UCINY should respond to the processes taking place in
the yrmo began to emerge with clarity in these discussions. For example, some
tobich oso expressed the view that UCINY should try to recover control of and
access to places where important bahluts dwelled and that, being in private
hands, have become increasingly difficult to access or are being destroyed—
recall Don Ramon's intervention previously. This, they argued, was very dangerous for the entire health of the yrmo. Echoing what they felt Natura had
been offering through its interventions, other community members, like
Calixto, wanted UCINY to lobby the state to compensate for the historical loss
of territory in the form of development projects, educational programs, jobs in
the state apparatus, and more favorable (and better enforced) wage scales in agribusiness enterprises. Others wanted UCINY to secure a few more "productive"
tracts of land so that family-based agricultural activities could be expanded—
something not possible with projects such as Natura's carbon credit one, that
precluded those kinds of activities. Some of those concerned with obtaining compensation in the form of development projects or new tracts of land
voiced their opposition to UCINY spending time and resources on an unrealistic and unnecessary strategy of recovering "lands" they deemed "without
value" (that is, the places of mostly "ceremonial" importance). Reflecting their
perception of the unworkability of some concerns, they argued that the government would never respond to these demands but would be more likely to

agree if UCINY demanded "productive lands" and development projects, subsidies, scholarships, and the like. Yet, those who deemed access to these places, and the existents that dwell in them, necessary for a good life could not simply cast aside the practices and obligations that bring into being the yrmo. They refused and felt that it was deeply wrong to assume that any form of compensation to people in the communities could make up for interrupting or severing the relations that constitute the yrmo as an emplaced collective.

The divergences that became evident in these discussions did not come as a surprise to the leaders, for they existed among themselves as well. For this reason, the last stage of defining a strategy for UCINY involved a group of around thirty female and male elders who were tasked with providing the leaders with guidelines on how to respond to the processes that were affecting the yrmo while articulating the heterogeneous visions of a good life that had been made explicit in the process of community discussions. The elders were invited to discuss among themselves first and then, with the help of an Yshir facilitator, generate the guidelines on how UCINY should proceed. It must be pointed out that many of the elders involved had grown up in the 1940s and 1950s, during a time when, although under pressure, infrastructures of emplacement were relatively stronger in the communities. It is thus not surprising that their advice to the leaders reflected the eight-like movement I discussed in the prelude: carefulness about the negative consequences of imposing a supposedly common vision of a good life on everyone was paramount. I was not present in those deliberations, but the Yshir facilitator—my colleague Andres Ozuna Ortiz, a linguist—later explained to me what transpired. I highlight the central points. He said that after several hours of conversations, the elders told him that, in their view, and regardless of its details, any strategy that UCINY could pursue should have as its overarching concern "keeping good relations within the yrmo." They further explained to him that "because nothing stands by itself but all things are related, all things and standpoints should be respected." Finally, they emphasized that actions that deny these relations should not be allowed because they endanger the yrmo.

I must stress that I am paraphrasing a conversation that was already a condensation (and translation) of discussions that mobilized a conceptual universe that is communicated largely by referencing the oral tradition that everyone in the Yshiro community associates with the tobich oso. Andres, who is also a tobich oso, and many of the participating elders were aware that these notions could not be communicated exactly in those terms to the rest of the communities, for they could generate adverse reactions among Yshiro who associate "cultura" with "devilish things" or "backwardness." So, what the elders and Andres did was draft a set of guidelines in a language that could be accepted by everyone while at the same time addressing the central concerns that arise from understanding the yrmo as an emplaced collective. The guidelines stressed that whatever strategy UCINY decided to follow, it should be mindful that "all aspects of community life are interconnected" and therefore should consider the needs of everyone and carefully avoid actions (coming from within or without the communities) that disregard this relationality. What is remarkable about this exercise is that the elders were not as concerned with asserting and imposing a certain version of the yrmo as with generating practices that would enhance the principles that they see sustain the yrmo. For this, they "translated" the principles of emplacement into a language that could instigate the practices they hoped for, even if these practices had different referents as a frame of justification. In other words, they staged a translation as controlled equivocation! And, in effect, following those guidelines, the Yshiro leaders finally agreed that recovering as much of the yrmo as possible could be established by the federation as a "common good"—which does not disregard its grounding in the uncommon, I would add!

The agreement did not come easily, though. I was present at the final deliberation among the leaders and saw that some of those who were strongly invested in demanding "development projects" in compensation for the loss of territory agreed to take a wider approach reluctantly and only after it was pointed out to them that privileging their concerns would likely result in UCINY losing the support of many tobich oso, some of whom, as I mentioned before, had been accompanying the leaders to meetings with external agencies in Asunción. While they are not a majority, the tobich oso have clout in the federation: as I have been signposting throughout, they are who appear at the front of the representations of indigeneity as identity politics when UCINY must garner public support for its demands, including the demands of those Yshiro who call the tobich oso backward! Faced with these arguments, the guidelines from the elders, and (some would say) the intervention of the bahluts mobilized by tobich oso, those leaders were eventually convinced that recovering the yrmo was the strategy UCINY should follow and sustain as a central requirement that Natura should abide by to work with UCINY. While implying a particular allocation of efforts and resources, this strategy did not preclude pursuing, with circumstantial allies within both the Natura and Humanitas networks, the realization of the heterogeneous visions of a good life that existed in the communities. Thus, even if not only by them, the life project for the Yshiro that UCINY is still championing under the equivocal rubric of "recovering the yrmo" ended up being tractioned by and expressing the principles of emplacement that characterize this emplaced collective.[27]

Whether this life project will contribute to intensifying the actualization of these principles through practice, and consequently strengthen the yrmo as an emplaced collective, is an open-ended question. In fact, as I have shown elsewhere, the colonial history of the yrmo as an emplaced collective is littered with events that have at times weakened and at times intensified the practices of emplacement through which it comes into being.[28] In a way one could look at that history as the sporadic foregrounding and backgrounding of the bird in relation to the rabbit in our ubiquitous figuration of equivocal entanglement. For example, there was a time between the late 1950s and the 1980s when, because they had to be hidden from missionaries and other agents of modernization, many of the practices and relations that constitute the yrmo as an emplaced collective diminished in intensity. So, its presence became less conspicuous, less real, or changed its value for many, not least for the predecessors of the Yshiro families who nowadays are the most assiduous "modern practitioners" in the communities. But since the 1980s, some of those practices have intensified (particularly those that involve existents such as the bahluts), making the presence of the emplaced collective yrmo more evident, albeit for some observers and commentators, only as culture. This "foregrounding" of the emplaced collective was hand in hand with the establishment of self-governed communities and the reactivation of the male initiation ceremony, which had not been performed since the 1950s; but it was also connected with a change in the standpoint of many who came into contact with this emplaced collective. As "Indigenous culture" shifted from being something to be eradicated on the way to modernization to something to be tolerated and even encouraged within the multicultural framework of human rights (promoted by Humanitas since the 1970s), some of the yrmo's infrastructures of emplacement were boosted. I draw two important points from this. First, although not necessarily by design, the standpoint of those who encounter emplaced collectives like the yrmo (that is, what they "see" in, and how they respond to, these collectives) does play a role in whether infrastructures of emplacement are strengthened or weakened. Second, the possibility of further strengthening infrastructures of emplacement depends on taking advantage of the gaps produced by the interruptions that interscalar vehicles extending the modern collective sometimes impose on each other. I begin from the last point to then return to the first.

Given the multiplicity of concerns they pick up and carry, the various interscalar vehicles through which the modern collective grounds and extends itself are far from always mutually consistent. Not only are there different versions of the "same" vehicles—for example, human rights to development are not always congruent with human rights to culture—but also they may carry different and mutually antagonistic visions of the "global common good." This less-than-perfect consistency between vehicles contributes to the complex topology through which they have to transit, sometimes with interruptions that open gaps where life projects can become relatively stabilized. For instance, "recovering the yrmo" was successfully (re)staged as a common life project, at least in part, by mobilizing the potency that multiculturalist versions of human rights have contributed to the (equivocal) symbols of ethnicity embodied by tobich oso. In a manner of speaking, the entire process could be seen as human-rights-as-multiculturalism interrupting and containing the capacity of human-rights-as-development to undo a previously (and relatively) stabilized (small) common good. The interruption opened a space to enact the controlled equivocation "recovery-of-the-yrmo" as a common good that might strengthen practices of emplacement. However, the flip side of containing one version of the global common good by mobilizing another version is that infrastructures of displacement continue to further their grip on how the place is made, to the point where it becomes extremely difficult to tease out an emplaced collective from what appears to be simply a local version of the global—one more station along the railway I call the one-world world effect of the modern collective.

Against this background, a life project that hinges on the idea of recovering the yrmo ends up being experienced (including by many Yshiro) as the "Yshiro communities" seeking to recover their "traditional territory" by mobilizing their rights to "cultural difference." What is easy to lose sight of in such experiences is that the categories of (human) "community," "territory," and "culture" designate sets of practices and relations that also (that is, equivocally) participate in the constitution of the yrmo as an emplaced collective. And here we get back to my first point: since the standpoint of those who encounter an emplaced collective like the yrmo plays a role in whether principles of emplacement might intensify or weaken, an effort is required in order not to miss the equivocation at play. This is important not to dispel the equivocation, which is impossible, but in order to refuse the idea that the only response to the interpellation of infrastructures of displacement is through other infrastructures of displacement that entrench the universal effect. Put in other words, keeping an eye on the equivocation is critical to remaining faithful to the pluriverse manifesting through the recalcitrance of emplaced collectives.

Being Faithful to the Pluriverse

The notion of faithfulness to the pluriverse builds on Rancière's depiction of "the political" as being grounded on a distinction between "the police" and "politics":[29]

> Politics is generally seen as the set of procedures whereby the aggregation and consent of collectivities is achieved, the organization of the powers, the distribution of places and roles, and the systems for legitimizing the distribution. I propose to give this system of distribution and legitimization another name. I propose to call it *the police*.... I now propose to reserve the term *politics* for an extremely determined activity antagonistic to policing: whatever breaks with the tangible configuration whereby parties and parts or lack of them are defined by a presupposition that, by definition, has no place in that configuration—that part of those who have no part.... This break is manifest in a series of actions that reconfigure the space where parties, parts, or lack of parts have been defined. Political activity... makes visible what had no business being seen, and makes heard a discourse where once there was only place for noise; it makes understood as discourse what was once only heard as noise.[30]

In this formulation, politics stands for the absent ground of society (i.e., there is no foundational reason for a community to be ordered in one particular way rather than another). The police, in contrast, stands for the always-contingent instantiation of an order—a "partition of the sensible," as Rancière calls it—where constituents, with their roles and their parts, are recognized.[31] Politics and the police are inextricable from each other, for politics proper (in Rancièrian terms) only occur as a disturbance of the order of the police. It is the inability of any given order to escape its own contingency, paired with that order's obstinate attempts at suturing itself against such contingency and the excesses implied by it, that propels the dynamic between politics and the police.[32] This is because any attempt by the police to closure its order will unavoidably generate "wrongs," insofar as there will always be something not accounted for, something that, in exceeding a particular order, indexes an alter-order. This alter-order is always present, albeit only as potentiality haunting the established order or, in Rancière's words, as a presence that dwells in the order of "the virtual."[33]

Within the order of the police, the wrong is not usually perceived as such. Recall that the police is fundamentally an aesthetic order; it is a particular "partition of the sensible" that distinguishes what is visible from what is not, what can be heard as speech from indiscernible noise. Thus, how does the wrong of a given order become visible and audible? Through politics understood as "a matter of performing or playing, in the theatrical sense of the word, the gap between a place where the demos exists and a place where it does not."[34] Or, put in other words, through the act of performatively staging the excess, the potential "other" to the instituted (but contingent) order. A good example, which I borrow from Eric Swyngedouw, is Rosa Parks sitting down on the wrong seat of a bus in the segregated South of the United States, thereby simultaneously staging a potential alternative order and exposing the "wrong" of the instituted one.[35] This staging initiated a political sequence whereby others embraced and intensified this refusal to give up a seat in a bus, transforming it into one of the bloodlines feeding and giving shape to a general demand for civil rights that could not be negotiated within the established social order but rather required (at least to some extent) its remaking.

As with any theatrical play, how a potential public might perceive and respond to a particular staging of excess is uncertain. Refusing to give up a seat in the segregated South could have appeared simply as a disobedient action that was efficiently dealt with by police. If the habitual command of policing forces ("Move on! Nothing to see here!") to onlookers of that event had been successful, Rosa Parks's disobedience would have been a nonevent, would have left no trace in the public transcript.[36] But, in this case, the staging of excess was effective because it gripped a public that prolonged it and expanded it in a political sequence that eventually produced some changes. In fact, that "excessive event" remade what the public transcript was and what goes into it! In other words, the political sequence might be effective if there is a public that, seeing and hearing in the staging of excess the promise of a different order, declares fidelity to it. This fidelity is a bet on the political sequence and its capacity to realize the alternative orders suggested in the staging of excess.

Being faithful to the pluriverse thus signals a disposition to declare fidelity to excessive events manifesting the principles of emplacement that are, precisely, conducive to the pluriversal. It implies a bet on a political sequence that might steer political imagination away from a vantage point predominantly grounded through infrastructures of displacement. This is particularly called for in circumstances where, like the one we discussed about the Yshiro, a common life project is articulated *also* through entanglements with infrastructures of displacement. In such cases, it becomes very difficult to see that responses to the extension of infrastructures of displacement can involve something else than mobilizing other infrastructures of displacement. This stance is sometimes advanced as a normative injunction, sometimes as a sober description of an unfortunate state of affairs.

In its normative version, this stance is often expressed as skepticism toward claims that the life projects of grassroots movements embody alternatives to the dominant "global" (often conceived of as capitalism and/or neoliberalism), particularly when those movements use vehicles of the(se) global(s) to pursue their visions: *These are not truly political movements, they do not truly challenge the global order*, would say the skeptic. Local movements are seen as naively embracing Trojan horses through which the neoliberal global continues to be extended; consequently, the proposal is to actively confront this particular version of the global with another. This is a position echoed by some members of Humanitas who see Indigenous struggles for territory as one more component in the general struggle to substitute the capitalist order with a (singular) noncapitalist one. At best, they might accept the use of certain vehicles of the (neoliberal) global (such as human rights or environmental concerns) as tactical moves within a strategy veering for hegemony.

In its more "descriptive" version, confronting what I describe as infrastructures of displacement with other infrastructures of displacement is seen with a sort of resignation: What else could possibly be done? In effect, without sharing in the skepticism of those who want to replace one global order for another, other commentators and analysts related to Humanitas are very aware of the trappings implied by the use of vehicles of the global, albeit not necessarily in the terms in which I am casting them here. Indeed, they stress the perils of having to present the life projects embodied in many "Indigenous struggles for territory" through vehicles that make them hearable and seeable to modernist logics in general. It is absolutely clear that using those vehicles also further entangles those modes of existence with colonial logics.[37] And yet, despite awareness of the trappings, such moves appear unavoidable, a matter of real politics. As many of my colleagues and acquaintances (in UCINY, Humanitas, and elsewhere) would say, in the present circumstances, these are the vehicles available to carve spaces for the actual (as opposed to the Rancièrian virtual) excess of other modes of existence to which one might be faithful.

In this context, one aspect of being faithful to the pluriverse involves uncommoning by way of affirming and making evident that concerns that submit to other orders, other "common goods," can be traveling within interscalar vehicles of the global—such as human rights, the environment, and so on. As I have just done in this chapter, this often implies the effort of rendering explicit the pragmatism involved in advancing life projects by using the interscalar vehicles through which infrastructures of displacement get extended. This might sound like making evident the tactical dimension of such usage within a larger strategy, but in the case of the life projects of emplaced collectives, it is not exactly the same—precisely because there is no larger strategy! This point is well captured by the concept of *(r)existencia* or (r)existence that has become popular in some circles in Latin America.[38]

The term involves a play of words between *resistencia* (resistance) and *existencia* (existence) to foreground how certain modes of existence *are* against the grain or *are* in spite of modernization projects that are premised on making those modes of existence cease. As we have seen with the Yshiro life projects, (r)existence is often enacted as what may appear to be tactical exploitation of the gaps generated by contradictions and inconsistencies within and between interscalar vehicles through which the modern collective, as an infrastructure of displacement, grounds itself. And yet, there is no larger strategy that would make this *existing-in-spite-of* a tactic. True, as I have pointed out before, many analysts, commentators, and activists do see or want to enroll practices of (r)existencia as tactics within strategies oriented toward alternate versions of the global common good, which are considered the only "properly political" responses. But this is not the case with the (r)existence of emplaced collectives. In this point, and through the contrast it affords, Rancière's formulation of the "properly political" helps highlight the specific "politicity" of life projects.

Rancière seems to depict the space of the political as operating in one plane, where excess is always already part of the police order as its potential alter. If excess expresses a challenge to that order's partition of the sensible it is because it implies that different orders, which remain *virtual*, could be realized. As the case may be, the formulation does not consider that the challenge might come from another partition of the sensible that exceeds the one of reference, not only as a virtual possibility but as an actual occurrence. In other words, this conception of political space cannot envision a situation like the bird/rabbit image and its dynamic of asymmetrical invisibilization. Consequently, a notion of the "properly political" as specific moments in which excess ruptures the order of the police is not well equipped to grapple with situations in which excess travels in vehicles that transform it from noise into speech without ceasing to, in a sense, be noise—as when concerns for an emplaced collective are heard and seen as, but are *not only*, the human rights of an ethnic group that seeks control of a territory (i.e., human and natural resources in a perimeter of land) by mobilizing their cultural difference. In a strictly Rancièrian formulation, this situation would not be properly political, insofar as no challenge to the established order seems to be happening. (And, in fact, such is the reading that some members of Humanitas had of UCINY's involvement with Natura). This, however, misses the "politicity" of life projects, for their intent is not to disrupt the order of the established assemblage of infrastructures of displacement so that another order of infrastructures of displacement (with a similar scalar orientation to the big) can emerge; life projects are simply not oriented that way. And it is precisely in their recalcitrant persistence against the pull of displacement and the big that they are profoundly political!

Recovering the yrmo, as a life project, does not require extending the particular order of the emplaced collective the term designates. The yrmo does not need to remain self-same while the circulation of vital energy that brings it into being travels through different articulations—it can travel perfectly well in different vehicles, as long as these vehicles enable it to keep doing itself as a specific place. Someone might say that when it travels as human rights to culture and thus curtails some forms of development, the yrmo is doing just this. Ultimately, this enables the yrmo to remain different from any other place. So, what is the problem? The problem is that an emplaced collective (r)existing in the gaps left between colonially imposed infrastructures of displacement is not the same as one that exists within an ecology of mutually nurturing infrastructures of emplacement. In other words, being a "small common" that constantly endures its simultaneous uncommoning and (re)commoning into the one-world world is not the same as being one that weaves and reweaves its own coming into being in mutual accommodation and articulation with other divergent, and relatively symmetrical, small commons constituting a pluriverse.

True, smallness is never a guarantee for such symmetrical articulations; these are always uncertain. However, the value of this uncertainty gets foregrounded in contrast with the certainty that these kinds of symmetrical articulations are extremely unlikely when the specificity of diverse modes of existence is subordinated to the colossal effort of sustaining one particular mode of existence that, veering for the big without restraints, makes the small unviable. But then, how is it possible to foster a space for that potentially productive uncertainty? I contend that a general strategy for this emerges by default if one follows the logic in the practices of (r)existencia of life projects *as if they were* tactics: interrupt infrastructures of displacement wherever possible. But, again, one must be mindful that in contrast to strategies that offer an alternative order as a horizon to inform tactics, a strategy that emerges from tactics only offers an opening to the uncertain possibilities of the small. This is not an offer many of us might easily take up, especially when the pull of the big no longer appears in the familiar garments of the story of the good life called modernization, but rather in those of the dangers brought about by the momentous challenges we all face.

Postscript

In May 2022, the most consistently sustained land use planning process in which Natura had involved the Yshiro communities was coming to an end, and a set of regulations derived from it were to be approved by the region's municipal government.[39] Through constant pressure and refusing earlier drafts, UCINY had been able to modify at least the language of the proposed regulations so that its "territorial concern" remained at the forefront. Articles had been drafted that committed the municipal government to provide support for the Yshiro's territorial claim by, for example, prohibiting logging in lands being claimed, setting no logging areas around watercourses, and controlling the use of pollutants in agriculture. The agribusiness lobby, which had remained aloof from most of the process, suddenly came alive and began to enroll some Yshiro families, whose livelihoods depend on the operations of nearby ranches, to front as an "Indigenous opposition" to the regulations. I was visiting the communities at the time and was able to hear from Calixto the argument the agribusiness lobby had used to enroll people like him. The story was that Natura was run by "foreign" interests that wanted to keep for themselves resources that belonged to the "locals," and therefore its land use planning was designed to prevent the Yshiro from using "their forest" and the "entrepreneurs" (such as ranchers) from "working their land" and creating the jobs that the Yshiro needed to "progress."

Considering the strong presence of Brazilian landowners and workers (and media) in the Yshiro area, it is not surprising that this argument replicated a typical line sustained by groups that in Brazil are called *ruralistas* (large landholders and their representatives, but also many rural poor), who have been staunch supporters of former president Jair Bolsonaro. As it is well known, Bolsonaro is a figurehead of what many analysts have called the global emergence of far-right populism and a constant denouncer of "global conspiracies" that seek to take control of "national resources" under the pretext of protecting the environment of the Amazon.[40] However, it is worth highlighting that these kinds of denunciations are not the exclusive turf of the far right; recall how my interlocutor from Humanitas criticized the activities of Natura. The Yshiro often heard these kinds of criticisms (directed against Natura) from several organizations that compose Humanitas. Thus, ironically, left-leaning interlocutors helped prepare the terrain that the right-leaning agribusiness lobby used to enroll some Yshiro in opposing the regulations. By the time UCINY could organize community meetings to inform that its demands were included in the latest draft of the regulations that Natura was going to present to the regional municipality for approval, newspapers friendly to the ruralist lobby publicized that there was "Indigenous opposition" to the regulations. With that, and their reach within governmental structures, in a matter of days the lobby had the central government halting the approval of the regulations.[41]

By July 2022, land use regulations that were relatively favorable to "recovering the yrmo" amid the expansion of agricultural extractivism became stuck "under study" (and have continued thus) in the capital city. In August of the same year, we learned that an environmental impact assessment study for mineral prospecting in the area had been requested to the Paraguayan ministry of the environment by a US-based "lithium and critical minerals" exploration group.[42] Thus, a new wave of (now green) extractivism seems to be on its way, adding one more stroke to paint a scene in the ethnographic terrain where we find several elements that remit to the debates on momentous challenges that concern me. In effect, we have here fixes to climate change, the scramble for resources needed for the much touted technological "transition" to a green economy, emerging right-wing populism, and disputes about the appropriation of "commons" defined at different scales, to mention just the most evident. Nowadays, these are the elements that compose dominant stories about the good common life, which, as I have argued, mostly adopt the shape of negative proxies, the successor stories of modernization. These are the stories with which life projects must increasingly grapple while trying to sustain and develop infrastructures of emplacement. These stories are the grounding infrastructures through which displacement (and its effect, the one-world world) continues its expansion.

Big Stories

In the prelude, I characterized emplaced collectives on their own so that we could have some references to navigate the entangled ethnographic terrain we were to visit in act 1. Here, I reverse the movement and pull from that entangled terrain the thread of successor stories of modernization to characterize on its own a modern collective that, I will argue, is starting to lose some aspects of the relatively familiar shape I sketched in the introduction. Drawing out the traces of this shift from the political imaginations that successor stories express, and raising some questions about its significance for the dynamics between emplacement and displacement, is the aim of this chapter.

To scrutinize the political imaginations expressed in successor stories of modernization, I read North Atlantic discussions about the Anthropocene through Latin American discussions about *lo común* or "the common." There are a few reasons for approaching political imaginations through these discussions, and especially through their mutual resonances and dissonances. For one, the Anthropocene figures prominently among the momentous challenges "the world" faces, and it is a key element in many successor stories of modernization. In effect, just speaking of the Anthropocene (or cognate but contending labels) conjures modernization and its effects. Also, discussions about the Anthropocene explicitly raise the question about the fate of modernization: Is it truly over or can it, or some aspects of it, be saved? For the moment (in mid-2024), a consensus seems to have settled in governmental circles (spanning state and nonstate actors) that a new lease on life for modernization, what I alluded to before with the term *modernization fixed*, is possible. In this context, the most prominent (as distinct from mainly academic) discussions about the Anthropocene have now started to turn around "transitions." Questions about exactly from what and toward what we are (or should be) transitioning, who will be the agent(s) that drive the process, and who will pay its costs are central to these discussions. These questions signal the ongoing and arduous task of defining a common cause or problem that can rally a collective agent that will act (in common) upon it.

Here enter Latin American discussions about lo común or "the common," a concept that is related but more expansive than the English term *the commons* in that it centers on the shared root with terms such as *community, communal*, and, more generally, with the very question of what makes something to be or become *in common*. Latin American discussions on the concept are particularly attractive because having developed amid struggles primarily hinging on the scale (understood as the extension) of the common, they contrast with Anthropocene-related discussions that have tended to focus more on the scope of the common. By this, I mean that they have been more focused on what sorts of things or concerns are considered worthy of being included and/or excluded in commoning—that is, they have focused on the political process of constituting a common (cause, agent, world) and on how the play between inclusion and exclusion is processed. The contrast between discussions of lo común and the Anthropocene helps to foreground the blind spots produced by the primacy of their respective foci, either in terms of scale or scope, and the importance of keeping an eye on their intrinsic connection. Indeed, attending to such a connection allows us to identify both changes and continuities in the modern collective as these get expressed in the political imaginations that pop up in debates about momentous challenges. I will want you to have these changes and continuities present when, in act 2, we continue our exploration of the challenges that a politics oriented to emplacement and the small will have to grapple with in the entangled terrains of practices.

In the first section, I begin by presenting an overview of modernization successor stories expressed through various narratives about what the Anthropocene challenge entails. Taking as a starting point the apparent consensus in governmental circles about the need for "transitions," I move on to discuss diverse reactions to such a view and what political imaginations those reactions reveal. In the second section, I signal that the way in which "transition" initiatives begin to manifest in Latin America is quickly encountering a long-standing and well-grounded tradition of debates that express different figurations of the common with diverse, sometimes mutually competing scales. With that discussion as a lens, I then reread Anthropocene narratives to elicit how concerns for scope and concerns for scale connect within each of them, giving shape to divergent political imaginations. I close by highlighting the importance of noticing how the emergence of cosmopolitics as an alternative to reasonable politics is heralding transformations of the modern collective that we need to keep in sight as we return to the analysis on the ground.

Successor Stories

The various successor stories that have emerged concerning the Anthropocene thesis constitute what Noel Castree has aptly called the "Anthropo(s)cene": a space occupied by the epistemic communities that "are today speaking most audibly for the Earth, present and future."[1] Looked at closely, the stories in the scene are very dispersed, as each of them grapples with the legacies of modernization in slightly different ways. To map out these stories I use two criteria: what kind of challenge they think the Anthropocene poses, and what kind of politics they think is appropriate to meet it.[2] On this basis, I discern a series of narrative clusters composed by successor stories, which, without being identical, more closely resonate among themselves than with others. I call these the *consensus*, the *dissensus*, and the *compositionist narrative clusters*.

THE CONSENSUS NARRATIVE CLUSTER

The problem of biodiversity loss associated with deforestation was the first Anthropocene-related phenomenon that governmental agencies (backed by international organizations) tackled in the Yshiro area, and along came a series of fixes such as national parks, biodiversity conservation areas, and land use planning. Soon after came climate change and one of its solutions—trading carbon credits through Reducing Emissions from Deforestation and Forest Degradation (REDD) projects—and more recently the next manifestation of another solution to the problem: a new wave of extractivism in search of lithium and other critical minerals. What all these initiatives share is that they are on-the-ground, practical expressions of the consensus narrative cluster about the Anthropocene, which, being closely associated with international governmental institutions, is the dominant one in the Anthropo(s)cene. To some extent, this cluster sets the tone for the other two, for the latter are compelled to get across their versions of the Anthropocene problem (and its possible solutions) using this cluster as a foil.

How does this cluster conceive the Anthropocene problem? The website Welcome to the Anthropocene, hosted by, among others, the International Geosphere–Biosphere Programme, the International Human Dimensions Programme, and the Stockholm Resilience Centre, offers a good example. The visitor to the site can follow an Anthropocene timeline that, beginning with the first appearance of the genus *Homo* 2.5 million years ago in "a period characterized by barely recognizable influence from our early ancestors (Homo Habilis) on the environment," illustrates the increasing impact of our species as it culturally evolved from hunting and gathering to agriculture and then to industrialization, always in pursuit of its well-being.[3] The narrative is a familiar one. At each step in this process of cultural evolution, "we" humans increasingly transformed the natural environment without much awareness of or concern for the consequences. With the advent of industrialization and the explicit quest for modernization in the 1950s, this process intensified in speed and magnitude to a point where the consequences have now reached a scale and character that jeopardizes the very survival of the human species; welcome to the Anthropocene![4]

Not surprisingly, at the center of this narrative cluster sits Earth system science, the cradle of the Anthropocene thesis, and a varied set of international institutions and programs, such as the International Panel on Climate Change (IPCC), the United Nations Framework Convention on Climate Change, and the various research and advisory bodies most directly connected to them, whose roles straddle research, advising, advocating, and setting the "global" policy agenda.[5] In general, for the approaches that compose this narrative cluster, above anything else, the Anthropocene has revealed a problem of design in the modernization project: insufficient (albeit potentially ever-perfectible) knowledge about how the Earth's natural systems work and (crucially) a system of governance that is often ill-suited to respond effectively even when solidly based information is available. Thus, for several years, the key activity of this cluster was building a solid knowledge base to make an argument about the "reality" and multidimensional character of the problem while simultaneously grappling with the fact that, even when the information mobilized enjoyed the highest levels of consensus among scientists, it was not eliciting effective responses from the existing system of governance. For example, in 2009, the Earth System Governance Project diagnosed that the (then existing) governance of Earth systems (treaties, agreements, and so on) did "not ensure the sustainable co-evolution of natural and socio-economic systems" and posited that a central challenge ahead was "the question of how integrated systems of governance can support a co-evolution of nature and human societies that leads towards sustainable development."[6]

The statement illustrates how this narrative cluster has conceived the response to the challenge posed by the Anthropocene. The crucial concepts here are "integration" and "sustainable development." The first connects to the idea of undue differentiation into parts of a single system, the Earth. Thus, the integration of scales, actors, policies, and, above all, knowledge of the natural and social systems (through the sciences that study each) has been and continues to be evoked repeatedly in this narrative as a necessary step in the right direction. The second concept remits to a normative orientation informing in which sense the Anthropocene constitutes a problem. When all is said and done, the Anthropocene is a problem because it jeopardizes humanity's well-being understood in developmentalist terms.

Although there are important "pockets of resistance," as we shall see, in the last few years a variety of state, corporate, and international organizations seem to have come around to the idea that a solution to the problem involves pursuing a carbon-neutral global society by the end of the century, as recommended by the IPCC. This is what Bringel and Svampa are calling the "consensus of decarbonization."[7] Quite central to generating this "consensus" have been approaches that paint the Anthropocene not only as a challenge but also as an opportunity to be embraced.[8] The trajectory of discussions that brought into being ideas like a green New Deal in the United States and the green deal in the European Union is instructive in this regard.[9] From being conceived as a potential obstacle to economic growth, climate change slowly became the springboard to relaunching a new era of economic growth and prosperity based on technological innovations that will allow a transition to a green economy. The idea of a "transition" (especially toward "clean energies") that promises to relaunch economic growth has also helped to bring "developing countries" into the "consensus" as it removed (mostly, de jure) a source of concern for them—namely, that the transition would impede their own development. In effect, the promise of investments in projects related to green energy from the Global North has made many (often indebted) governments in the Global South very receptive to new waves of (now "green") extractivism, which, like the one searching for lithium in the Yshiro area, take advantage of the groundwork done by previous waves. In this context, the Reason Police would say that green extractivism is the reasonable solution to the unwanted effects of previous forms of extractivism because the latest one comes equipped with better knowledge and procedures (like environmental and social impact assessments and participatory planning processes) that are avowedly designed to avoid unexpected negative environmental and social consequences, to mitigate the expected ones, and to ensure benefits are better distributed.[10]

In sum, within this narrative cluster, the problem posed by the Anthropocene is that "humanity" cannot continue to pursue the common good promised by modernization as it has been doing—that is, without fully understanding and managing the consequences of its actions. To correct this problem, better knowledge and a better system of governance are needed. And to achieve these requires the participation of "all parts" of the system through their spokespersons. Thus, the natural sciences and the social sciences are called to speak for natural and social systems in front of an assembly formed by a variety of recognized institutional actors (including the various tiers of the international system of governance, corporations, and NGOs) that in aggregate are taken to represent the "humanity" that will respond to the Anthropocene challenge. The challenge is thus defined like this: How can we mobilize the consensus about the problem and its solution that has emerged among these various actors/stakeholders and across scales so that they can act coherently and in concert? International agreements, new green technologies, carbon markets, biodiversity conservation areas, and similar institutional and/or technical fixes are examples of some of the mechanisms that supposedly will instantiate these coherent actions to manage humanity's ultimate commons: planet Earth. The assumption engrained in this way of conceiving the Anthropocene problem and its solution is that the political community (humanity) can be articulated via the consensus enabled by the "facts" about an already-existing common world or reality that are revealed by the natural and social sciences. Thus, the kind of politics the Anthropocene requires are definitely within the space of "reasonable politics" where, under the vigilant eye of the Reason Police, reasonable claims will be allowed into the political process while unreasonable ones will be excluded.

THE DISSENSUS NARRATIVE CLUSTER

I borrow the notion of *dissensus* from critics who have warned that the constant invocation of necessity as the ground for consensus—in the face of economic globalization, terrorist threats, or, in this case, ecological doom—renders political choices superfluous. The critique largely hinges upon a notion of "the political" that, by contrast, makes evident that the dominant forms of conceiving the governance of the Anthropocene (as those expressed by the first narrative cluster) are "postpolitical." Albeit in different forms, the postpolitical critique operationalizes Rancière's distinction between the police and politics, which I discussed in act 1. Recall that, in this author's formulation, politics stands for the lack of transcendental foundation to any particular social order while the police stands for the always contingent instantiation of an order (or "partition of the sensible"). There is always tension between the police and politics, for the latter haunts the former with dissensus—that is, with the possibility that the partition of the sensible could be otherwise. Politics occurs when this tension erupts and cannot be negotiated within an established social order but rather requires its remaking—that is, a repartition of the sensible. The label of postpolitical applied to the dominant modes of contemporary governance signals that dissensus in this strong sense is disavowed, either as inexistent or as irrelevant in the face of urgent matters which must be accepted by all. Now, while the dissensus critique of consensus, or the postpolitical order, emerges from a specifically anticapitalist stance, I find it useful to more generally characterize Anthropocene narratives that, without always being left leaning, see the defense of the order(s), or partition(s) of the sensible, implicit in (and implicitly advanced by) the consensus narrative cluster as "the problem."

The (anticapitalist) postpolitical critique maintains that in presenting the phenomena the term *Anthropocene* refers to as being caused by the activities of the human species, the consensus narrative cluster glosses over the fact that human groups contribute to them, and are affected by them, unequally. More importantly, these inequalities are inherent to the socionatural configuration called *capitalism*, which is itself the cause of those phenomena, and hence the Anthropocene should more properly be called the Capitalocene.[11] In this version of the Anthropocene, the increasing human impact on the Earth system is not a side effect of the "natural (cultural) evolution" of humans but part and parcel of a particular socionatural formation (capitalism) predicated on the uneven appropriation of humanity's commons—which is, in many cases, understood as the sum total of all the processes that make life on Earth possible—and the uneven distribution of the socioenvironmental consequences of this appropriation. Through its parasitic nature, capitalism cannot but continuously erode its own and, more generally, all conditions of existence.[12] The main premise subtending possible "solutions" in this way of conceiving the Anthropocene problem is well voiced by Slavoj Žižek when he says that "one can solve the universal problem (of the survival of the human species) only by first resolving the particular deadlock of the capitalist mode of production."[13] How to resolve this particular deadlock then becomes the key.

For some commentators within this narrative cluster, overcoming the dominant "consensual framing" that depicts the Anthropocene as just requiring a techno-managerial response, like a transition to green energies, is of paramount importance. For example, Swyngedouw points out that "the fetishist invocation of CO_2 as the 'thing' around which our environmental dreams, aspirations as well as policies crystallise [*sic*]" is a perfect example of the Anthropocene turned into a postpolitical issue.[14] The proliferation of CO_2 is treated as an anomalous side effect that can be attributed to a particular "technical" failure in the capitalist system rather than to the normal operations of the system itself, thus what is required is a "fix," the shape of which will emerge from the consensual participation of all recognized stakeholders. In this way, "the ecological problem does not invite a transformation of the existing socio-ecological order but calls on the elites to undertake action such that nothing really has to change, so that life can basically go on as before."[15] Counterproposals, like the Pacto Ecosocial del Sur and postdevelopment (in South America), or degrowth (mostly in Europe), among others, position themselves along these critical lines with respect to the "consensus of decarbonization."

From the point of view of many of these counterproposals, the vital and rather immediate challenge is overcoming the traps that capitalism lays down to smother dissensus and the potential emergence of "real" change—that is, of change that is properly political in the sense that it disrupts the established order. Of course, as reflected in the mutual criticism between members of Humanitas and Natura in Paraguay that you may recall, the question of what might constitute real change and how to achieve it generates heated debates between those who espouse an incremental approach and those who think time has already run out, or between those who put their bets on state action and those who put it in bottom-up popular mobilization or even violent activism, and everything in between.[16]

From these perspectives, then, what makes the dominant consensus narrative cluster appear as sustaining a postpolitical order is, first, the presumption that the current "partition of the sensible"—including the definition of the Anthropocene problem, its recognized spokespersons, and their proposed solutions—accounts for all that matters, and, not less important, that this "partition of the sensible" is presented as having no realistic alternative. Countering this consensual framing is thus crucial in order that "the matter of the environment in general, and climate change in particular [get] displaced onto the terrain of the properly political"—that is, of open dissensus, where the conflict between different visions about the right way to live on Earth, which is inherent to any discussion on transitions, is not brushed under the rug.[17]

As I pointed out, this critique to consensus (or postpolitical) narratives of the Anthropocene came originally from the left; however, more recently we have seen the so called populist right mobilizing similar arguments. But in this case, it is not capitalism, per se, but a "globalist liberal order" and the privileges of its elites that (its critics say) the consensus seeks to preserve. It is true that the most prominent voices of this populist right on the international scene (such as Donald Trump, Jair Bolsonaro, or Marine Le Pen) have often peddled out-right negationist positions with regard to Anthropocene phenomena, claiming that these are hoaxes that "globalist elites" use to justify policies that control "the people" and, if not their very souls, their national or "local" resources (as the Brazilian ranchers in the Yshiro area argued). But this is changing. As environmental crises become more evident, populist right movements have been moving from simply negating the crises to reframing the key in which they must be understood. In effect, analysts who have been paying attention to these movements signal the emergence of voices within them that recognize environmental crises are unfolding but reframe them along their usual concerns with the purity and survival of the nation and the risks that "outsiders" (immigrants, the "unclean," and global elites and their international institutions, like the environmental NGOs that work in South America) imply for it.[18] Populist right politicians start to also pay attention to this. For example, at least as far back as 2014, Le Pen was already saying, "When you are a patriot, you are an environmentalist; when you are a globalist, you cannot be an environmentalist."[19]

One particularly interesting aspect of the populist right's critique of consensus is that, by eschewing an apparent consensus based on expert knowledge, it contributes to the contestation of the authority of the Reason Police. It does so by echoing (from another angle, so to speak) the left's critique of how the components of what I call the Reason Police (i.e., Science, Capital, and State) are variably subservient to each other and to the status quo. Aside from how they label this status quo (globalist-liberal for the populist right and neoliberal for the left), the critiques differ in that the former would rarely directly denounce Capital, while the latter would be less inclined to denounce Science, and both are ambivalent about the State, which appears alternately as a potential tool or enemy for both agendas.

Now, what connects these otherwise strikingly divergent understandings of the Anthropocene problem within the dissensus narrative cluster is questioning the way in which the dominant cluster seems to smuggle the protection of a given order, a status quo, under the pretense of a consensus on what the problem is about and how to tackle it. Across the board, the dissensus narratives claim to reveal the "real problem" underneath the appearance of consensus and then attribute various degrees of self-mystification or bad faith to those who do not accept the urgency of this "real problem." In this way, dissensus narratives put in evidence that far from being a technical matter, how the problem is defined along with its solutions always implies different visions about the right way to live on Earth. This putting in evidence might involve either questioning that there is a problem that calls forth the "solutions" that are being proposed or questioning the adequacy of "solutions" that (on purpose or not) do not tackle the "real problem," but all dissensus narratives see the need to actualize their version of dissensus in the form of a relatively coherent collective subject as a first step that can thwart or alter the plans to defend (or further advance) the established order. To the extent that its criticisms are buttressed by a claim of having access to the "real problem," this cluster also embraces a form of reasonable politics. And yet, at the same time, the cluster also makes evident how the authority of the Reason Police to sort between what can be included and what must be excluded (as unreasonable) in politics begins to falter. The much-touted arrival of a post-truth era is but a superficial symptom of this, which became more manifest when the repression of disobedient "irrationality" during the COVID-19 pandemic targeted an unusual cross section of strange bedfellows ranging from alt-right sympathizers to back-to-the-land lefties.[20]

THE COMPOSITIONIST NARRATIVE CLUSTER

The third narrative cluster would not deny the role that capitalism or globalization play in the planet's predicament but stresses that the premise upon which the "solutions" imagined in the previous narrative cluster sits is fundamentally wrong. Clive Hamilton, for instance, argues that the assumption that the "natural system" will get fixed once capitalism is overcome and the proper "social system" is in place is a non sequitur when the stable natural system that we have known during the Holocene no longer exists.[21] What has replaced the natural system is an unknown whose logic, behavior, and trajectory can be as capricious as that of any willful agent: "In the Anthropocene we begin to see that the earth as a whole is not an entity that takes kindly to being governed."[22] This entails that the human-centered notion of politics that informs the two narrative clusters discussed so far is ill prepared to properly face the Anthropocene challenge, not least because it cannot account for the role of nonhumans as political agents. The compositionist narrative cluster hinges precisely upon this problematic.

In this narrative cluster, the Anthropocene is largely seen as the consequence of what, following Bruno Latour, we may call the "modern constitution" that established a fundamental divide between nature (i.e., the external reality composed of nonhumans) and culture—namely, the human perspectives on that reality.[23] According to this constitution, humans could dispute their perspectives (and that was politics), but nature (the objective reality) was independent and impervious to those disputes. Precisely because of its alleged independence, nature or reality was implicitly assumed to provide the stable grounding and stage for human political community, or at least the limit for its manifold contingent manifestations. Ultimately, whatever a given political dispute could be about, reality would impose itself as a limit. As I pointed out earlier, the assumed exteriority of nature became the engine of the modernization project and is the grounding for reasonable politics. However, the consequences of treating nonhumans under the label of nature as an exteriority independent of the human drama have piled up in the form of environmental imbroglios to the point that the very assumption of exteriority has become untenable. Thus, rather than the paradise promised by modernization, what we have is the Anthropocene.

I would argue that if it were to use the Rancièrian terms discussed previously, this narrative could say that the term *Anthropocene* marks a political event in which the modern partition of the sensible has been called into question, where the part that had no part (i.e., the nonhumans) is intruding into the exclusively human political assembly with its vitality and agency, making evident the "wrong" of its exclusion.[24] Academic buzzwords such as *posthumanism, multispecies, more-than-human assemblages, vital materialism*, and *agential realism*, among others, reflect the conceptual work that this questioning of the modern partition of the sensible prompted.[25] The underlying diagnostic in many of these tropes was well captured by Bennett early on: "Why to advocate for the vitality of matter? Because my hunch is that the image of dead or thoroughly instrumentalized matter feeds human hubris and our earth-destroying fantasies of conquest and consumption. It does so by preventing us from detecting (seeing, hearing, smelling, tasting, feeling) a fuller range of the nonhuman powers circulating around and within human bodies. . . . The figure of an intrinsically inanimate matter may be one of the impediments to the emergence of more ecological and more materially sustainable modes of production and consumption."[26] The diagnosis implies a prescription: if the situation labeled "Anthropocene" is connected to the exclusion of nonhumans—that is, the part that had no part in the prevailing "political order"—then responding to that situation involves making them part of the order. However, it is important to stress here that this prescription goes well beyond the integration of nature and society often invoked in the consensus cluster, for the diagnostic that emerges from these narratives involves a questioning of these very categories and a redistribution of agencies beyond the human. Thus, the problem some call the Anthropocene is conceived by others as the emergence of the threatening face of Gaia. Isabelle Stengers calls this an intrusive event that "questions the tales and refrains of modern history," generating a major incognita: "The answer we, meaning those who belong to this history, may be able to create as we face the consequences of what we have provoked."[27] Understood in this way, the challenge that the Anthropocene poses is to imagine the procedures, the material-semiotic apparatuses, and the affective dispositions needed in order to take into account those agencies. "Composition," or the cognate but slightly differing "composting," are the terms Latour and Donna Haraway, respectively, propose to designate the "efforts to assemble a political body able to claim its part of responsibility for the Earth's changing state."[28]

In contrast to the consensual "reasonable politics" of the first narrative cluster (which pivots around the expectation that the parochial interests and perspectives of human subjects will be superseded by the unhindered flow of "matters of fact" about an already existing world) or the dissenting "reasonable politics" of the second cluster (which pivots around the need to see through postpolitical distractions in order to tackle the "real" problem), composition pivots around the challenge of articulating "matters of concern" that gather together heterogeneous assemblages composed by a variety of (human and nonhuman) agencies.[29] And here we go back to the contrast I highlighted in the introduction between reasonable politics (associated with the two previous narrative clusters) and cosmopolitics (associated with this one), where the former stands for a politics concerned with either potentially compatible or competing perspectives on an already existing factual world while the latter is concerned with "the building of the cosmos in which everyone lives, the progressive composition of the common world."[30]

The compositionist cluster is *somehow* also present in the ethnographic terrain visited in act 1. I qualify its presence because, for the moment, it only appears as the resonance that I marked before when I said that the politics of emplaced collectives (embedded in the "recovery of the yrmo") poses the fundamental political questions of how to live together well, or how to compose a common world, as an experimental one, thus being a cosmopolitics avant la lettre. In this sense, the cosmopolitics of the compositionist cluster also assumes the uncertainty of the results of this experimental question and remains open to it. From the compositionist standpoint, in principle, the only requirement for "something" to legitimately be part of the cosmopolitical task of building the common world is that it be an issue, a matter of concern that gathers a public, an assembly. This traces a distinction in "the scope" of the politics of the three clusters, which is marked by the different ways in which reasonable politics and cosmopolitics constitute what is common—that is, in the way each does commoning.

For the reasonable politics prevailing in the consensus and dissensus narratives about the Anthropocene, exclusion is a requirement of commoning. In effect, exclusion involves filtering the false and the unreal so that we (humans) can come to an agreement and work with or over an already preexisting common reality. For compositionists, in contrast, the emphasis on exclusion is precisely part of the problem, for there is not a single (common) real to which we can arrive by filtering out the erroneous and unreal. The work of commoning is much more complicated, as it requires, at the very least, being careful with exclusions (and associated destructions) that might further provoke Gaia, to use Stengers's evocative image. Thus, compositionist narratives offer a more open and generous, if tentative and uncertain, path for politics understood as the arts of gathering and holding collectives together. However, even within the compositionist cluster this generous opening in the scope of cosmopolitical commoning will vary in relation to whether analysts are more concerned with building a common world with nonhumans or with the exclusions that this commoning will necessarily entail. We will return soon to this, but for now, let's turn our attention to discussions about lo común, which will reveal how concerns for scope connect with concerns for scale.

Lo Común and Its Various Figurations

As the consensus of decarbonization solidifies and new waves of green extractivism are set in motion, long-standing debates on "the commons" have regained public visibility in several countries in South America, particularly in the so-called lithium triangle (Argentina, Bolivia, and Chile).[31] How these *bienes comunes* (commons), coveted by transitions agendas, are going to be managed and appropriated is a question that appears regularly in the news and scholarly analyses.[32] Discussions often reflect a familiar script that pitches self-defined progressive antineoliberal agendas against self-defined antipopulist ones. Both agendas claim to have the best plans to mobilize the national commons in pursuit of the common good and accuse their adversaries of (mis)appropriating them for their own private or spurious benefit. This back and forth often takes place in a terrain where "local communities" must contend with the denial of their (small) commons by both dominant agendas—a denial that the latter justify by invoking the "greater common good." In any case, these debates keep a particular figuration of the commons in the center of mainstream public attention, one that follows a long tradition where, together with its antithesis of enclosure/dispossession, the concept refers mainly to ways in which human communities manage and appropriate "resources." However, just beneath the surface of these relatively narrow debates on the "commons" simmers a more expansive and very sophisticated set of debates about lo común (the common), which have been ongoing in Latin America since the 1990s.[33] These debates on lo común delineate slightly different figurations of the common, which, while not necessarily contradicting each other, do draw scales that are often in tension with each other and have been quite central to discussions of the common in this setting.

The problematization of the commons, understood primarily as a common pool of resources, is a good starting point to discuss these different figurations of the common. The work of Elinor Ostrom and associates, often invoked in the consensus narrative cluster as that which must be cared for, exemplifies this first understanding.[34] Critics assert that this figuration, set alongside the notions of the private and the public, makes the idea of the common simply another form of managing and appropriating resources, thus rendering it amenable to be captured as another governance mechanism to keep capitalism going.[35] This, many argue, runs counter to the radical meaning of the concept, which designates above anything else a form of sociality, "lo comunal" or the communal form, that is "against and beyond capitalism."[36] Along these lines, Linebaugh says that to "speak of the commons as if it were a natural resource is misleading at best and dangerous at worst—the commons is an activity and, if anything, it expresses relationships in society that are inseparable from relations to nature. It might be better to keep the word as a verb, an activity, rather than as a noun, a substantive."[37] Considering this emphasis on practices, rather than speaking of the commons, many commentators prefer to talk of commoning and refer to the common as the emergent "results of social production that are necessary for social interaction and further production . . . *the practices of interaction, care, and cohabitation in a common world.*"[38]

Feminist scholar Silvia Federici explains that "if commoning has any meaning, it must be the production of ourselves as a common subject. This is how one must understand the slogan 'no commons without community.'"[39] Here, common-as-sociality begets another figuration, the communal-common, which is what many would tend to first picture in their minds when the word *community* is invoked—that is, a relatively circumscribed group of people who can somehow be distinguished from other groups. Federici, however, further clarifies that rather than simply referring to "a grouping of people joined by exclusive interests separating them from others," community refers to "a quality of relations, a *principle of cooperation and of responsibility to each other and to the earth, the forests, the seas, the animals.*"[40] In this point, commoning starts to resonate with the view in compositionist narratives—and, I would say, emplaced collectives—of communities/collectives as entanglements of coemerging existents. My own use of the term *commoning* builds on this conceptualization to propose it as a generic term for practices that bring together divergent existents to form a collective.

But the figuration of common-as-sociality precipitates yet another (related) figuration of the common: common-as-life-itself. In effect, building on the feminist insight that, albeit analytically and politically disavowed, domestic labor of care and nurturing is the key site for society's reproduction, the common-as-sociality appears as coterminous with the reproduction of life itself.[41] Following Raquel Gutierrez Aguilar, one could say that in this formulation, the communal is to capitalism and the state what the domestic sphere is to the private and the public spheres—that is, the site of unrecognized but critical labor that sustains the capacity of the two other actors/spaces to produce their forms of value.[42] From this standpoint, the ultimate "value" that the communal form of (more-than-human) sociality produces is life itself. This understanding of the common-as-life-itself grounds a critique that resonates with some narratives of the dissensus cluster that see this "value" (the sum total of the processes that make life possible on Earth) as being parasitized by the market and the state forms of sociality through processes of appropriation geared toward their own self-expansion. Thus, rather than being simply in a relation of antagonist exteriority with capitalism and/or statism, the common (or better, commoning) is conceived with a double valence: (1) as a general and always ongoing activity (an infrastructure) that produces life, the "value" being captured by capital and/or state; and (2) as a set of concrete practices of (re)existence that prefigure a political horizon where this capture will be transcended and the- (aforementioned) "principle of cooperation and responsibility to each other" will unfold unfettered. However, as we will soon see, there are disagreements about both the degrees of autonomy that the communal form retains vis-à-vis capitalism in the contemporary world and whether the state form might, or should, play a role in the realization of the common as a political horizon to be realized.[43]

As advanced, the figurations of the common that emerge from these discussions (i.e., common-as-resources, common-as-sociality, communal-common, and common-as-life-itself) do not negate each other; rather, they operate as tonalities of the concept. However, depending on what tone is stressed, and with what intensity this is done, invocations to the common can draw different scales, sometimes in tension with each other.

Let's begin with the common conceived as a pool of resources. This conception involves the *resourcification* of that which moderns call "nature"—that is, nature is conceived as a series of self-contained "things" to be administered by humans. I argue that there is a strong correlation between the resourcification of the "natural common" and the establishment of the "national" as the proper scale of the "greater common good." In effect, resourcification makes possible the partitioning of the common in ways that render it pliable to be mobilized in scaling operations—that is, in practices that weigh the worth between different common good(s) in terms of greater and minor, acceptable and unacceptable. For example, land conceived as resource and partitioned into hectares of fertile soil to do agriculture might be part of a common managed by a community of peasants for their common good, which is recognized as acceptable by the nation-state. But such a conception of land also makes it possible to single out other resources that are under the soil as being part of the national common and needing to be managed by the nation-state on behalf of the greater common good. And if to achieve that greater good the state must destroy the (minor) common of the peasants, no problem—a replacement to their source of livelihood, in addition to the benefits they will receive from the fulfillment of the greater good, should compensate! Of course, as we have pointed out before, existents and collectives that do not operate on the basis that they are simply composed of humans and resources might refuse to accept that some sort of benefit will offset a change in the web of relations that characterizes their mode of existence. In these cases, we see governments of all ideological stripes mobilizing the kinds of scaling/weighing operations that paint opposition to extractivism (or its fixes) as irrational and unacceptable precisely because they run counter to the greater common good.[44] Obviously, central to the whole operation is denying autonomy to the minoritized commons; from the point of view of the state they cannot but be a (minor) component of the grater national common.

Now, just as resourcification enables national governments to deny the autonomy of and minoritize any common "from below," it also enables them to counter claims that might limit the autonomy of and minoritize the national common from above. This happens when the commons, even though it still involves nature and its human stewards, is conceived not as resources but in ways that are closer to the commons-as-life-itself—for example, as biodiversity, as a planetary life system, and so on. All these things can be claimed as part of a global common. We have seen earlier how right-leaning governments (like Bolsonaro's), and the ruralist lobby in the Yshiro area, denounce claims of concerns for an "environmental" global common as the subterfuge of foreigners who seek to appropriate the national commons. But, as I pointed out, these kinds of arguments are also mobilized by left-leaning governments and commentators. For example, in 2011, Bolivian vice president and prominent leftist intellectual Alvaro Garcia Linera fustigated a coalition of environmentalists and local communities opposed to the construction of a road in a national park in Bolivia in remarkably similar terms: he argued that environmentalists played into the hands of transnational capitalist interests that claimed the Amazon as a hotspot of biodiversity and global commons in order to appropriate it for themselves.[45] Notice that, in the process of denouncing foreign interests, governments also double down on denying autonomy to minoritized (small) commons, which, as in the Yshiro case, might be traveling in interscalar vehicles like "biodiversity conservation" and associated regulations for land use!

This sort of balancing act through which the common-as-resources can be minoritized "downward" and defended "upward" is not necessarily in contradiction to conceptions of the common-as-sociality that begets life itself. For example, Garcia Linera has also argued that actualizing the potentialities of the communal as a horizon of emancipation requires popular movements to gain control of the state to "create expansive communitarian relations that, first at the national, then continental and finally planetary scale, can trigger the wealth of communal forces constrained and drowned by capitalism. After all, the real community will be universal, planetary, or it will not be."[46] In this view, the communal plays the double role of an existing negative form (e.g., practices of survival in resistance to capitalist enclosure) and a potentially positive form (life in its plenitude), but only fully realizable as a universal. Here, the State appears as a crucial instrument in the passage of the negative to the positive form of the communal, and, thus, it is not surprising that grassroots opposition to government's extractivist designs (conceived as a vehicle toward the expansion of the communal) were derided by Garcia Linera as misguided at best and counterrevolutionary at worst. However, critics have pointed out that far from contributing to the realization of the common, these moves by self-proclaimed progressive governments only reconstitute a State form that not only remains subservient to global capitalism but also prolongs the operations of coloniality, repressing and subordinating the diverse forms that the common adopts in the region.[47]

References to the coloniality of the State, which represses and subordinates the diverse shapes of the common, are connected to what I see as a slight variation in the figuration of the communal-common, where the communal not only appears as distinguishable groups (i.e., as communities) but also as irreducibly heterogeneous modes of existence. I draw insights from the research collective led by Raquel Gutiérrez, Mina Navarro, and Lucia Linsalata, to discuss what this variation, which I call *the properly communal common*, entails.[48] The properly communal common overlaps with the other figurations of the common I have discussed but also diverges from them to the extent that the latter are not necessarily inimical to the scaling operations that produce a national or a global common. The properly communal common, in contrast, does postulate a certain scale beyond which speaking of the common would no longer be accurate (I subsequently just use *communal common* to refer to this figuration of the common).

According to Linsalata, the common names a variety of organizational experiences whose propelling associative logics (those that produce common) might be similar but have radically different trajectories:[49] "The common is produced in an autonomous Zapatist community, but also within a network of critical consumers in Italy; common is produced in an Aymara community in the Bolivian highlands, but also in a community garden in New York city."[50] Amid this heterogeneity, the proper scale of the common could not be defined a priori, for each trajectory defines its own appropriate scale. However, retaking works by Ivan Illich and Leopold Kohr, Linsalata argues that the proper scale of the common can be conceived as a matter not of size but of proportion. Proportion refers to the appropriate fit between the scale of a community and its way of producing that which is common to it. For the common to be properly common, it must be produced in "close personal relations." Linsalata clarifies that closeness does not only or always mean physical, but rather that relations must be "personal and not anonymous as capitalist relations are."[51] According to her, close personal relations imply empathy with the other, which enables a disposition to meet and reach agreements. The cultivation of closeness in relations helps a community to self-limit the potential expansion of the spatiotemporal scale of the common because it is within these close relations that the members of the community can participate in the discussion about what can be accepted and what should be excluded from the common: "When a community loses the collective capacity to establish the limits of what should be accepted or excluded from its commoning [i.e., loses its closeness], the production of the common tends to dilute, loses its shape, can be easily coopted, it becomes something else."[52]

Following on the logic of the argument, it seems that the subsumption of the communal common under the (so-called) national or global common could conspire against "close personal relations," and, thus, it would end up turning the former into something other than a true common. This argument goes hand in hand with a defense of the heterogeneity of communal commons and the idea of (re)existence—that is, of small commons persevering in the uniqueness of their constitutive relations against the grain of forces that seek to reconstitute them as minor components of a bigger common. In this sense, the argument to some extent speaks to how the scalar orientation of different figurations of the common might impinge on what they include or exclude (i.e., their scope). Some of this we saw with the tobich oso seeking ways to persevere in their close relations with other-than-yshiro existents, which, like the pitin'bahlut (spirit owner of the "anteater"), contribute to coconstitute the emplaced collective yrmo.[53] This (r)existence went against the grain of attempts to remake these close relationships in ways that would univocally make tobich oso, pitin'bahlut, and their relationship into other existents (i.e., "Indigenous peoples," "natural resources [or biodiversity]," and "cultural beliefs") that would fit into a national or global common—that is, into not a proper common, according to Linsalata.

While, as we have just seen, arguments defending the heterogeneity of communal commons somehow speak to the relationship between scale and scope, they only go so far in this regard. The heterogeneity of commons (in relation to each other and to bigger commons) is largely conceived of in these analyses as arising from human agency. In fact, nonhumans tend to fall largely off the analytical radar; they seem to play no part in this heterogeneity. This is palpable in the use of "close personal relations" when discussing what distinguishes the proper (good) communal-common from the national or global (not-quite) common. Recall that, according to Linsalata, the communal-common ceases to be such and becomes something else—the national or global (not-really) common—when a community loses the capacity to define what is accepted and what is excluded from its commoning. The limit beyond which this capacity is lost is marked by the presence or not of close personal relations, which are defined via the opposition between anonymity and empathy. However, anonymity neither is the opposite nor prevents empathy. Anderson's classic argument about the role of the printing press in the formation of "imagined communities" is a reminder that, mediating the intervention of certain nonhumans, one might develop profound empathy for, and be moved to action by, a variety of big and rather indistinct entities such as the nation and, more recently, species at risk of extinction, women struggling against patriarchalism, racialized communities, and so on.[54] So, if the opposition between anonymity and empathy is not good enough to define closeness, and despite protestations on the contrary, we are left with physical proximity as the basic criterion to do it. The problem is that lurking behind this is the figure of the human in its imagined "natural" state, without nonhuman mediators—that is, things/infrastructures (ranging from cell phones to political parties, but also from lovable endangered animals to gods, and all the way to visions of a good life) that make the various actual versions of the human and their variably scaled commons possible. It is not surprising, then, that stories about the defense of the communal commons often convey the image of small communities of humans, with their own cultures, negotiating and struggling with each other and with bigger communities of humans (personified by the state, corporations, or whatever) over their respective jurisdictions over a living space (i.e., a territory) and its scale. In these discussions, we do not usually get a sense of how certain nonhumans might push against and redraw human-defined scales and with what consequences.[55] In other words, an important aspect of the connection between scope and scale still remains little attended.

Scoping and Scaling: Commoning Anthropocene Narratives

With the elements we have drawn from Anthropocene narratives and discussions on lo común, let's now see how scope and scale play in tandem within the figurations of the common implicitly advanced by modernization's successor stories.

For the consensus narrative, the dominant figuration of the common seems to be that of a planet-sized pool of resources, plus its (better- or worse-informed) human managers who face the challenge of building efficient institutions to manage it sustainably. What I have called the *issue of scope* (i.e., what kinds of things or concerns are to be taken into account in the constitution of the common and how) is actually a nonissue, because in general we are dealing with one and the same "thing" everywhere (i.e., a version of the one-world world), even if in particular this thing may be broken down into components of different sizes. This means that matters of scale are conceived also as relatively uncontroversial. In effect, although Earth systems science complicates easy definitions of global and/or local "things," when it comes to governance, the tendency in practice is to operate with the conventional scalar imagination of nested units according to which, in general terms, large-scale domains encompass smaller ones, and in the spatial terms of (conventional) geopolitics, the global encompasses the national, which encompasses the local. Such a view normatively addresses the potential conflict between scales with versions of the subsidiarity principle. This is the idea that decisions should be delegated to the smallest jurisdictional unit (whether this is a group of nation-states, private owners, a community of users/managers, a municipality, or a mix of these) able to handle them for the benefit of the global common unless doing so might generate conflict between "units"; in such cases, decision-making should be "passed up" to a higher-level administrative unit.[56]

The status of the common in the dissensus narratives, in turn, seems ambivalent. Conceived as coterminous with reality, a natural order, or life itself, the common appears as already there, a given that is unproblematic except for the fact that a global capitalist or liberal system is increasingly putting its very existence (or its naturalness) into question. In this guise, there would seem to be no fundamental differences from the consensus narratives when it comes to issues of scope; in effect, even if presented simply as the fundamental principle subtending its existence, we are still dealing with a version of the one-world world. However, once issues of scale enter the discussion, it becomes evident that things are a bit more complicated. To begin with, since the "dissenting" diagnoses of momentous challenges point to "the global system" as the problem, the common is not simply figured as reality, a natural order, or life itself but rather as a set of repressed and/or vampirized forms of life (whose proper scale, depending on the commentator, should be the national, the communal, or even the familial).[57] For some analysts this implies that life itself—or, in a more right-leaning version, the natural order of things—can be fully realized only if the global (capitalist or liberal) system ceases in its capture. In this line of thought, and to the extent that it can be used as an instrument, the nation-state can act as a buffer, protecting the national or communal commons from attempts to encapsulate them into larger entities; perhaps it can even rearticulate them to bring about the full realization of the proper subtending common on a planetary scale. Not all analysts and commentators who would otherwise agree with the general drift of dissensus narratives concur with the all-too-common privileging of the nation-state as the proper scale of the common, not even as a halfway step toward full realization. For some of these analysts and commentators, often associated with stories about the defense of the communal common, this is because when it comes to actualizing a common, rather than life itself or a natural order, what is at stake always and foremost are very heterogeneous modes of existence. This has some points of resonance with the compositionist notion that the common world does not already exist and rather must be composed out of radical heterogeneity. This resonance, however, comes with some dissonances that are rather illuminating about how compositionists figure the relation between the scope and the scale of a common.

As we have seen, in arguments about their defense, the heterogeneity of communal commons hinges on human agency and nonhumans tend to disappear, thus somehow sidelining an important connection between scale and scope. In contrast, the conception of heterogeneity in compositionist narratives always includes the agency of nonhumans. And yet, the relation between scope and scale also receives little consideration. Indeed, while paying close attention to the role that the agency of nonhumans plays (or should play) in the composition of the common, compositionist narratives are not as attentive to how the scale of those nonhumans might impinge on the way commoning is done (scope). To fully discuss this, I must return to the slight divergence I mentioned before between versions of compositionism that are more preoccupied with composing the common world with nonhumans and those that are more preoccupied with exclusions of all kinds.

As we have seen, compositionists in general challenge reasonable politics by removing the presupposition that the common (world) is always already there. With nature gone, compositionists tell us, the proper political work of composing the common world can truly start. Here, the term *composition* replaces terms such as *delegating representation, persuasion/coercion,* and *obedience,* which, borrowed from Latour, I used before to describe how (human) group formation is achieved. Likewise, the terms *matters of concern* and *matters of fact* come to displace the humanist and transcendentalist undertones of "the several" and "the one," respectively, to describe the contrasting moments through which cosmopolitics will circle between the chaosmic sea of the pluriverse and the possible common world to be composed (see figure 5).

Notice that the pluriverse here figures in a slightly different manner than in the cosmopolitics of emplaced collectives that we saw in the prelude, where it needs to be cultivated. In his compositionist manifesto, Latour points out that, as the modernist conceit of a transcendent Nature lies in ruins, the *pluriverse that was there all the time* becomes visible (for moderns) and constitutes the ground from which compositionism has to start.[58] The term *composition* "underlines that things have to be put together (Latin *componere*) while retaining their heterogeneity," and, thus, compositionism takes up from universalism "the task of building a common world; from relativism, the certainty that this common world has to be *built from utterly heterogeneous parts that will never make a whole, but at best a fragile, revisable, and diverse composite material.*"[59]

As we can see, the image we obtain as the horizon sought by Latour's compositionism is a "designed" fragile and revisable common world.[60] Latour has been rather explicit that his is a project of recalling modernity (in a similar way as a company recalls a faulty product to redesign it).[61] This explicitness makes remarkably visible that the challenge of cosmopolitics for his version of compositionism remains, as it is the case for reasonable politics, located on "commoning": the movement from the several to the one—or, better in Latour's case, from matters of concern to matters of fact, from the pluriverse to the common world. The crucial challenge is figuring out what devices and procedures are required to turn the pluriverse into a proper common world. In other words, while the pluriverse (that sea of multiplicity constantly spouting out matters of concern) might become visible (again), it still appears

Political Circle Turns into Cosmopolitical Circle

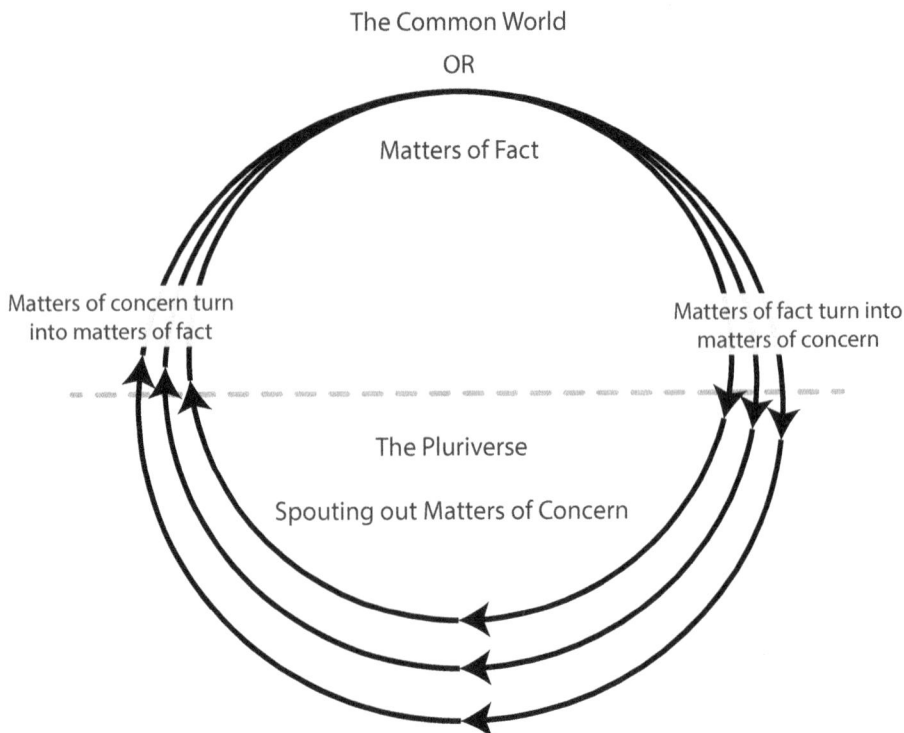

The Common World

OR

Matters of Fact

Matters of concern turn
into matters of fact

Matters of fact turn into
matters of concern

The Pluriverse

Spouting out Matters of Concern

FIGURE 5. The cosmopolitical circle. The "materials" with which the common world (a cosmos) should be composed are gathered from the cosmos of the pluriverse. The One remains the horizon. Drawing by Steve Chapman.

as the issue that needs to be somehow handled; it remains a problem. Why this should have been the case in the first place is never directly addressed; rather, the rationale tends to rest on the crises that modernization has produced. To rehash succinctly the Latourian story line about the point: assuming a transcendent Nature as the already established common ground, moderns ignored the pluriverse that was the actual ground of existence and aimed to bring into their imagined common world (i.e., modernize) all the collectives they encountered—kicking and screaming, if need be. The result has been a catastrophe of planetary proportions, the Anthropocene.

For many compositionists the damage modernization has caused is already so big and the forces that sustain it so large that they cannot but share Latour's conviction that "smallness is not an option" for its inventors—or, I will add, its inheritors.[62] In effect, the urgent task of addressing the crises produced by modernization demands that a "good" (i.e., crafted through due process) big story like "the common world" be composed, by all collectives: "To be on planet Earth at the time of the Anthropocene is not the same thing as being 'in nature' at the time of its modernization. Cosmopolitics is now the common situation for all collectives. There is no common world, and yet it has to be composed, nonetheless."[63]

Without necessarily buying wholesale the Latourian vision of a "common world," compositionists across the board would agree that modernist practices turn the pluriverse, or Gaia, as many are calling this "partially cohering systemic whole," from being hospitable for an enormous variety of existents into a badly messed-up jumble unlivable for most of them.[64] Crucial to the making of this unlivable jumble is precisely modernity's ignorance and/or denial of the pluriverse, which nevertheless keeps reasserting itself as that which exceeds (but also is rejected and excluded by) attempts at collecting it (or rounding it up, to follow with the image of the circle) into a One, be this a one-world world, the whole, the global, or what have you.

Versions of compositionist narratives that lean toward Haraway's image of a more haphazardly piled planetary compost, rather than Latour's "designed" common world, tend to pay more attention to those excesses, to what might be excluded in processes of commoning. And it is from such a standpoint that sympathetic commentators, like María Puig de la Bellacasa, have highlighted the exclusionary (and colonial) potential of a cosmopolitics that, too eager to compose the common world, might conclude too quickly that the concerns composing "a problem" (momentous challenges, for example) are readily visible.[65] I contend that this potential intensifies when a veiled humanism mentioned in the prelude seeps back into cosmopolitics. This veiled humanism appears when concerns about the agency of nonhumans are expressed in terms of, How can we humans take into account nonhumans on their own terms? And the answer is: by listening to their assumed spokesperson—namely, the natural sciences. This might be implicit in the constant return to those sciences to chart how nonhuman agency manifests in political dramas or explicit in calls to recognize that these sciences provide a way to access the world in "our" absence.[66]

Aside from missing the STS lesson that it is always an assemblage who speaks, the privilege that some compositionists grant to the natural sciences as spokespersons for nonhumans has a further potentially problematic consequence. While opening themselves to the question of living together with nonhumans, these compositionist versions do not pay enough attention to the consistent tendency that the nonhumans of natural sciences show to veer toward the largest possible scale (i.e., universal) and the little space they leave for existents (such as spirit masters, ancestors, or even simply densely storied landscapes, lives, or relations) whose very being cannot be verified by those sciences. Attention to these issues should raise the question to any project of composing *a* common world of how radically heterogeneous commons, each containing variably scaled entities, might relate with each other and with what consequences. For example, how practices associated with an "emplaced" existent like the pitin'bahlut might relate to those associated with the (perhaps slightly less emplaced) *yurumi* of Guarani-speaking Paraguayan peasants, and both to those associated with the (rather universal) *Myrmecophaga tridactyla* of wildlife biologists. I worry when this question is not present in these projects, and especially when the empty space of this unaddressed question is filled with the urgency of composing a common world and the presumed "big" scale of the "Anthropocene problem" (and its possible "solutions"), because I believe that in these moments practices that constitute the one-world world are lurking nearby.

Cosmopolitics, Commoning, and the (Postnatural) Big

As we have seen in act 1, for a collective to sustain an orientation toward emplacement and the small nowadays implies the arduous task of (r)existence, which must be undertaken against the grain of modernization stories whose material expressions on the ground involve a constant attempt to include small commons into increasingly bigger commons that have the one-world world as the final horizon. In this interlude, I have tried to underscore some shifts that follow from the emergence of modernization's successor stories. Of the latter, the predominant ones would be largely (but not exclusively) versions of what I have called *modernization fixed*—that is, stories that, as we have seen with the consensus and dissensus narratives, acknowledge the momentous challenges while operating within the same (modernist) logic of reasonable politics in attempting to respond to them. Thus, commoning, as the key political gesture of these stories, reiterates the circular movement of politics that I discussed in the prelude, a movement that through a mix of coercion and persuasion attempts to gather the Several (humans) into what is supposedly the only (transcendental) common—be this conceived as a (natural) planet, reality, or the natural order of things—and excludes anything that does not fit into it. True, the Reason Police's loss of authority to determine what is included or excluded in the political process is not a minor occurrence, for it creates the possibility of unlikely synergies between "unreasonable claims" that are otherwise radically heterogeneous from each other (a point to which I will return in the postlude). However, the usual orientation of reasonable politics toward displacement, expansion, and the big remains there. The important question is, How does the cosmopolitics that emerges within the compositionist cluster fare in this regard?

In the previous section, I argued that versions of compositionist narratives that are more concerned with commoning the common world with non-humans are likewise oriented to the big—although in this case the big (the common world) needs to be composed and will always remain provisional and revisable, and thus relatively open and generous. My impression is that the closer advocates of the common world remain to Latour's original com-positionist proposal (and especially its material semiotics' underpinnings), the harder it is to easily fall into rushed exclusionary and colonial gestures sympa-thetic commentators have warned about. However, here is where my character-ization of the Anthropo(s)cene as a set of narrative clusters is key, for neither compositionist nor consensus and dissensus narratives remain impervious to each other; in most cases, they actually mix and modify each other. In this re-spect, it is versions of compositionist narratives variously mixed with dissensus and consensus narratives that have gained more traction among a wider public straddling academia, policy advising, and journalism. This, I would argue, is an index of important changes that the modern collective is undergoing.

Regardless of the clusters I have delineated, in general, narratives of the Anthropocene foreground, in one way or another, the entanglements of that which modernity held separate—nature and culture—giving way to the per-vasive notion that "we" live in a postnatural world. In this context, postnatu-ral figures, versions of naturecultures, proliferate. The treatment of "things" as "more-than-human" or as "multispecies" assemblages within various posthu-manist strands of scholarship and beyond is one of the most ubiquitous forms in which these figures appear in contemporary analyses and discussions. It is within this milieu that the versions of compositionist narratives more con-cerned with composing the common world with nonhumans end up relying primarily on the natural sciences to bring them into politics. Allegedly, in this way, we move closer to a postnatural form of accounting that includes all the relevant agencies (i.e., human and nonhumans), and the assembly can now get on with the cosmopolitical work of composing the common world.

In these cases, rather than implying the generous opening one might associ-ate with cosmopolitics, the bringing of nonhumans into politics signals a shift in the existents/infrastructures through which the modern collective grounds itself, but not necessarily in the way it does so. In other words, a shift from the nature/culture divide to a seamless human/nonhuman assemblage may index changes in the collective but not in its orientation toward displacement and the big. It might even be the case that the collective is ceasing to be strictly modern but perseveres in its reliance on infrastructures of displacement and their coloniality. This is why delinking the notion of coloniality from the specific form that it adopts as modernity is becoming a necessary move; it helps to attune analytical sensibilities to how coloniality might find expression in political imaginations that, qua grounding infrastructures, complement an emergent postnatural order of power. Such order might implicitly or explicitly disregard the significance of existents that refuse to fit in an emerging understanding of the one-world world as a big postnatural human/nonhuman assemblage. An eventuality that, as I indicated previously, has been considered to some extent by compositionists more concerned with exclusions. Puig de la Bellacasa's call for the staging of "matters of care" is an example of a potential remedy to such quick exclusions.[67]

Riffing off the Latourian "matters of concern" but attending more closely to Stengers's call to not lose sight of those with no power to represent themselves or—apposite to our interest in (r)existing small commons—who do not want to take part in the composition of the common world, Puig de la Bellacasa's "matters of care" offer a way of tempering the exclusionary potential of a cosmopolitics oriented to such a pursuit.[68] The notion of matters of care underlines that in deeply stratified worlds, "erased concerns do not just become visible by following the articulate and assembled concerns composing a thing, nor does generating care happen by counting the participants present in an issue"; rather, making visible certain concerns, and generating care for them, requires the active work of critics.[69] Seeking to foster new attachments and care for heretofore absent participants and concerns, matters of care index a disposition to actively remain open-ended in order to avoid and counter hasty exclusions of that which might be considered less important and/or sacrificeable in the process of commoning a common world. After all, it is precisely the careless exclusion of heterogeneous reals that, according to many compositionists, has messed up the planet!

Those intensely preoccupied with these exclusions may thus be more attracted to Haraway's suggestion that the stories that are needed should be less self-assuredly expansive and, like her Chthulucene, aspire to be "just *big enough* to gather up the complexities and keep the edges open and greedy for surprising new and old connections."[70] These versions of compositionism are less eager about the need to compose a big story like the common world and more concerned with making sure that the very conditions of possibility for flourishing on Earth are not bulldozed in its pursuit. As a way of preventing the problems that may come with having the (big) common world as the horizon, big enough stories might be a helpful tool for a cosmopolitics oriented toward emplacement and the small, but only insofar as the plainly big does not trickle back into those stories through the demands of postnatural figures of the big! Let's now see how such thing might happen on the ground.

ACT II

Being Careful with Atiku, Killing Caribou
(The Science Question in Cosmopolitics)

If man, by dint of his knowledge and inventive genius, has subdued the forces of nature, the latter avenge themselves upon him by subjecting him, in so far as he employs them, to a veritable despotism independent of all social organisation. Wanting to abolish authority in large-scale industry is tantamount to wanting to abolish industry itself, to destroy the power loom in order to return to the spinning wheel.—FRIEDRICH ENGELS, *On Authority*, 1872

The big is a demanding god. Its gifts come with strings that attach, compellingly. That much was clear to Friedrich Engels when he derided those he called "anti-authoritarians" for seeking the abolition of authority, being as it was an unavoidable prerequisite in the organization of large-scale industry. Suitably, the railway was one of the examples Engels used to make his point: if you want a working railway, he argued, you need "a dominant will that settles all subordinate questions."[1] Although Engels was referring most immediately to humans (a manager or a committee) when speaking of a dominant will, he was also pointing to the very capacity (and requirement) of the railway to subordinate any other consideration to its own purpose, to its intention. And that capacity/requirement was directly proportional to its scale! Indeed, if for Engels the scale of the industry was equivalent to the degree of nature's subjection to the genius of "man," that subjection could only be sustained by the reciprocal—and "scaled up"—subjection of "man" to this (henceforth) anthropogenic nature. The bigger the industry, the stronger the subjection. In making the point, however, Engels is clear: subjection to the demands of an increasingly anthropogenic nature was the rightful price humanity had to pay to progress from the primitive spinning wheel to the power loom.

Engels's evocation of a vengeful and despotic anthropogenic nature strikes an eerily resonant note with the various Anthropocene narratives discussed in the interlude, although accepting the inextricable entanglement of Anthropos and Geos might appear in the latter not as the price of progress but as the only basis on which life itself can now persevere. As we saw before, these narratives underwrite the pervasive notion that we live in a postnatural order, where postnatural figures proliferate in scholarly tropes of "more-than-human" or "multispecies" assemblages. But aside from scholarly tropes, postnatural figures also manifest in situations that spark the formation of hybrid forums—that is, the actual and ongoing experimentations with what Bruno Latour called "Parliaments of Things."[2]

Hybrid forums are relatively formalized instances where an assembly comes together to dispute and discuss options involving a matter of concern (a thing) and where the spokespersons claiming to represent components of that assemblage include, in addition to nonhumans, experts, politicians, technicians, and interested laypersons. More attuned to the multiplicities and uncertainties of the post-natural world of the Anthropocene, these forums are said to offer a response "based on collective experimentation and learning" to momentous challenges.[3] Thus, whether formalized or not, these forums have been touted as prefiguring more open and democratic forms of socionatural organization than the ones associated with the technocratic "dominant will" that transpires through reasonable politics. Here, I want to probe this promise, informed by the insight Engels offers—namely, that the big (the always extending infrastructures of displacement) exercises its "despotism independent of all social organization." At the center of this probe hangs the question of whether and under what conditions science (with a capital *S* or not) might be enrolled in enacting a cosmopolitics for emplacement. I would argue that the question is particularly pertinent amid the emergence of a postnatural formation of power in which the coloniality associated with infrastructures of displacement might find even more compelling justifications for its operations.

To conduct my probe, I will revisit (and expand on) ethnographic materials I have worked with before.[4] These involve an equivocation similar to previously discussed ones, which I illustrated by reference to the bird/rabbit image. In this case, the "site" of the equivocation is atiku/caribou. To progress quickly, let us for the moment say that *atiku is* for the Innu of Nitassinan *where caribou is* for Euro-Canadians of Labrador. Atiku and innu coconstitute, along with other existents, the emplaced collective nitassinan (or nutshimit).[5] As a collective, nitassinan is entangled with, but exceeds the continental portion of, the Canadian province of Newfoundland and Labrador. Invited by a group of Innu elders and hunters I met while I was interviewed for a position at Memorial University, I have been intermittently dwelling in this site of equivocation since 2009.[6] Coming from the communities of Sheshatshiu and Natuashish, this group of Innu was concerned about the declining numbers of atiku that could be found in the area. In addition, they also worried about how governmental wildlife management agencies, who had expressed concern about the decline, might respond to it. As with other equivocal situations I have discussed previously, the matter of concern at play here seemed to be the same for all involved, but it was not.

I begin with an inquiry into what is "caribou," the thing at the center of the governmental concern, as this will also provide some pointers to understand why its grounding in nitassinan compounds the concern that the Innu elders and hunters with whom I have worked have about atiku. I will then move on to discuss how atiku and the practices or infrastructures of emplacement from which it emerges have persevered against the grain of the imposed infrastructures of displacement that come along with caribou. In the following section, I argue that in persevering against the grain, atiku became invisible as a divergent multiplicity until a conflict made it evident again. This conflict helps me to center the question of what role science might play in cosmopolitics, which I address in the subsequent section. I conclude by revisiting the strategy that I saw emerging from the Yshiro life project of recovering the yrmo—that is, interrupting infrastructures of displacement whenever possible. I argue that the strategy needs to be accompanied by an offer of viable alternatives that will enable those of us who feel interpellated by the demands of different figures of the big to convert away from them.

Caribou, from Game Animal to Post-Natural Figure

What is caribou? This question opens a 2008 landmark publication, *Caribou and the North: A Shared Future*, that sought to bring into the public eye the need for urgent actions to ensure the survival of caribou from Alaska to Labrador.[7] The authors explain that answering this is not as straightforward as it may seem, for even if all caribou (and reindeer) are one species (i.e., *Rangifer tarandus*), there are many "types" of it. Starting with this question thus underscores a crucial challenge that has accompanied the production of scientific knowledge on caribou since its inception: how to properly classify a remarkable variety of different forms of the same animal.[8] Why is this classification important? Because "a good classification system . . . captures the full diversity of the wildlife species being classified, *at a scale that is meaningful for both conservation and management purposes.*"[9] I surmise that the quote unwittingly underlines how caribou obtains within a set of concerns that are intimately connected with the processes and infrastructures through which a changing modern collective continuously grounds itself in places.

To substantiate my point, I propose to briefly explore "caribou" as a "thing," an assemblage whose genealogy can be fruitfully traced back to at least the eighteenth century and the emergence of what Mary Louise Pratt has described as a shift in Europe's "planetary consciousness." One of the characteristics of this shift was an orientation toward "the construction of global-scale meaning through the descriptive apparatuses of natural history."[10] Central to these apparatuses was the Linnean classificatory project, which—aligned with practical concerns about ordering, taking stock, and, ultimately, controlling resources—pulled diverse existents out from the particular "tangled threads of their life surroundings" and rewove them into "patterns of global unity and order."[11] That orientation to the construction of patterns of global unity and order, inherently entangled with a will to accumulate and control, has accompanied caribou through the transformations it has undergone as it adopted the shape of a natural figure and then of a postnatural one.

MODERNIZING THE NORTH AND CARIBOU (SCIENCE)

Regarding its transformations, it is illustrative that while the word *caribou*—which comes from the Mi'kmaq *qalipu* (literally, the action of kicking snow aside)—was widely used by European settlers, explorers, and naturalists by the turn of the eighteenth century, it was generally considered a simple synonym for, or a type of, deer.[12] Even as the term *caribou* made it into the emerging Linnean classification, the earliest game laws seeking to control its access in Newfoundland still called it "deer."[13] The point may seem superfluous, but it offers a baseline to grasp the significance that the ever more precise classification of caribou will subsequently acquire. To put it bluntly, the state of affairs, when these early laws were passed in the mid-nineteenth century, made it so that just knowing caribou as a kind of deer, a "game animal," was good enough for governmental purposes and regulations.[14] The knowledge base for these early regulations was largely drawn from anecdotal but relatively common experiences of European settlers and their descendants with "deer," rather than from a systematic "science of caribou." In fact, to speak of a science of caribou for the period between the mid-nineteenth century to the turn of the twentieth is a misnomer, for the way of knowing caribou was still taking shape out of the entrails of the generalist methods of natural history—that is, collections and reports from travelers, trading-post managers, and governmental and/or institutionally sponsored "discovery" expeditions. (Incidentally, it is worth stressing that, as General Belaieff did in the Chaco, all of these "actors" relied greatly on the infrastructures of emplacement made available to them by people indigenous to the places being reported about.)

To the extent that they contributed to shaping the imagination of Canada as an untamed wilderness, the "true North, strong and free," these reports had an enduring legacy in the affective constitution of caribou as one of the "most iconic symbols of Canadian identity and pride."[15] Unsurprisingly, many of these reporters were spearheading processes of modernization that would eventually trigger the earliest efforts to conserve the very "wilderness" they were helping to "tame." In effect, without diminishing in the least their genuine curiosity about the matters on which they were reporting, few of these travelers and expeditions (or their sponsors) had the advancement of "science" as their only goal; most were at least also surveying potential riches to be developed in the North. In this, we see a glimpse of how the Reason Police began to be ensembled and deployed in the North. Indeed, the entanglement between economic development, state control, and the development of "a science of caribou" would only intensify through the twentieth century.

Given some of its habits and characteristics, caribou turned out to be a rather "uncooperative scientific subject."[16] Showing diverse morphology across regions, displaying variable patterns of habitation (sedentary versus migratory) within the same region, and moving across enormous distances through places hard for researchers to reach, the more the latter would try to see beyond its description as a type of deer, a game animal, the more caribou would appear as an incognita calling forth more research. And the impetus to look closer would come to a large extent from development projects geared toward modernizing the North. Thus, the coming into being of contemporary caribou, and concerns associated with it, were punctuated by (1) the introduction of domesticated reindeer in Alaska and the Yukon and attempts to domesticate wild caribou to create a ranching industry; (2) the emergence of professional bureaucracies that, far from remaining strictly preservationist, embraced a productivist vision of wildlife management; and (3) the expansion and intensification of extractive industries in the North. Let's look into each moment a little closer.

A truly colonial multispecies social-engineering endeavor, the attempt to create a reindeer and caribou ranching industry in the early twentieth century sought to domesticate and render productive in one swipe both humans (northern Indigenous peoples) and nonhumans. Yet the way reindeer and wild caribou responded to the project made the clarification of "intraspecies" boundaries more necessary: wild caribou had a penchant for mating with and luring away the reindeer they encountered! Aside from reducing domesticated herds, the mixing of domestic and wild stock posed a problem that required the delimitation of specific herds, spatial ranges, and their mutual relations—first, because the preservation of "pristine wilderness" was, along with productivist visions, an important component of the emerging wildlife management bureaucracies, and second, because in both livestock and wildlife management, the "carrying capacity" concept was, at the same time, gaining enormous weight. This only intensified the importance of tracing clear boundaries, as the concept required an unambiguous definition of the unit doing the carrying (a delimited area of land, for example) and the one being carried (a herd, for example). The practical need for these boundaries, and the calculations they could enable, propelled the pursuit of ever more fine-tuned investigation of caribou characteristics (i.e., how their morphological and behavioral features should be used to group them as subspecies, types, or herds) and the factors (predators, food, weather patterns, and so on) composing the capacity of a given area to carry a herd.

Increased state presence in the Arctic and sub-Arctic at the onset of the Cold War gave researchers access to capital-intensive technological resources such as aerial surveys and radio (and later satellite) collars. This made it possible to overcome what had long been an insurmountable obstacle to research: the enormous spatial range that caribou inhabited. With these technologies, it was now possible to track the movement of caribou, establish ranges, delimit herds, and count and track variations in their numbers. In this way, through the first half of the twentieth century, caribou became relatively stabilized as a "techno-scientific artifact" characterized as a single species, comprising several types, forming particular herds that inhabit particular ecological zones (tundra, forests, mountains). Given its position in the "food web," this techno-scientific artifact has recently become also an indicator species to which scientists turn when they want to check the health of the various sub-Arctic ecosystems.

A TECHNO-SCIENTIFIC-LEGAL-CORPORATE
ARTIFACT

A professional state bureaucracy—receptive to academically trained personnel's ideas and university connections—grew alongside the drive to produce more fine-grained knowledge of caribou (as well as other wildlife species) for management purposes. Legislation seeking to align "human practices" to the more or less elusive purposes of wildlife management also began to expand from the early decades of the twentieth century onward. In turn, new industrial developments encountering that legislation elicited new questions about caribou, and thus further research. In effect, in the face of growing legislation that protected habitats and species, corporate extractive industries (and their backers in government) that had been moving to the North since the late 1950s had to be able to argue that their activities did not, or could find ways not to, infringe standing legislation. But what did science know about how caribou (among other species) were affected by industrial activities? And if these activities were to have negative effects, what did science know about possible technical solutions to mitigate them? This knowledge gap was the corridor through which corporate extractive industries introduced themselves as an important player in caribou science (and northern science more generally), for they would sponsor—solely or jointly with universities and governmental agencies—further studies that could answer such questions.[17]

The participation of corporate interests in northern science (including caribou science) became further legitimized from the 1970s onward with the emergence and consolidation of environmental assessment guidelines, regulations, and legislation.[18] According to these, and as part of the process to obtain governmental permissions to operate, project proponents (corporations) would have to produce environmental impact assessment studies, often through hiring expert consulting firms. Environmental impact assessment processes also reshuffled the role Indigenous peoples played in caribou science. While they had participated from early on, lending not only the word *caribou* but also on-the-ground support and information to naturalists and, later, wildlife managers and biologists, their understanding of caribou was taken to be clouded by cultural beliefs and thus unfit to stand on par with scientific knowledge. But from the 1970s onward, and in the wake of strong opposition to intended massive development projects, several court rulings paved the way for the gradual recognition of aboriginal rights in Canada, including the right to have their cultures respected.[19] By the mid-1980s, cultural beliefs could no longer be simply sidelined from understandings of what caribou is

and how it must be managed. Thus, under the rubrics of cultural value and/
or Traditional Knowledge, culture became a new thread in the constitution of
caribou. The inclusion of this thread is perhaps the clearest index of caribou's
shifting from being a natural figure to becoming a postnatural one.

Although its status as a "natural" entity (that is, transcendent and ultimately independent from human perspectives) remains an enduring and
consequential assumption (as we will soon see), in practice, caribou has become ever more explicitly treated as a multispecies or more-than-human assemblage, the more or less stable outcome of those hybrid forums I mentioned
earlier. The North American Caribou Workshop, which has been meeting
regularly since 1983, is an occasion where this kind of forum, and the assemblage that constitutes it, turns remarkably visible. Described by organizers as
"the largest technical conference of its kind dealing specifically with caribou
biology and management," the workshop is attended by the proverbial stake-
holders/spokespersons incessantly being invoked in calls to protect caribou:
biologists, wildlife managers, representatives from environmental NGOs, outfitters and hunters' associations, corporations, and Indigenous groups.[20]

To the workshop come the "inputs" (latest information, discoveries, research
methods, evaluations, concerns, and best practices) of various institutions
and publics (universities, corporations, governmental offices, environmental
NGOs, interest groups, the general public, and so on) concerned with caribou.
And true to its name, in the fairly cooperative setting of the workshop, the latest iteration of caribou is more or less cobbled together. This then travels back
through concerned publics and institutions, reshaping their practices in ways
that become visible again to the outside observer when, in the face of a proposed development project or policy modifications, impact assessment processes (another hybrid forum) are conducted. Generally, and especially if there
are strong controversies between different stakeholders, these assessments
instigate further research, which, in the words of the authors of *Caribou and
the North*, "is needed to better understand [in each case] thresholds of human
harvest, as well as our industrial footprint with its corresponding deterioration
in habitat quality. How much of this can be tolerated by caribou, and what are
their minimum protection needs?"[21]

As a postnatural figure, caribou continues to emerge within concerns inherently linked to the question of how to overcome challenges to displacement
and expansion. It remains a postnatural figure of the big. True, caribou cannot
be reduced to any one of the threads that I have accounted for here. For instance, caribou science does not boil down to the utilitarian curiosity of "How
can we use them?"; in fact, I would venture that the question of how we can

live together has always been more prominent for many practitioners. Yet even the latter question is never asked in a vacuum. Utilitarian and legal concerns actively shape it and contribute to weaving caribou into a "pattern of global unity and order" as a big techno-scientific, legal, and corporate artifact. Thus, while caribou is irreducible to any one of them, disentangling the threads that constitute this pattern is not easy. This is brought into sharp relief when we consider how, with the backing of the Reason Police, caribou has come to interrupt atiku, the other character in our story.

Hunting Atiku: A Persevering and Careful Worlding Practice

Atanukana (or atenogens) are a category of Innu stories that recall events before innu became differentiated from beings that moderns would categorize as animals. Savard quoted an Innu storyteller explaining that these are stories that must be passed on so future generations will understand what is important to know.[22] Not surprisingly, given what was discussed in the prelude about emplaced collectives, what is important to know about atiku begins with the relation established by a male innu who went to live with the atiku, married one of their females, turned into atiku himself, and eventually became Kanipinikassikueu, or atiku-napeu (*the atiku master*). Since then, Kanipinikassikueu ensures that atiku will give themselves to innu hunters so that their families can live. However, this generosity is not guaranteed. As many other-than-innu entities that compose the emplaced collective nitassinan, atiku have full personhood and a will of their own, so hunting is not mainly about outsmarting but rather about enticing these fully volitional beings and their leader to be generous with their bodies. This is achieved through practices that show respect for and recognition of these altruistic acts. Among these practices are very detailed protocols to dispose of the bones of hunted atiku (from which new specimens will regenerate), the injunction to not waste any part of their bodies, and the requirement that meat be generously shared among innu. Other prescriptions, like keeping atiku in one's thoughts through storytelling, singing, and drumming (on a drum made with atiku skin), and celebrating a mokoshan (ceremonial meal) at the end of a collective hunt, are geared to receive the blessings that this relationship generates for the general well-being of nitassinan or nutshimit.[23] In short, hunting atiku is quite central among the careful practices that world the emplaced collective innu are with—that is, hunting is part of the infrastructures of emplacement from which nitassinan obtains.

(R)EXISTING AGAINST INFRASTRUCTURES
OF DISPLACEMENT

Similar to what we saw in the Yshiro case, and as it has happened with many other careful practices, hunting has adapted to and become entangled with the infrastructures through which the modern collective became grounded where nitassinan is. The establishment of fur trading posts in nitassinan from the eighteenth century onward had a profound effect on how hunting took place, not least through the introduction of new technologies and its progressive entanglement with faraway markets. This also modified the way innu moved in nitassinan, as they began to include regular visits to trading posts in, or close to, the places known as Sheshatshiu and Utshimassits. Although careful practices have continued, the erosion of the infrastructures of emplacement that made them possible has been relentless, particularly since Newfoundland and Labrador joined the Canadian Confederation in 1949. If until the mid-1940s a European observer could describe the life of the Innu as "dictated by the hunt," a decade later government officials warned that the days "of [the] primitive hunting economy are numbered" and that Indigenous peoples in Labrador had to be prepared for "the industrial society now ready to burst upon them."[24] And burst upon them it did!

In 1954, the air base that had been established during World War II in Goose Bay (thirty-five kilometers, or about twenty-two miles, from Sheshatshiu) was expanded to become part of the Cold War nuclear deterrence strategy. In the same year, railway tracks were laid, and mining operations began in the Québec–Labrador border area. In 1967 began the construction of the Upper Churchill Falls hydroelectric generating station, which, by its conclusion in 1974, flooded an area of 6,527 km² or 2,520 square miles. Starting in 1981, the Goose Bay air base became a center to train NATO's jet pilots in low-level flying (with over seven thousand sorties per season). In 1992, the Trans-Labrador Highway was constructed between Labrador City/Wabush and Happy Valley–Goose Bay. In 1995, the discovery of rich nickel deposits in a place called Emish (Voisey's Bay) resulted in over 270,000 mineral stakes being claimed over nitassinan. In 2006, the provincial government announced its intention to build another multibillion-dollar hydroelectric project on the Lower Churchill River, which is soon to enter into operations. And these are just the major developments, which, in turn, prompted myriads of smaller ones (from the construction of recreational cabins to industrial forestry) that took place throughout the entire period (see map 2).

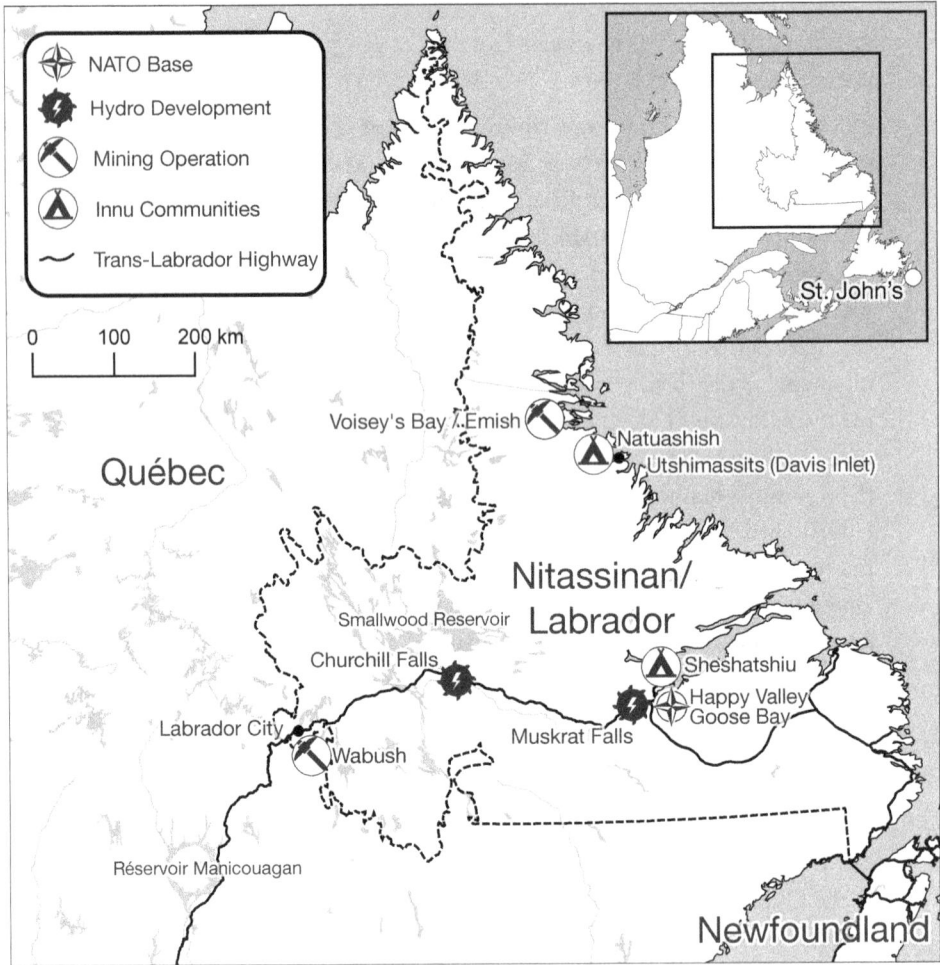

MAP 2. The Innu communities in Nitassinan. Only major developments are marked in the map. Map by Steve Chapman.

Extractivism not only greatly changed the landscape but also—as had been envisioned by governmental agents—brought an end to the hunting economy on which Innu families relied. This pushed the Innu to gravitate more and more toward permanent settlements, which, paradoxically operating as infrastructures of displacement, the government prepared for them. In the settlements the Innu were provided welfare support as long as their children attended school.[25] Aside from forcing Innu families to live for larger periods of time in settlements, schooling and more or less explicit pressures to turn

Innu into self-reliant individuals participating as wage laborers (and, more recently, entrepreneurs) in the extractive economy ended up interfering with the enactment (and intergenerational transmission) of the careful practices that constitute nitassinan. Innu political organizers, as well as anthropologists and commentators, have extensively documented the terrible toll settlement took on Innu well-being, pointing out how, in the span of one generation, the Innu were brought to "a state of destitution and humiliating dependency," their communities suffering from a variety of "social pathologies" ranging from high rates of diabetes, obesity, and suicide to widespread alcohol and drug abuse and family violence.[26] The response to these effects by social services was with the systematic removal of Innu children from their families and communities.

It is instructive to dwell for a moment on what the "social" dimension of these "pathologies," and governmental responses to them, implied (and still imply) for the Innu. This is what my Innu translator, the late Paul Pone, told me about a conversation I witnessed in 2010, where elders were discussing why their communities were in the shape they were:

> So that's the reason why they are blaming the animals [spirit masters].
> They [the spirit masters] are probably saying, "Where are the innu in
> nutshimit? Where are the people that spent a lot of time in nutshimit
> before?" Now we don't spend a lot of time in nutshimit, so the animal
> spirits themselves are speaking. Etienne [one of the elders] says, "I sort
> of blame [them for] what has happened, what's happening to our com-
> munity here." He said the animal spirits are mad at the Innu, and he is
> saying this is the animal spirits showing they are mad because innu are
> not in the country, they are not in tents, and they are saying, "Where are
> the innu?"

As is evident, elders identified the weakening of "social" relations with animal masters (central among them Kanipinikassikueu) as the most proximate cause for what analysts described as "social pathologies"! It is no surprise, then, that staying in nutshimit has transformed from being a regular feature of life to being a lifeline for many Innu. The importance of this lifeline is underscored by the efforts and resources Innu invest in sustaining life in nutshimit against pressures and incentives to live a "productive" life anchored to settlements. For instance, many families continue to use a large proportion of earnings from wage labor to buy equipment and supplies (snowmobiles, tents, rifles, ammunition, satellite phones, and so on) that make it possible to sustain some of the practices of emplacement that generate nutshimit/nitassinan under the present conditions. Likewise, since the late 1970s, Innu governing bodies have been using governmental support payments (and, more recently, royalties accrued from impact and benefits agreements associated with extractive industries) to keep an outpost program, which helps families go to hunting camps by floatplanes.[27] Moreover, protest hunts (i.e., hunting atiku in defiance of governmental rules and restrictions) have become a recurrent form of direct action Innu organizations (on both sides of the Newfoundland/Québec provincial border) use to draw attention from governments and publics to their otherwise unattended concerns. Innu hunters seldom miss opportunities to participate in these out-and-out practices of (r)existence, protected by their political organizations and their lawyers. In summary, and as in the Yshiro case, again we see that practices and infrastructures of emplacement have persevered, entangled with, but also against the grain of, the infrastructures and practices of displacement that ground modernity where nitassinan is. But let's take a closer look at how this has played out in the encounter between atiku and caribou.

FOLDING ATIKU WITHIN CARIBOU (COLONIALITY
IN ACTION)

While not completely unconnected to them, for a time, the Innu could avoid some of the practices that constituted the assemblage from which the techno-scientific artefact "caribou" would eventually emerge, such as the collection of specimens. For example, a visitor to the fur trading post at North West River (across from where the contemporary community of Sheshatshiu sits) observed in 1860 that the Innu who came to barter "skins for articles of English manufacture" would "on no account, bring in the entire body of the carabboo deer," and further explained: "There is a superstition current amongst them, that whoever brings one of these to the white man will meet with dire misfortune, and that his hunting-grounds will be destroyed. Mr. Smith [the local trader] informed me that although large bribes have been offered for specimens, they have proved unavailing, the Indians declining to bring in even the head or horns."[28] By the mid-twentieth century, the full panoply of practices that constitute caribou would become ubiquitous and harder to avoid for the Innu. Game laws, which evolved alongside caribou science, could be more easily enforced as Innu families gravitated toward permanent settlements where rangers could catch "poachers" red-handed. Almost anyone in the Innu communities can tell a story about rangers confiscating meat and hunting implements, for it has become a constant occurrence since the late 1960s. Throughout, the justification has been the protection of caribou, as "biology and herd management" indicate it should be done.[29] Some Innu took these claims in good faith and even collaborated with wildlife managers and biologists conducting "caribou studies and surveys"; but for others, this justification for governmental interference rang hollow, and more so after 1974, when the Upper Churchill hydroelectric project submerged under its reservoir atiku's calving grounds and migration routes![30] Subsequent developments followed the same pattern of disregard for atiku, amid governmental claims of caring about caribou. And this would remain the case even as, in the process of shifting from being a natural to a post-natural figure, the caribou assemblage purported to include atiku in its composition. Let's look into this.

Uninformed of what was going to happen, the Innu could do little to defend themselves and nitassinan from the consequences of the Upper Churchill hydroelectric project, but by the time NATO's low-level flying training began some six years later, they had become better prepared. In the mid-1970s, the two Innu communities within the province had created a political organization, nowadays known as Innu Nation, and took the first steps in a land claims process.[31] Thus, when NATO's low-level flying in nitassinan started in the 1980s, Innu Nation launched an intense protest campaign, with support from human rights and peace movement organizations. This included international tours, occupation of the base's runways (which resulted in the arrest of men, women, and elders), and protest hunts. I will not dwell on the details of the conflict, which gained unprecedented public visibility and has been extensively analyzed.[32] What interests me about this event is both that it marks the beginning of caribou's shift from being a natural to a postnatural figure in Labrador, and that it shows the role that coercion played in stabilizing this latter figure.

Besides the shock that the sudden noise of a twenty-ton jet bomber flying close to treetop level at over nine hundred kilometers (about 559 miles) an hour produced in people (especially children), the Innu constantly remarked that, terrorized by the jets, atiku abandoned their calving grounds, strayed away from their migration routes, lost weight, and hurt themselves or died while running in panic.[33] These concerns eventually led the government to form an Environmental Assessment Panel to look into the effects of low-level flying. The expert panel released a preliminary statement in 1989, concluding that the activities would not have significant adverse effects if they were carefully monitored and managed. The key to careful monitoring and management was an arrangement that combined satellite collars to track caribou and information advanced by "land users" as to where they planned to be at any point in time so that jets could avoid both. Of course, the participation of the Innu was central for this to work. However, Innu Nation rejected the conclusions of the statement and the invitation to participate in the monitoring project, as well as any further studies to improve it. They wanted low-level flying to stop.

Considering the training of NATO pilots a sizeable source of revenues and jobs, a majority of the public in Labrador supported the activity.[34] According to low-level flying supporters, science had shown that with monitoring, the activity's impact on the health of animals and humans would be minimal, hence Innu refusal was unreasonable.[35] Thus, low-level flying continued despite Innu opposition, and protestors continued to be arrested when involved in direct actions. This experience started to become internalized as a tension (that continues to exist) within the Innu communities at large and within their leadership in particular: How far should the Innu oppose a government-backed project that would nevertheless go ahead? What hurts the Innu and nitassinan/nutshimit more—remaining an outsider and opponent to modernization projects or becoming a participant in order to gain some control over them while deriving as much "benefit" as possible? Asked in the context of the construction of new roads, logging, and mining developments, the answer to these questions from the mid-1990s onward began to tilt the balance within Innu Nation toward leaders who saw in formal land claims negotiations a more promising path than direct action to defend Innu and nitassinan, although direct action was never totally abandoned, as we will see.

The government's simultaneous imposition of a project that disrupted the assemblage composing atiku and the invitation to the Innu to participate in a techno-institutional arrangement to manage the project's impacts on caribou underscores the role coercion plays in the constitution and stabilization of caribou as a postnatural figure. In effect, while in the context of this conflict, a majority of Innu steadfastly refused to participate, the "lesson" about the costs of outright refusal did sink in for many in the Innu Nation leadership who, in the face of subsequent extractive developments, were less inclined to go that route. And with Innu Nation acquiescing to participate in arrangements to manage caribou, even if grudgingly, atiku seemed to become a component of this postnatural figure—although not for very long.

Atiku's Divergent Multiplicity and the Coloniality
of Caribou Multiple

As a postnatural figure, caribou is also a figure of multiplicity, to some extent analogous, and thus comparable, to "the body multiple" that Annemarie Mol discussed in her now classic book by that title.[36] Mol showed how, in a Dutch hospital, the practices of radiologists, clinicians, and pathologists perform different versions of atherosclerosis, and then how this multiplicity is singularized (i.e., made to hold together as a single "thing"), even if temporarily, for the purpose of deciding on an intervention.[37] In the caribou case, it would be so-called stakeholders who enact slightly different versions of caribou. Elsewhere, I have explored this analogy in order to probe the extent to which cosmopolitics can, in practice, avoid the trap of reasonable politics.[38] Briefly, and in the terminology used in this book, my probe involved two initial premises: (1) that commoning as conceived in the cosmopolitics of compositionists can be seen as Mol's singularization; and (2) that the atiku/caribou case affords contrasts with atherosclerosis that are useful to illuminate some aspects of compositionists' singularization/commoning that are not often foregrounded. Let's begin with the contrasts.

First, while atherosclerosis cannot be "seen" without the obvious mediation of expert practices, caribou appears as *self-evidently* out there, as if it holds together by itself and preexists the various practices of knowing it. In its most qualified version, this perception reinforces the generalized and enduring assumption (discussed earlier in the book) of a "world without us" and its significance. In its most assertive version, this perception reinforces a series of modernist assumptions about the basic stability, orderliness, and givenness of a world/reality that is independent of and prior to knowledge practices and which consequently calls for a specific way of knowing epitomized by the scientific method. Thus, and this is the second contrast with Mol's atherosclerosis—whose multiple versions are, in principle, symmetrical—what I have called the *technoscientific* version of caribou (i.e., the one most immediately emerging from the practices of caribou biologists) dominates when it comes to specifying what this "thing" is and, hence, how humans have to manage it. The important point of contrast to draw from this is the following: the symmetry between versions of atherosclerosis means that it is always uncertain how they will hold together in different circumstance. In contrast, in the case of the caribou multiple, the dominance of the technoscientific version of caribou means that reasonable politics and its coloniality constantly creeps up, even if with some subtlety.[39]

As the Innu learned during the low-level flying conflict, coercion appears justified in the eyes of many publics when the limits of "reasonable practices" (as defined by the techno-scientific version of caribou) are transgressed. Aside from its association to reasonable politics, I argued that coercion is crucial to the very constitution of a type of multiplicity that characterizes caribou and, more generally, other postnatural figures, a multiplicity I labeled *diffractive*.

This is the kind of multiplicity that has been more commonly addressed in science and technology studies (STS) analysis, centered on technoscientific controversies gathering publics that agree that each of them has a legitimate voice and is entitled to contribute to the issues that concern them. But these publics also often operate on the assumption (in their either qualified or assertive versions) that something (called caribou, atherosclerosis, or whatever might be) sits "out there" at the center of it all. This makes diffractive multiplicity more pliable to singularization. In contrast, atiku underscores another kind of multiplicity, a "divergent multiplicity" that is recalcitrant in the face of attempts at singularization. I illustrated this point with the trajectory of the caribou multiple from its stabilization after the low-level flying conflict to its disruption by a recent conflict, which I will summarize below.

THE UNHEARABLE AND UNSEEABLE ATIKU

The coercion the Innu experienced during the low-level flying conflict contributed to channeling their concerns about what was taking place in nitassinan into the space of hybrid forums, which subsequently began to sprout around proposed policies and projects involving "natural resources." Typically, these forums would include impact assessment studies producing recommendations (for both mitigation and compensation) and the ensuing establishment of a monitoring committee or comanagement board in charge of administering them. Since the late 1990s, these studies have come with the explicit mandate that they should give "full consideration to traditional ecological knowledge."[40] But what does this mean? Revealingly, in the environmental impact studies of the two largest developments launched after that mandate became effective, a mine in a place called Emish-Voisey's Bay and another hydroelectric power generator, now on the Lower Churchill River, "Innu traditional knowledge" (or TEK) about caribou (and any other aspect of "the environment") was treated as if it involved two different domains. In effect, elements of TEK that could supplement scientific knowledge—such as empirical observation about migration routes, seasonal behavior, and so on—were included in sections dealing with impact on the environment, while elements attributed to culture, such as the importance of spirit owners, the fully volitional character of atiku, and so on, went to sections dealing with "social or cultural" impact.[41] Not surprisingly, when it came to proposing measures to protect caribou, the studies focused on the first kind of knowledge to recommend actions such as accommodating development activities to seasonal movements of the herds, restricting vehicles to designated routes, engineering slopes on roads at caribou crossing paths, and the like.[42]

In this way, the divergent multiplicity of practices that went under the label "Traditional Knowledge" were made to hold together with technoscientific practices so that the impact assessment processes could singularize and stabilize a caribou workable for a partic u lar intervention— that is, one pliable to the calculation of, to cite the authors of *Caribou and the North* again, "how much of this [development] can be tolerated by caribou, and what are their minimum protection needs." As we will see, *the caribou* referenced here renders irrelevant the concerns about atiku that, through the studies, many Innu expressed.... For example, regarding the mine:

> "This is shared Innu and Inuit land, but the wildlife also own the land as much as anybody else." (Nympha Byrne)
> "This was our grand fathers' land. Now we have taken their place to look after it with care.... Elders mention that we have animal masters, and we should be careful of them. The young people do not understand the meaning of these caretakers for our people. If an animal is not well taken care of, or if you take more than you can have, elders know that is not right for the masters." (Ann Rich)
> "The white people just damage the land, especially the animals who are very sacred to us. When I hear that the boat capsized near Nain, that might be the sign the animals are angry at us." (Penash Rich)

Regarding the hydro development:

> "I don't like the idea of damming the Muskrat Falls [located in the Lower Churchill River]. What I know about Muskrat Falls, there's a hole in the falls somewhere. Probably the spirit in the spirit world used that waterfall for a reason, whoever being lives in that hill. Probably the spirit that lives in the mountain prob ably will destroy the dam itself, somehow.... I think that the animal beings who live in that mountain will destroy the dam." (Pien Penashue)[43]

As can be appreciated, these interventions foreground the animals and their masters' agency, will, desires, and capacity to feel offended and retaliate— that is, they highlight the concerns and objections these entities would have about the projects. One could venture that from the vantage point expressed here, the purpose cited above that the authors of *Caribou and the North* assign to research—and, by extension, to impact assessments—might have sounded something like establishing how much disrespect atiku and other powerful entities could take on and how to make sure the projects did not go over the limit!

Innu were acutely aware that the mitigation measures proposed by experts had no relation to being careful with atiku; they were aware of an equivocation and aware that their interlocutors did not know this. The late Innu Nation leader Ben Michel made the point eloquently in one of the meetings related to the mine project:

> You tell us about the regulations you will follow because these are the laws of the governments, but what do you know about me, my father and mother sitting here. Do you think these regulations will solve anything? I don't pretend to understand all that was spoken here. This language of geologists and mines, I don't understand it although I'm fluent in English. How do you expect these people to understand it? We have values different from Europeans who see the world as a commodity. . . . Can you tell me that your regulations from St. John's will protect the land in the way my parents view it? I don't think they can ever understand you because their values are so different from yours. . . . Through my schooling, using a foreign language, I was made to understand things the way you do. I am a full-blooded Innu, but I am bringing foreign values to my parents. They are telling us, "Stop, we are going the wrong way." . . . I know you're listening, but I don't know if you're hearing. If I was to come and try to change your way of life, make you Innu, it would be difficult for you. That's what you're asking a whole people to do.[44]

Expressing himself in a second language, Ben Michel mixed the different emphasis that the terms *listening* and *hearing* usually have for native English speakers, but the confusion turns out to be felicitous if we connect it with Rancière's notion that the order of the police (the Reason Police in this case) determines what is hearable. In this light, Michel's remark underscores that the concerns of atiku (and other nitassinan entities), voiced by innu, could not be "heard" in the order being extended through measures to mitigate the impact of mining on caribou (multiple); they were just noise. The point is made even clearer when we consider instances where it is emphatically demonstrated that these concerns are not being heard, precisely because it appears that they are being listened to!

AN ONTOLOGICAL CONFLICT BECOMES EVIDENT

The Lower Churchill hydroelectric project was presented in the 2007 energy report of the Newfoundland and Labrador government as a precursor of what today we would call a transition to decarbonization. In effect, the justification of the project hinged on using the revenues from offshore oil extraction to build a solid energy supply (and commodity to sale) based on electricity.[45] From very early on in the process of evaluating its possible impacts, atiku concerns seemed to find echoes in the concerns that biologists and wildlife managers (from governmental and nongovernmental agencies) raised regarding the lack of attention that the proponents' environmental impact study had paid to the George River caribou herd.[46] This was an issue that by the time the studies were carried out (2010–11) had already become a growing public concern.[47] In effect, by then, experts everywhere were sounding the alarm that caribou herds were in dangerous decline throughout the circumpolar North.[48] Studies pointed out that from Alaska to Labrador, the species was "showing up on species-at-risk lists as 'endangered,' 'threatened,' or 'of special concern.'"[49] Two herds of Labrador's sedentary caribou were already in these categories, and biologists and wildlife managers feared the George River migratory herd was going in that direction as well.[50] The herd had dropped from eight hundred thousand members in the 1990s—making it the largest in the world—to 74,000 in 2009. What impact would this megaproject have on this trend? biologists asked. As before, Innu also raised concerns about how the project would affect atiku, but (again) their concerns were not exactly the same as those of biologists.

Biologists ventured a combination of natural population cycles, climate change, increasing industrial activity, and loss of habitat as the most likely primary causes for the decline in caribou populations, but they also began to consider that while not per se one of the causes, given the status of the herd and of its habitat, hunting now could tip the herd in the direction of extirpation. The Innu elders and hunters with whom I started working in 2009 saw the decline in population as a symptom of the deteriorating relationship between the younger generation of innu and the atiku master. According to these experts, Kanipinikassikueu was not releasing atiku because younger people had not been properly taught, and thus did not follow, the practices of carefulness (expressed through hunting) that prompted its generosity toward innu; a concerted effort was needed to properly teach these practices to the younger people. In short, while biologists and Innu experts agreed that the situation was very concerning, neither the definition of the situation nor the responses needed were the same for each party. The equivocation became evident when, in 2013, the government passed a total ban on hunting, which the Innu have since refused to abide by.[51]

Although several consultations and discussions have been put in place, and the Inuit of Labrador (represented by the Nunatsiavut Government and the NunatuKavut Council) have accepted the argument that the ban is necessary to respond to the population decline, the Innu "perspective" cannot be brought into compliance, and they consistently and openly refuse the measure. Aside from Innu hunters being prosecuted, and Innu Nation and the provincial government having entered into a protracted court battle, their unyielding stance has earned the Innu a barrage of vitriol from the larger public, accusing them of self-centeredness (they are only concerned about asserting their "Aboriginal rights," no matter what) and questioning both their authenticity (i.e., their declaimed spiritual bond with the land is bogus) and their rationality (i.e., their stance just does not make sense). These reactions only underscore how the impact assessment processes (among other instances of relatively formalized hybrid forums) had entrenched among non-Innu interlocutors the "uncontrolled" (or unrecognized) character of the equivocation that *caribou* and *atiku* are just different words for the same thing—even though Innu had constantly tried to render the equivocation visible and hearable. Now, hitting right on one of the most crucial practices that constitute atiku (and, by extension, nitassinan), the hunting ban was the proverbial straw that broke the back of the caribou multiple.

Based on the analysis of this conflict, I argued that we can see in it how the divergent multiplicity of atiku disrupts the relatively civil process of singularization that (purportedly) characterizes hybrid forums, a point that extends to a cosmopolitics hinging on diffractive multiplicity. Moreover, I argued that this disruption underscores that coloniality is inherent to diffractive multiplicity. In effect, being quite recent and obvious, the coercion that inaugurates and sustains caribou multiple appears as a glaring sign that diffractive multiplicity, in general, cannot be obtained without it. In other words, the difference between the singularization of atherosclerosis and the singularization of caribou boils down to coercion being more evident in the latter case because, in contrast to the former one, divergent multiplicity has *not yet* been fully evacuated or tamed. In this sense, the atiku case gives us a whiff of "the smoke of the burned witches," to which Isabelle Stengers refers, and which hangs over the Dutch hospital, where civil procedures of singularization (of atherosclerosis) are "heirs of an operation of cultural and social eradication—the forerunner of what was [and continues to be] committed elsewhere in the name of civilization and reason."[52]

The corollary of all this is that, hinging on diffractive multiplicity, the cosmopolitics of Parliaments of Things (such as hybrid forums), rather than fully circumventing reasonable politics, only slows it down. In part this is because the drive to singularization (or commoning) ultimately overrides cosmopolitics' apprehensions about exclusions. As Latour put it, when the multiplicity at stake is not amenable to singularization and stabilization within the common world, the entities that express it must be excluded and viewed as insignificant.[53] This led me to raise the question of whether another cosmopolitics, one that hinges on divergent multiplicities, is possible—and, if so, what that would entail. I will come back to this question later, but first, I must tackle a potential objection some readers might raise to the corollary I draw from the caribou/atiku case with regards to cosmopolitics. The objection would be that my example does not quite serve the purpose of exploring cosmopolitics, precisely because science still retains its privileges in defining what caribou is: it is Science with a capital *S*. They could argue that this is not a necessity, that science can be otherwise. Divested of its privileges, it could be but one among other equally valid ways to get to know or perform caribou. Moreover, in truly cosmopolitical fashion, these various ways might converse or rub against each other as they go on conforming a common world. To this I will respond that while I am willing to be convinced otherwise, I see a substantial obstacle for this to be possible—namely, that science (with or without a capital *S*) has a little problem of scale to contend with.

A Little Problem of Scale

The little problem of scale that science confronts is intimately related to the fact that its entities, even in their postnatural guise, are woven into patterns of global unity and order and thus, as I suggested in the interlude, veer toward the largest possible scale: they are what they are everywhere (i.e., they are universals). To generate these universals (even if negotiated ones) requires constant extension through and maintenance of infrastructures of displacement and their associated coloniality. Now, while I contend that divergent multiplicity disrupts the smooth extension and maintenance of these infrastructures (thus making evident the coloniality of the entire enterprise), there are many who think coloniality is not necessarily inherent to science, that it can deal with divergent multiplicity otherwise. But can it? And if so, under what conditions? I will frame my subsequent discussion in reference to a commentary a scientifically trained acquaintance made about what transpires in the caribou/atiku conflict, which helps highlight why some of these arguments about the pliability of science to the demands of cosmopolitics are unpersuasive for a political ontology concerned with divergent multiplicity.

SCIENCE PLUS AS (SCHOLARLY) HYBRID FORUM

By way of introduction, let me explain that my acquaintance works in a governmental conservation agency and, while not directly involved in it, is familiar with various aspects of the caribou/atiku conflict.[54] Her commentary came amid a friendly but heated discussion where I expressed my concerns about the ban, to which she responded thus:

> I know corporations and their mega-development projects are the main culprits; don't you think I know that? But this is not the place to be discussing a change of civilization; that is a larger, global struggle that will take a generation. But right here, right now, under the present circumstances, the ban on hunting is like giving CPR to a patient that is flatlining. Of course, CPR will not address the root causes of the patient's problem, but it will give us a chance to still have a patient with a problem to treat at all! I fully take your point that the Innu might lose part of their way of life and culture if they don't hunt. But, with the ban and all, the Innu will still continue to exist; without it, caribou will not. I do not know how to express this to you as you are not Canadian, but it really hurts to think that there might come a time when we do not see caribou any longer. Look, even the Inuit understand this and contribute their knowledge in the effort to save it. I do not understand how the Innu, who say they care so much for caribou, cannot see that if we don't take these kinds of urgent measures, this species, as many others, will not survive. If we keep closing our eyes to the harsh things that need to be done, all of us, including the Innu, will go the same way soon, and the entire planet too!

The way in which this commentary stages and scales the caribou problem finds echoes in a series of analytical moves that characterize the scholarship that seeks to grapple with divergent multiplicity while preserving an important role for science in cosmopolitics. One move, which I have mentioned before, is the singling out of a big set of entities categorized as "humans" and the simultaneous tracing of another big category of "out-thereness"—that is, the nonhumans with which humans relate but which exceed that relation. These are the things (in our case, the caribou) by themselves and for themselves; in short, the world without us. Another move involves setting the nonhuman as a sort of "third party" in quarrels between contending "human practices" that end up being treated as perspectives. In effect, while human groups might have different and even contending relations with or practices of a nonhuman, qua human perspectives they will be exceeded by "the perspective" that the nonhuman will have of itself, its situation, and its self-worth. A final move turns this "third party" into a luring site for both curiosity and moral affirmation. Curiosity, because humans' descriptions of, or relation with, nonhumans can never be exhaustive.[55] Moral affirmation, because a truly cosmopolitical ethos implies that we (humans) should strive to hear what nonhumans have to say on their own or, at the very least, should recognize their intrinsic worth (beyond their relation to us) and act accordingly. The corollary of all these moves is the call to pay close attention to nonhumans on their own, which in practice within this scholarship tends to be answered by appealing (mostly) to the natural sciences.

One of the reasons I am uncomfortable with scholarship that enacts these moves is because they can be deployed to restage the hierarchy among "human perspectives" that characterize reasonable politics—precisely what my acquaintance does in her intervention. Indeed, she situates "all of us, including the Innu," in a common domain (human) that is set apart from caribou (nonhuman), an animal whose critical condition requires an urgent intervention, even if at the cost of one human culture. Then, she signals that if the intrinsic worth of this (iconic) animal is not enough to mobilize us into sacrificing what might be a unique but ultimately dispensable marker of human difference, the risk to our common human condition, and the entire planet, should do it. Now, in my acquaintance's argument, it is implicit that the science behind the ban is not just one more perspective—although, in multiculturalist fashion, she also points to how this knowledge is now open to other perspectives (the Inuit's traditional knowledge), insofar as they are not disruptive of what science indicates needs to be done! In the scholarship I am discussing, there is nothing as blatant as this in terms of setting a hierarchy among human perspectives, although something of the sort resurfaces with their staging of a "meta-frame" that I call *science-plus*.

In a recent contribution seeking to build bridges between multispecies and ontological approaches, where the latter have criticized the former's reliance on science, Anna Tsing argues that it is wrong to assume that "learning about nonhumans reduces one's knowledge base to science," and she gives numerous examples of learning about the nonhumans she is interested in also from mushroom pickers, farmers, and so on.[56] As we will see, this response misses the central point of the concern raised about the role of science in accounts of more-than-human assemblages, and thus leads to analytical moves similar to those outlined previously. In fact, it seems as if the concern expressed were about the lack of inclusion of nonscientific (human) perspectives in these accounts. Thus, in describing how this should not necessarily be a problem, the fundamental distinctions between humans and nonhumans, on the one hand, and human perspectives on those nonhumans, on the other, is reiterated. This leaves the door wide open for the staging of a meta-frame or standpoint (science-plus) that, purporting to encompass divergent multiplicity, ends up paying little attention to its analytical and political consequences—that is, to the point at the heart of the original concern with an overreliance on science in accounts of more-than-human assemblages. Let us consider this in more detail.

In a revealing passage about how one does not need to be reduced to science-based knowledge of nonhumans, Tsing says about a series of entities (dogs, snails, rice plants, and ghosts) that populate a farm: "These organisms, as with ghosts, are both objects of farmers' cosmological reckonings and makers of worlds on their own. *It is in that double status that we get to know them.*"[57] We see here traces of the analytical moves discussed before. First, the farmers' cosmological reckonings (a human perspective) are established as distinct from the "objects" as makers of worlds on their own. Second, other human perspectives are aligned on the human side of the divide. In effect, although not explicit, the shadow interlocutors of farmers' cosmological reckoning are other reckonings, those of the natural and the social sciences. (Incidentally, this is made explicit in another programmatic statement by Tsing and her collaborators, where the label "cosmological reckoning" is replaced by "nonsecular cosmologies" to designate the knowledge of lay "Others" that can stand side by side with the secular "ecological models" of the natural sciences and the secular "political economies" of the social sciences.)[58] But then, we have a third move: having all human perspectives lined up as equally valid "reckonings," the ethnographer aggregates them in order to know the objects as both "reckonings" (of others) and as makers of worlds "on their own." This science-plus is implicitly advanced as a metaframe, a superseding vantage from which a more textured way of getting to know nonhumans can obtain. In effect, the bringing together of perspectives within the encompassing meta-frame of science-plus is implicitly assumed to redress to some extent the lack of exhaustiveness of each perspective on its own. However, the argument is not that with this meta-frame we truly get to know the "objects" on their own but that we get a more nuanced grasp of their (to use my terms) *diffractive* being. In this sense, it might not escape readers that the aim of science-plus has a similar ring to that of hybrid forums (such as environmental impact processes in Labrador), which, by way of attending to a variety of spokespersons/stakeholders, promises a more democratic method for addressing the multiplicity of postnatural figures. The difference is that hybrid forums are compelled (by their very practical purpose of guiding interventions) to singularize this multiplicity, while science-plus can satisfy itself by registering the diffractive multiplicity present without having to grapple with the disruptive potential of the divergent multiplicity that might be at stake (albeit muted) in a situation.

It must be stressed that dealing with divergent multiplicity was not the problem that originally concerned the scholars who have been giving shape to what I call science-plus. This scholarship was concerned with producing compelling stories of power-infused post-natural entanglements involving humans and nonhumans, not of entanglements involving collectives in which this particular distribution of agencies is neither the only nor the most relevant. Thus, my point is not to criticize an apple tree for not giving oranges; rather, what I seek to highlight is that oranges do not hang well from apple trees. Let me put it in these terms. As I have said, it seems that when political ontology raises as a problem the difficulty that science has in conceiving of spirit masters and other similar entities as anything other than cultural beliefs, science-plus misunderstands that the problem is about inclusion, that nonsecular cosmologies (represented by these entities) are not taken into account in the descriptions of more-than-human assemblages that science-plus undertakes solely on the basis of science. The response, then, is to include these cosmologies in the description, on the assumption that even if they run counter to (natural or social) scientific understandings, they can all be rubbed against each other to produce the more textured vantage (science-plus) of the ethnographer. What is missed here is that the sharpness of contrast, which spirit masters or ancestors afford, seeks to make evident a more general point that exceeds the presence or not of nonsecular cosmologies in a situation. The point is about the impossibility of "peaceful" synthesis, singularization, or the staging of a meta-frame or superseding vantage *outside conditions like the one in Mol's Dutch hospital*—that is, a situation in which divergent multiplicity has either *not yet manifested* or has already been successfully suppressed or evacuated by coloniality.[59]

Now, it should be emphasized that what I have just said does not mean that working articulations are impossible when it comes to divergent multiplicity; controlled equivocations that enable the balanced articulation of divergent modes of being as the one represented by the bird/rabbit figure are certainly possible. Thus, the point of emphasizing the impossibility of synthesis or meta-framing is never to lose sight of the fact that, as Stengers puts it, when it comes to divergent multiplicity, "ontological clashes would have to be anticipated everywhere, as no issue can any longer be considered a matter of free deliberation."[60] And here we finally come to why the resonances between my acquaintance's arguments and this scholarship strengthen my worries about claims of the pliability of science to cosmopolitics. Either by more or less explicitly ranking different "knowledge practices" and affirming that science knows best after all, or by considering that divergent practices can be instrumentalized to generate the superseding vantage point or meta-frame of science-plus, both positions scale themselves above the fray. In this way, they shortcut one of the tasks that political ontology considers of the utmost importance: the laborious attention to unrecognized divergences (or the uncommon) and the search for ways to articulate antagonistic ones without activating the coloniality inherent to a standpoint that assumes itself to be above the fray. I see this as critically important because, as I argued in the interlude, I fear that when this attention wavers, the one-world world finds fertile soil to ground its infrastructures of displacement. This worry becomes even more acute as an emerging formation of power consolidates the Anthropocene (under its various guises) as the "big postnatural problem" everyone must face.

POSTNATURAL ENTANGLEMENTS AND GEONTOPOWER

A recent work by Nigel Clark and Bronislaw Szerszynski on "planetary social thought," which also arises from a concern with postnatural human/ nonhuman entanglements, engages more thoroughly with the challenge posed by the divergent multiplicity of—to keep using the terms of science-plus— "cosmologies" that have neither humans nor nonhumans.[61] In a nutshell, Clark and Szerszynski argue that the mutual imbrication of planetary multiplicity (nonhuman agencies) and earthly multitudes (human agencies) shows up in how some of the always as-yet-to-be-determined potentialities of the former become realized through the practices of the latter—or, what is the same, the imbrications manifest in how "the Earth speaks through us" in practice.[62] Consequently, the phenomena subsumed under the term *Anthropocene* can thus be seen as one way the Earth speaks through one (let's say, modern) version of earthly multitudes; it expresses the joining of a particular set of potential planetary dynamics—for instance, the capacity of carbon to accumulate in the atmosphere given the right conditions—with a particular set of human agencies, such as the fortuitous emergence and expansion of "capitalist modernity" and "carbon democracy."[63]

As is often the case with science-plus, the main narrator (or spokesperson) for planetary multiplicity is geological science, which discloses how multiplicity and self-differentiation are constitutive of the Earth. But unlike science-plus, planetary social thought understands that the different cosmologies that express earthly multitudes cannot be simply rubbed together with the story told by this particular spokesperson (i.e., geosciences), for they each "offer their own pathways into the multiplicities proper to material existence."[64] In other words, for Clark and Szerszynski, it is not that earthly multitudes (including "cosmologies" and geosciences) "represent" in different ways or have different perspectives on planetary multiplicity; rather, they are the latter's actualized expression. The authors recognize that there is, however, a logical tension between the multiplicity of the planet as "narrated" by (other) earthly multitudes (or what science-plus would call *cosmologies*) and the story of planetary multiplicity "narrated" by geosciences. In no small measure, the tension spans from a recognition of the mutual irreducibility of these narratives, and the scientific one's implication in the brutal suppression of the others through colonialism. For Clark and Szerszynski, this is problematic not only in ethical terms but also in practical terms, for it has reduced the very repertoire of pathways through which planetary multiplicity can express itself, thus increasingly locking the planet in a process of self-differentiation that doesn't bode well for many extant forms of life. And it is precisely in grappling with this tension while wanting to remain faithful to the empirical findings of the geosciences that the authors reach out for what, within these sciences, makes it possible to advance the wager that "'divergent worlding practices' inhere in the world itself without giving Western science the first or last word in articulating these enactments."[65]

The story that planetary social thought tells is powerful and compelling on many accounts, and I will have more to say about it later. Here I want to push the envelope a bit more following a thread that is left a bit dangling: the practical implications of divergent multiplicity's irreducibility, particularly when it erupts as antagonisms that involve science. Let me put it this way: declaring "our" geoscience-based stories about planetary multiplicity symmetrical to those of other earthly multitudes does not address science's ongoing practical involvement in suppressing other pathways of planetary multiplicity, as evidenced by conflicts such as those around atiku and caribou. In effect, these kinds of conflicts are profoundly connected with the expansion and maintenance of the very infrastructures of displacement that make it possible to tell a geoscience-based story of planetary multiplicity! Think how just the instruments required to tell such a story (satellites, telescopes, ice core drills, and so on) depend on electricity and minerals produced by hydroelectric dams and mines just like the ones established in nitassinan, never mind the wider assemblage of infrastructures and practices (from governments to impact assessment studies) that make the latter possible. Thus, even if we accept Clark and Szerszynski's wager that, in principle, science does not have the first or last word in articulating how divergent worlding practices inhere in the world, in practice, we find that it expresses a form of planetary multiplicity that is not simply in tension with other expressions of that multiplicity but tramples on them. And this trampling promises to become even more acute as the centrality of science (particularly the natural sciences) increases amid the surfacing everywhere of a postnatural formation of power that Elizabeth Povinelli has baptized "geontopower."[66]

According to Povinelli, "Biopower (the governance through life and death) has long depended on a subtending geontopower (the difference between the lively and the inert)," which the conditions labeled "Anthropocene" now make more evident everywhere.[67] In the context of tropes of planetary extinction, the fundamental difference between Life and Nonlife becomes increasingly more prominent as a basis for contemporary formations of power than the distinction (and tensions) between Life and Death. In other words, the logic, justification, and denunciation of practices of governance gain traction in relation to the tensions that run along the line dividing Life from Nonlife. And as we have seen with science-plus and planetary social thought, that line is traced primarily with the narrative fodder of the natural sciences.[68]

I contend that in the context of geontopower, and not withstanding openings to "alter-narratives," the privileging of scientific narratives further orients postnatural figures toward the big. In effect, if in biopolitics the pair "life and death" and the governance of populations pivot around each other, then in geontopower, the pair Life and Nonlife has as its counterpart a series of correlative "targets" that, including but also exceeding the notion of population, are increasingly larger: entire species, ecosystems, the earth systems, and the planet. This increase in the "size" of the "targets" of governance is accompanied by an increase in the extension of the infrastructures required to care for and pay attention to problems that affect them. Again, think of the size and density of the infrastructures required in the twenty-first century to know and care for caribou as an indicator species for subarctic ecosystems compared to those required in the early twentieth century to know and care for it simply as a game animal. And let's not even compare either of these with the infrastructures required, under the right circumstances, for being careful with atiku![69] Finally, but no less important, the shift in scale brought about by geontopower has a correlate in terms of affectual intensity. For many, the stakes attached to the governance of these large-scale issues cannot be higher. As my acquaintance conveyed, what could be more compelling than, for example, saving the scant population of a species at risk of extinction in order to sustain the integrity of one of the ecosystems that keep our common planet Earth alive? Recalling how usually "moderate" commentators (and perhaps even ourselves) reacted to those who resisted vaccination through the COVID pandemic should bring home how compelling the "size" of a problem might become in making coercion appear as a reasonable response to stances deemed "unreasonable."

The density, extension, and complexity of postnatural figures operating as infrastructures of displacement are of such magnitude that the word *despotism*, which Engels used to describe how the big exercises its demands on "all social organization," seems too blunt and imprecise. These demands operate in so many ways, both blunt and subtle, their tendrils reaching so deeply that their effect is better grasped by words such as *attachment* and *obligation*, both made intensely acute by the feeling of urgency that comes along with geontopower. And it is precisely these affective tones associated with figures of the big in their postnatural guise that constitute a formidable challenge for the task of sustaining, creating, and re-creating infrastructures of emplacement oriented to the small.

Given its centrality in the narratives that bolster attachments to figures of the big, the question of whether science can play anything but a colonial role in relation to the divergent multiplicity of emplaced collectives, and the infrastructures that ground them, comes clearly to the fore. My gut answer would be that I see little sign of this being plausible. In this regard, I am tempted to paraphrase what Povinelli says of late liberalism and apply it to science—that is, in a context where many argue that changes "will have to be so significant that what we are will no longer be," science "says that we can change and be the same, nay, even more of what we already are."[70] And yet I am warned by those who, like Stengers, call for us not to give in to a clash that seems all but assured without exploring the possibility of turning science practitioners into allies. (Of course, this call is even more compelling for those who, like me, are casting their lot with the vision that in principle appears the weakest.) Can science be without figures of the big? Is another science possible? What infrastructures might be required for suspension or betrayal of its attachments to these figures to become a possibility? These are questions for which, in lieu of a proper answer, I can only offer a hunch born from practical experience, read through a cinematic analogy.

Science Interruptus

As I advanced before, my probing of compositionist cosmopolitics through the caribou/atiku conflict led me to raise the question of what it would entail to enact a cosmopolitics that hinges on divergent multiplicities. For our research team (composed of academics and Innu community-based experts), this was a thoroughly practical question that prompted us to explore the purposeful staging of a controlled equivocation that could enable atiku and caribou to hold together symmetrically while avoiding the hunting ban. One way in which we have done this is through our proposal to wildlife managers that a limited hunt of atiku be allowed to the Innu communities, under their strict "traditional" protocols. The pitch is that the amount of work required to follow the protocols, and their enforcement by Innu Nation (with the backing of Elders), would have better results in terms of addressing the biologists' concerns than a ban that no Innu will ever abide by and that is nearly impossible for governmental agencies to effectively enforce. In other words, a restricted hunt would cater to Innu concerns with keeping a relation with Kanipinikassikueu and to biologists' concerns with keeping tabs on how many and what kinds of caribou are being hunted (male, females, calves, healthy, unhealthy, and so on). A homonymic practice with two different referents.

In 2012, before the ban was passed, on-the-ground wildlife officers (i.e., the ones who must confront, in practice, their limited enforcement capacity) promised to give serious consideration to the proposal, but soon after, under public pressure, the decision was made higher in the provincial ministerial hierarchy to pass the ban (and since then, the refusal to entertain our proposal has remained constant at that level). Nevertheless, a few years later, our team was engaged by staff from the regional office of the federal (as opposed to provincial) agency in charge of wildlife—i.e., the Canadian Wildlife Service (CWS)—who found our approach to the conflict worth exploring and have since collaborated with us in modestly advancing our proposal and making it more robust. In effect, CWS financed our team's project to develop a methodology for conducting a cumulative impact assessment of atiku that could be symmetrical with the cumulative impact assessments of caribou produced by biologists and wildlife managers to inform their policies. This project also involved translation as controlled equivocation, although in the form of a study that foregrounds the divergences between atiku and caribou and thus seeks to evaluate the impact of various developments on atiku, based on a set of criteria that differ from those used to evaluate impacts on caribou.

I will not dwell further on the details of either of these "projects," for what interests me here is what made them worthy of serious consideration by our interlocutors. In the first case, the main reason was expressed quite openly by the wildlife managers working on the ground; for them, it was readily apparent that a total ban on hunting could not be effectively enforced across the vastness of Labrador. In addition, and especially if entire communities were bent on disregarding it, they feared that the consequence of the ban would be like dimming their surveying capacities: they would have no community collaboration to keep tabs on the numbers and status of animals being hunted. In the second case, the willingness to give serious consideration to our ideas was a bit more complex. Besides recognition of the unenforceability of the ban, the conflict between the province and the Innu sounded a dissonant note in the context of the Canadian federal government's promotion of "reconciliation."

The word *reconciliation* purports to express the state's recognition of, and commitment to redress, damages that its colonial policies inflicted on the Indigenous peoples inhabiting what is nowadays Canada.[71] Strong debates, particularly among Indigenous peoples themselves, surround the concept and the work it actually does (e.g., Does it open new possibilities for more respectful relations between Indigenous and non-Indigenous peoples, or is it a cosmetic change that seeks to keep the status quo? Are these alternatives always mutually exclusive?). But beyond these debates, and often disregarding them, what is clear is that the concept has permeated in uneven and often superficial ways into Canadian public discourses and the policies of institutions, from governmental agencies through the private sector to universities. To put it candidly, even if they are unclear on what it might entail in practice, many Canadian institutions are keen on pursuing reconciliation—or at least wish to avoid appearing to interfere with it, if possible. This "spirit of reconciliation," which is actively promoted within federal government agencies, animated the regional CWS office to open up to our project. Indeed, after we made a public presentation of our "atiku project" for CWS personnel, a participant told me as much:

> We will need more of these kinds of conversations if we are going to get our work done while advancing the reconciliation agenda. I understand we have our data and models, but in my humble opinion, riding roughshod over Aboriginals to impose them is ethically wrong, but it is even more so in practical terms. Look, the provincial government has now been entangled in a court battle with the Innu for, what, five years? Do you know what a drain of resources that implies? What the heck! They could have hired two technicians during these years with the money they are paying lawyers! And to top it off, I don't think the judge will rule against Aboriginal rights. So, when all is said and done, and if they can at all, their [the provincial government's] guys in Labrador will have to rebuild the bridges with the Innu that their bosses burnt . . . and the caribou will be gone anyway.

Notice that, as with the province's ground personnel ("their guys") in Labrador, for my interlocutor, the attempted imposition of the ban is problematic more on practical than on ethical terms. Not only will it not achieve what it intends (the caribou will be gone anyway), but it also will worsen the conditions for doing anything else (the bridges of collaboration will be burnt). Yet rather than being attributed only to the government's limited capacity to enforce, on the ground, an intervention based on "scientific data and models," the ban's impracticality is correlated with the capacity that "Aboriginal rights" might have, in the context of reconciliation, to short-circuit the operations of the Reason Police; that is, of the state's usual legitimation of the imposition of science-based solutions that are as little disrupting as possible of the status quo that privileges extractivism.[72] In other words, the arrangement of elements (actors, legislations, general public sentiments, and so on) in the situation is such that they at least slow down the play of reasonable politics and open a space for the staging of translations as controlled equivocations.

We have here again a situation in which infrastructures of displacement (in this case, the practicalities of enacting the "laws" of science and the legislated "law") are driven to interrupt each other, creating gaps where infrastructures of emplacement may gain a grounding. Science, however, is a reluctant ally in a cosmopolitics that hinges on divergent multiplicity. It might be willing to forgo the demands of its "data and models" only when it cannot proceed as usual—that is, when it is cut down to the size of the situation and cannot simply apply the general rules associated with its postnatural figures of the big. So, as in the Yshiro case we saw in act 1, interrupting infrastructures of displacement (including science as usual) wherever possible appears as an important "strategy" to foster spaces for emplacement.

However, this is not enough, for it puts the problem "out there." It leaves science's practitioners as adversaries, already clearly distinguished from "us," when we want to both try to turn them into allies and acknowledge that even if attempting to escape from their grip, "we" are also subject to demands from and obligations toward figures of the big. And here is where my cinematic analogy might come in handy. It involves a scene in Zacharias Kunuk and Norman Cohn's film *The Journals of Knud Rasmussen*, which dramatizes from the Inuit point of view the "conversion to Christianity in 1922 of Avva, Igloolik's last shaman and his family."[73] The scene comes close to the end of the movie when, after surviving a harsh winter journey with no luck catching animals to eat, Avva's starving group arrives at Igloolik, a village they left years ago and whose inhabitants have now converted to Christianity under the leadership of Umik.[74] "We eat after we pray," Umik tells Avva: "The hunters bring their meat first to me, and we eat all together after my sermon. Will you join us?" Avva is thus driven to decide whether he and his family will convert to Christianity, and thus survive starvation, or will remain attached to his animal spirit relatives and succumb to it. In the scene I am interested in, we see

Avva telling the spirits (which, throughout the movie and without ever being directly addressed, appear as silent, fur-dressed characters, always close to him) that they have to go now, that they have to leave him alone. The spirits start to cry his name as they move away, turning their gaze back to him, only to hear again Avva's pained and fearful cries that they have to go so that he can take in the Christian spirit; this goes on until the spirits disappear into the horizon.

Rather than a "one-reality" version of conversion, according to which someone realizes their beliefs are unreal and therefore converts to the "truth," what the scene shows is that within a purview of multiple reals, conversion could involve very painful but thoughtful decisions about the kinds of attachments and obligations that, in certain circumstances, one might or might not be willing or able to honor.[75] This kind of conversion does not require denying the existence of our demanding "relatives" but rather gauging (as far as one can) the effects that maintaining or severing relations with them may have. Avva came to a crossroads where responding to the demands and obligations of his animal-spirit helpers was no longer viable, as far as he could see in that moment. It is true that, in part, this crossroads was imposed by the particular demands of a Christian spirit that vied for exclusive fidelity. (One requirement for conversion, conveyed by Umik, involved eating parts of an animal forbidden by spirit helpers.) But even if tremendously restrictive and jealous, this "big" spirit offered an alternative to starving. I wonder if a sort of inverse situation to the one depicted by this movie might be necessary to push us away from displacement and its orientation to the big. Maybe the strategy of interrupting infrastructures of displacement wherever possible must come alongside the building of infrastructures that, providing alternative forms of grounding, are in one way or another more inclined to emplacement and offer something of a refuge from outright displacement and the big. In other words, the increasing unviability of the one-world world effect, which interruptions might make evident, may need to be responded to with viably small stories.

POSTLUDE

Viably Small Stories for the Displaced

Any intelligent fool can make things bigger, more complex, and more violent. It takes a touch of genius—and a lot of courage to move in the opposite direction.
—E. F. SCHUMACHER, "Small Is Beautiful," 1973

I began writing this book because I felt that in trying to respond to momentous challenges (defined in particular ways), the dominant stories about how to live together well seem to be caught in a vicious circle. In effect, qua grounding infrastructures, these political imaginations re-produce and expand what I have come to see as constitutive of these challenges—namely, the relentless expansion of infrastructures of displacement and their one-world world effect. Informed by critical voices that have questioned the assumptions underpinning these dominant imaginations, I set out to explore ways to cultivate imaginations that, emerging from a political ontology that makes room for emplacement, could break the circle. Thus, true to one of the most common meanings attributed to the term *political ontology* as an account of the elements that "comprise political reality," in this postlude I connect various threads of my discussion throughout the book to offer a schematic overview of the elements that comprise the "reality" within which a call for emplacement makes sense as a response to momentous challenges.[1] The purpose is twofold: to situate this proposal more clearly among other political imaginations that also seek to respond to these challenges and, based on what we have glimpsed in acts 1 and 2, to explore some questions that arise from the hurdles that a cosmopolitics of emplacement will have to likely face. I hope this will help move the discussion about emplacement forward.

Between the Universal and the Pluriversal Effects:
A Political Ontology

I have argued that the reasonable politics that characterize the modern collective involve the enactment of a story about the good life, the story of modernization. This enactment entails a movement in which divergent modes of existence are first conceived as human perspectives on a universal external reality; then these "human perspectives" are more or less forcefully rounded up, ranked, and finally driven to conform to the dictates of the Reason Police, which is none other than the (self-) authorized spokesperson of this allegedly universal external reality, the one-world world that supposedly preexists and is common to all human perspectives. As we have seen, the plausibility of this one-world world qua universal is an effect of successful extensions of the infrastructures of displacement through which it gets grounded and takes place. Thus, since its "reasonability" depends on being able to invoke a plausible one-world world, which in turn depends on constant extension, the reasonable politics of modernization ends up having a specific scalar orientation; it can only go big(ger).

I also argued, and we have seen examples of this in acts 1 and 2, that coloniality (i.e., the constant work of suppressing and/or taming expressions of pluriversal multiplicity) is crucial to the extension of infrastructures of displacement that constitute the one-world world. I further pointed out that in the face of momentous challenges, which are very much its collateral effects, the story of modernization gives way to a variety of successor stories. Some of these stories (which I grouped under the banners of consensus and dissensus narratives) remain resolutely oriented to the same horizon of a preexisting common world and prolong the "methods" of reasonable politics when seeking to address the challenges. Other stories (which I grouped under the banner of compositionism), give way to a cosmopolitics that centers the very process of constituting a common world as the issue at stake in politics, in general, and as a response to the momentous challenges, more specifically. This is an extremely fruitful move, for it expands the scope of politics beyond the narrow confines of reasonable politics. Yet, there is also some continuity insofar as certain versions of cosmopolitics still pursue the composition of *a* common world out of the heterogeneity of the pluriverse—that is, they carry on with an orientation to the big. Commentators have pointed out that this orientation risks the reintroduction of coloniality in the process of commoning the common world. I added that such risk is compounded when, advanced as the urgent response needed to tackle momentous challenges, this commoning of the common world primarily hinges on incorporating nonhumans recognizable for the sciences into politics.

One issue that stands out from this brief overview of some of my arguments is that the political imaginations (from the reasonable politics of modernization to the cosmopolitics of successor stories) that are involved in discussions of momentous challenges are predominantly focused on commoning as the answer to the fundamental question to which politics must respond. In effect, I surmise that if in general this question is enunciated in terms of "How can we live together well?" the implicit subtext in it is "despite our differences." True, the "differences" that need to be overcome are conceived in very dissimilar ways—as the parochialism of human perspectives, by reasonable politics, and as the unruly multiplicity of the pluriverse, by the cosmopolitics of compositionism—but while this variance is not trivial, it remains the case that when the question is posed in these terms commoning will necessarily appear as the logical answer, and the common as the necessary horizon of politics. This is even the case for those versions of cosmopolitics that might be somehow apprehensive about the project of commoning a "big" common world and are more enthusiastic about what, playing on Haraway's words, we could call "just big enough common worlds." For no matter how little or how much they are attracted to the big, for the cosmopolitics of compositionists the pluriverse is an immanent presence, and this calls for commoning as the quintessential political gesture. Indeed, whether as the starting point of commoning, or as that which exceeds all commoning, or as that which must be protected from hasty exclusions in processes of commoning, in whatever form it appears in the cosmopolitics of the compositionists, the pluriverse requires no effort to happen. Thus, by default, all the attention, all the concern, and all the relevant efforts end up being directed at commoning.

Keeping the shared concern with commoning in sight helps foregrounding a couple of "novelties" that the cosmopolitics of emplaced collectives contribute to the whole idea of cosmopolitics and to my political ontology. As I argued in the prelude, for the cosmopolitics of emplaced collectives, the fundamental challenge of (cosmo)politics can be expressed as, How can we go on together *in divergence*? Posed thus, answering this challenge requires something else in addition to commoning. It requires uncommoning through carefully tending to the heterogeneous multiplicity of place so that it is not diminished in the process of commoning. In this vein, it is important to stress that uncommoning is not just a defense that emplaced collectives have against being phagocytized into a bigger common; rather, it is primarily how they carefully reenact a livable pluriverse as place. And here we come to another insight the life projects of emplaced collectives offer us: rather than an immanent presence, the pluriversal is an effect that can be better or worse achieved depending on how uncommoning unfolds in its dance with commoning.

Taking in the novelties offered by the cosmopolitics of emplaced collectives, I propose that the various political imaginations discussed in the book (but more specifically in the interlude) can be located as extending over an entire spectrum of possibilities that stretch between the coordinates of the universal and the pluriversal. Each of these coordinates also expresses the epitome of scalar orientations toward the big and the small as horizons that, like attraction poles, lure, pull, and shape political imaginations. Figure 6 reflects how I envision this. It condenses the simultaneous moves of mapping various political imaginations and staging from where and why this book cut its problem in a way that calls forth a political imagination oriented to emplacement. In other words, it visually inscribes the political ontology I have sought to articulate here.

A few remarks are in order so that the diagram can be fully grasped. The diagram can be seen as analogous to the figure where, early in the book, I stretched the bird/rabbit illusion in opposite directions so that each figure could be made more discernible on their own. In this case, what becomes more discernible are the orientations that differentially shape political imaginations, even if neither of the poles is ever totally absent from those imaginations. It might also be helpful to think of this diagram as a yin-yang symbol. Notice that, as is the case with the yin-yang, in my diagram each pole contains the seed of its opposite. The pluriversal contains the seed of the universal as a propensity toward commoning—that is, a propensity toward gathering heterogeneous multiplicities into common groupings. Likewise, the universal contains the seed of the pluriversal as uncommoning, a propensity for divergences and multiplicities to exceed the formed common groupings. Also, notice that the practices that express these propensities get transformed as they move from one pole and get closer to the other. Driven by the intention (inscribed in grounding infrastructures) of rebirthing the heterogeneous multiplicity of place, uncommoning turns into carefulness toward multiplicities and divergences that are

A Political Ontology of the Universal and the Pluriversal

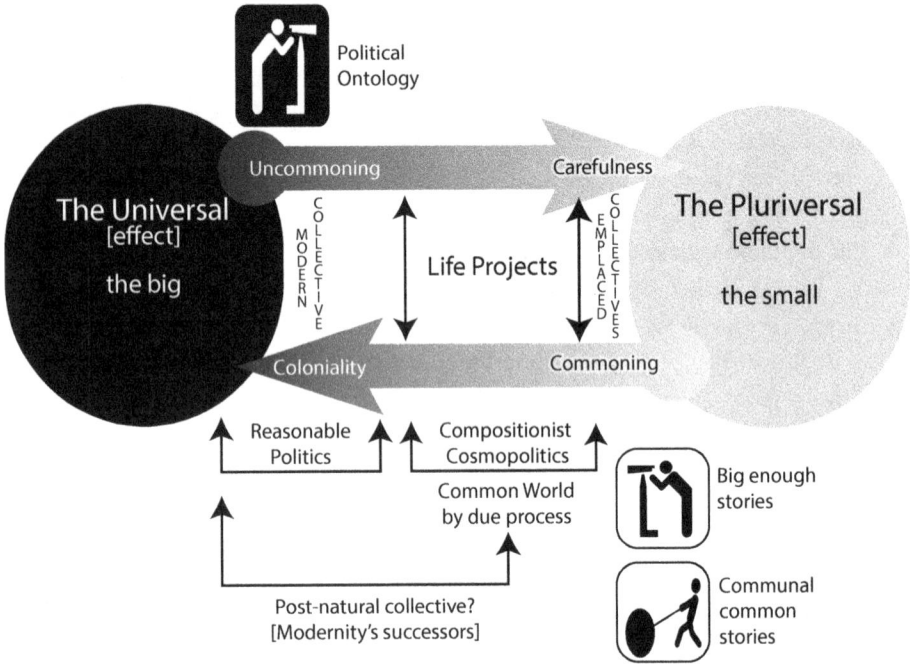

FIGURE 6. Setting the universal and the pluriversal (effects) as coordinates enables us to map various political imaginations vis-à-vis each other and to explain why it might be worth thinking of "momentous challenges" in terms of an imbalance between emplacement and displacement. Drawing by Steve Chapman.

crucial to spawning emplaced collectives. In contrast, driven by the intention (also inscribed in grounding infrastructures) of ensuring that the universal effect remains unchallenged, commoning turns into coloniality and relative carelessness toward multiplicities and divergences, thus begetting a "displaced" collective like the modern one, and possibly some of its successors, as hinted by the latter's positioning within the diagram.

With this diagram as a reference, speaking of the centrality of commoning in reasonable politics and the cosmopolitics of compositionism is tantamount to saying that the question of how to live together well is being conceived only along the arrow that goes from the pluriversal to the universal, from the small to the big. This, I contend, has a bearing on how a (cosmo)politics oriented to emplacement ends up appearing irrelevant or impracticable in the face of momentous challenges. In effect, in a scenario where uncommoning is missing, an orientation to the big ends up appearing as the only horizon, either to be reached or to be feared. But, before explaining further, a reminder of how I conceive scalar orientations is in order.

Recall that in the pragmatics of scale that inspire my use, the terms *big* and *small* do not imply a ready-made calculus of size; rather, taken together, they denote the directions in which collectives, by virtue of the ways in which their infrastructures ground them, might scale themselves. Thus, when I situate both reasonable politics and compositionist versions of cosmopolitics over the arrow of commoning that points toward the big, I am not implying that the latter will necessarily enact the big. In effect, some political imaginations (like reasonable politics or a cosmopolitics that seek to compose a common world through due process) might decidedly set themselves to enact that horizon. Others, like the cosmopolitics of big enough stories, might want to avoid hasty exclusions in practices oriented in that direction, and yet others, like stories about the defense of communal commons, might even resist its pull. Thus, the point of highlighting that these otherwise very different political imaginations are all aligned along an arrow pointed in that particular direction is to underscore two issues: first, that active uncommoning does not even figure in these political imaginations, and second, that such situation makes it easier for commoning to effortlessly slide from just grouping (i.e., the delineation of specific existents), to aggregation, and then to expansion, thereby turning all these imaginations into grounding infrastructures tilted toward displacement. What the politics of emplaced collective offers in this context is an active counterbalance to that tilt. In effect it makes the cosmopolitical question hinge not only on the challenge of commoning but also on the challenge of uncommoning.

Including uncommoning and an orientation to the small into the picture renders the pluriversal and the universal symmetrical in principle—that is, both appear as the effects of the joint doings of commoning and uncommoning. Thus, just as the universal effect can never fully stabilize itself as "the universe," the "pluriverse" is never always already there. And while speculating about the implications of absolute and final dominance of either pole is utterly futile (one cannot be without the other), degrees of imbalance between them can be conceived and problematized. This is precisely what I have strived to do throughout the book, first by setting the imbalance between poles (especially within political imaginations qua grounding infrastructures) at the center of momentous challenges and then proposing that a cosmopolitical imagination oriented toward emplacement might help to establish some balance. Now, it is worth stressing (again) that advancing this imbalance as a problematic worthy of attention is done from a standpoint that is not outside but rather within such problematization. This is why, in the diagram, I have included an icon that positions this standpoint, political ontology, within and along the other political imaginations. This is my way of indicating the closing of the circular argument that, as I said in the preface, is necessary to the exercise in bootstrapping that is essaying an ontology in writing. Thus, the icon labeled "political ontology" conveys that the diagram you are looking at represents the "political reality" (a political ontology) that is seen through the binoculars of the person depicted in the icon and which has been slowly staged in the book. If this staging has been cogent enough, you should now be standing "there" with the person in the icon, able to recognize the key features of the problem that I wanted you to perceive in the terrain where various political imaginations grapple with each other and which ultimately provide the rationale for making a bid for emplacement.

Life Projects and the Displaced

Insofar that they address the fundamental political question of how to live together well (or, as in the life projects of emplaced collectives, how to go on together in divergence), any political imagination involves invoking into being a certain "we" that will carry on its bidding. This raises the question of who might be the "we" that a political ontology for emplacement invokes. I have flagged at several points in the book that this political ontology is not intended to account for, give voice to, or guide those collectives that, like the yrmo and nitassinan, already have their own ways of articulating what I call *life projects*. Rather, inspired by them, it is generally meant for those who, with variable intensities, might feel somehow "displaced." This "we" is defined neither by identity politics nor by location in an urban or rural setting but rather by the perception that our modes of existence have come to depend on infrastructures of displacement to an extent that has become problematic, to say the least. But above anything else, the call is for those of us who feel trapped in constantly proliferating infrastructures of displacement, even as we try to generate more emplaced modes of existence.

At the beginning of the book, I mentioned that the political ontology I essay here partly stems from connecting the dots between my experience of living in displacement and my familiarity with profoundly emplaced modes of existing, which are persistently pushed to (r)exist by the very infrastructures that enable my displaced mode of existence. The connection had a particularly painful bite for me insofar as I have for many years been closely involved with efforts to advance life projects like "recovering the yrmo" that endure in the interstices created by pitching different infrastructures of displacement against each other. The painful bite I refer to is the realization that having life projects take shape in those interstices further entrenches the asymmetrical entanglement between emplacement and displacement in grounding infrastructures. In this way, life projects, and the (relatively more) emplaced collectives they might generate, end up appearing as an archipelago of small islands surrounded by the constantly encroaching ocean of displacement upon which, paradoxically, they become increasingly dependent. And yet, from the point of view of those invested in generating these interstices so that modes of (r)existence can be, it is often difficult to see what else can be done. But not knowing how else to sustain infrastructures of emplacement against the grain is just the flip side of the pervasiveness of infrastructures of displacement. And here is where, for me, the connecting dots also illuminate other paths, where the fractal nature of the "frontier" that I mentioned at the beginning of the book becomes patently clear, where the ever-expanding infrastructures of displacement that until yesterday to some might have appeared to be "their problem over there," reveals itself to be "our problem, right here." This "revelation" recenters the dominance of displacement as a problem that falls squarely at the feet of those of us who, even if for all the best reasons, keep extending it, not the least, through the political imaginations we enact. Hence, a central task that defines the "we" political ontology seeks to invoke is crafting our own life projects that could function as *viable* grounding infrastructures oriented toward the pluriversal and the small. I emphasize the word *viable* because it is this quality that inspires me the most in the life projects of emplaced collectives, for the true challenge is how to simultaneously be *small and viable*. I see life projects as stories of a good life that are viably small for the present circumstances of collectives, which, like the yrmo and nitassinan, (r)exist against the grain of ever-expanding infrastructures of displacement.

Saying that life projects are viably small stories means that they are crafted in such a way that their smallness cannot be taken as irrelevant to how other stories or visions of a good life, particularly those veering in the direction of the big, are being grounded. For example, the equivocal call to recover the yrmo where the yrmo appears as the traditional territory of the Yshir Nation is a life project that expresses the viably small in the current circumstances. Indeed, a few decades ago, the yrmo did not have to be a "traditional territory" nor did groups of yshiro-au-oso speakers have to constitute a nation to be a viable emplaced collective, a viable small common. But likewise, a few decades ago, a territory was an attribute of the nation-state, which did not need to pay attention to the presence of "primitive Indians" when establishing it. Life projects such as recovering the Yrmo are viable small stories in the sense that, by using available interscalar vehicles, they partially yield to the overwhelming imperative to move toward the universal and the big but never completely give in. Rather, as we have seen, they constantly pitch infrastructures of displacement against each other to open spaces where they can remain viable as small commons, thereby still giving plausibility to the pluriversal. Having said that, it is important to recognize that the challenge of telling viably small stories, of crafting life projects, is slightly different for those to whom political ontology's proposal is mainly addressed. In effect, depending on the intensity of our "being displaced," moving toward the pluriversal and the small might mean strengthening existing political imaginations that work as infrastructures of emplacement for some and refurbishing some imaginations that have the potential to go in that direction for others, and inventing them from whatever scraps might be gathered for yet others, one step at a time. And each of these positions must also grapple with those who for different reasons would outright reject the idea of the pluriversal, let alone the proposal to move toward it.

Those readers who have been primed through an engagement with the notion of cosmopolitics—be it through the works of compositionists or through familiarity with emplaced collectives in their guise as small communal commons—should, in principle, have no difficulties in following the logic of the proposal. In this sense, although in my diagram political ontology appears diagonally opposed to the cosmopolitics of big enough stories and stories of the communal common, the opposition must be understood as complementary. I'll explain. In contrast to political ontology, which has the universal at its back and its attention turned in the direction of uncommoning, these two political imaginations/stories have the pluriverse at their back and their attention aligned with the arrow of commoning. However, big enough stories are attending to the dangers that come with any movement in that direction, and stories of the communal common are trying to wrest the small communal commons from the attraction force of the universal and the big. In other words, even if their attention is turned in the direction of the big, neither of these stories is committed to it. Thus, political ontology and these stories are pliable, in conjunction, to eventually mimic the twofold attention that life projects of emplaced collectives give to both commoning and uncommoning in the process of grounding themselves. This is certainly a possibility. However, considering the present imbalance, I will argue that the active practice of un-commoning is what must take precedence for now.

As we learned in act 1, one form of uncommoning is affirming and mak-ing evident how infrastructures of displacement (or interscalar vehicles of the global) might lodge within them inklings of emplacement, and another one is interrupting infrastructures of displacement wherever possible. I am aware, however, that as Schumacher pointed out in the epigraph that began this chap-ter, moving in the direction of the small (i.e., to actively uncommon) is a very demanding proposition, one that, I would add, appears particularly difficult to accept for the inheritors of modernization. Indeed, engaging in an active practice of uncommoning requires navigating a series of interconnected hurdles that, even if in different ways, apply across the spectrum to all the displaced. Here it is worth recalling Latour's argument that "smallness is not an op-tion" for those who, previously invested in modernization, had been doing "the global"—or, in this book's terms, the one-world world. The argument is a good starting point to center something that connects some of the hurdles a call to uncommoning will have to sort through—namely, a reticence to "scale down."

Latour made the argument about the small in his book *Down to Earth* where, as I indicated in the preface, he sought to propose a new set of coor-dinates to orient politics in the face of what I have been calling *momentous challenges*. He proposed to abandon the vector running between the (for him, largely fallacious) coordinates of the global and the local and redirect what I call *political imagination* toward another coordinate, the Terrestrial. In his argument, the small appeared as a synonym of the local, understood as a self-contained place, the nation to which repentant globalizers now want to re-treat, xenophobically building defenses against the masses of displaced entities that modernization (cum globalization) created and that are flooding every-where. The Terrestrial he proposed as a vector involves his ever-present project of recalling the modern project of a common world to redo it through due process—a recalling that, according to him, has now been made even more imperative by the moral debts of the modernizers: "Yes, Europe was dangerous when it believed itself capable of 'dominating' the world—but wouldn't it be more dangerous still if it shrank down and sought, like a little mouse, to hide itself from history? How could it escape from its vocation of recalling, in all senses of the word 'recall,' the form of modernity that it invented? Precisely because of the crimes it has committed, smallness is not an option."[2]

Interestingly, the Terrestrial rehashes as moral imperative an argument that Latour had made before in terms of the scale of "the problem" being faced and of capabilities to address it. In effect, you might remember that for Latour, what seemed to justify recalling the modern project of a common world in the "times of the Anthropocene" was the scale of the messed-up jumble modernization made when it launched itself upon the planet. For him, there was no going back to a time before this messed-up jumble, the lethality of which could only be confronted by all collectives engaging the (badly designed) modernist dream of a common world to redo it (or compose it) through due process. Elsewhere, in his *Facing Gaia* (the Gifford lectures), Latour made a similar argument, doubting that so-called traditional people "who claim to be assembled, for instance, by Pachamama, the Earth goddess" would have adequate technologies, so to speak, to deal with the magnitude of the momentous challenges we face: "If only we could be sure that what passes for a respect for the Earth is not due to their small numbers and to the relative weakness of their technology. None of those so called 'traditional' people, the wisdom of which we often admire, is being prepared to scale up their ways of life to the size of the giant technical metropolises in which are now corralled more than half of the human race."[3] As we can see, Latour found the size of these collectives and the potency of their technologies wanting for the scale of the problem at hand; tackling it would require these collectives to participate in the composition of a common world with other collectives.

As discussed in act 2, it would seem as if in the postnatural times of the Anthropocene, a large capacity is required to heed the great moral imperative to address a big problem. In effect, what ends up weaving together Latour's technical and moral arguments about the best way to grapple with momentous challenges is this particular scalar orientation toward the big, which functions both as justification and horizon for his version of cosmopolitics. In a friendly critique, Eduardo Viveiros de Castro and Deborah Danowski have pointed out that what Latour did not seem prepared to accept was "that we [what I call the displaced], when the chips are down, might be the ones who will have to scale down our precious ways of living."[4] Of course, many more than Latour will have difficulties in accepting that we, the displaced, must indeed actively shrink to the size of a "little mouse" and understand that this is not hiding from history but rather taking our rightful place in the story of a pluriverse to come. However, delivered by perhaps the most a-modern of the modernizers, the arguments Latour mobilized to back up his reticence toward downscaling shed light on the tremendous hold that an orientation to the big has on us, the displaced. Having proposed another scalar orientation, toward the small, the first crucial question for me is, then, How might the hold that this scalar orientation has on us prevent us from embracing uncommoning and the crafting of life projects? And then, what can be done about it?

Can't Do Small without Doing It (Unless You Are Tricked into It)

Of the political imaginations we have visited, the most explicitly sympathetic to the idea of uncommoning and the small is the one associated with the defense of the communal common and notions of (r)existence. In effect, like what I did in act 1, stories about the defense of the communal common make evident (and greet) the constant work that many "small commons" undertake toward uncommoning the big common into which the state and capitalism seek to capture them. And yet, I will argue, such sympathy seems to depend on the common being defined with a degree of stability and certainty that only the universal and the big can offer. Recall that in the accounts of analysts like Lucia Linsalata, for a common to be properly common it must be produced in close personal relations. I pointed out that, despite affirmations to the contrary, the notion of close personal relations ends up invoking the figure of the natural human. It is true that, without paying attention to the role nonhumans play in them, the small communal commons most analysts tend to focus on appear indeed composed of humans that are physically close, but this is contingent on the "cases" that are being selected as representative of a common, not a feature that defines the common per se. Why is this important? Because there is a problem with implicitly extracting from a series of contingent communal commons a universal standard (i.e., the natural human) against which the common in general can be designated as proper (good and desirable) or not-a-common (bad and undesirable). Let me put the problem this way: if what ultimately justifies uncommoning is the mismatch between the scale of a natural human and the scale of the common that purports to encompass it, then, in the context of a postnatural order in which the "natural human" becomes a chimera, we would be left blind to distinguish between a good common and a bad common—and, consequently, to say when uncommoning might be necessary and how far we should push it. This problem is particularly acute for those who are positioned not as defenders of an already existing small common but as potential defectors from the big common I have been calling *the one-world world*.

The anxiety that the lack of a transcendent standard might produce among us, the displaced, constitutes a big impediment to embracing the proposal of moving toward the small. We, the displaced, are accustomed to having our sights set on figures of the universal and the big and, either as a horizon to be reached or to be repelled, what this pole entails is much easier to imagine than what the opposite pole entails. Herein lies, I believe, part of the enduring appeal and attraction that the big has on the displaced (even for compositionists). In effect, looking in the other direction only offers uncertainty; there is not a lot that can be said about it beyond the most immediate steps. With this, I am looping back to my point in act 1 that, when conceived more generally as a form of uncommoning or moving toward the small, (r)existence only offers uncertainties. I said that (r)existence can be likened to a tactic without strategy—that is, it involves actions done in the immediacy of what is perceived as challenges to a collective's mode of existence without necessarily having a point of arrival in sight. It is the perception of a lack of fit between the arising situation and the constellation of relations that (so far) constitute a given existent or the collective that triggers (cosmo)political actions—in this case, of (r)existence. This, however, does not mean the actions of (r)existence are merely reactive. Precisely it is because they are informed by and enact what I call *principles of emplacement* that, rather than simply being resistance, they constitute a form of (r)existence. The challenge is not simply to repel within an all-or-nothing alternative but rather to keep producing modes of being together in divergence: How do we (the tobich oso, for example) smuggle pitin'bahulut into the development projects Calixto wants? How can we (innu hunters) continue to be careful with atiku while you (wildlife managers) care for caribou? Can we go on together in divergence? Are these arrangements possible? Maybe not, and then we will need to engage each other as enemies.

I bring back this discussion to highlight two points. First, that uncommoning does not require a transcendental yardstick to tell us when it needs to be triggered or how far it must be carried out. Like the proverbial frog that, notwithstanding the myth, does not need a thermometer to tell at exactly what temperature the water becomes unbearably hot and must try either getting out of the pot or cooling the water, there are enough of "us" (existents of all kinds) who feel that a limit has been crossed, beyond which we cease to be meaningful participants in the definition of what should be accepted or excluded from the common we are with. True, things feel profoundly out of scale, out of proportion, and out of balance, although in relation not to a transcendental standard but rather to a variety of relatively contingent ones. But that is good enough to, at least, consider reorienting ourselves in the other direction! Now, and here comes my second point, since what characterizes us as displaced is precisely the relative lack of infrastructures of emplacement to inform our actions, to create our own life projects we will have to rely mostly on our faith in the pluriverse to initially overcome the anxiety of not seeing clearly what that horizon entails and yet actively move in that direction. Put in other words, while tobich oso might be engaged in uncommoning so that their (known) small common/collective can (r)exist along divergent modes of being, we the displaced will have to do it so that an unknown small(er) common/collective can come into existence. I am aware that putting our faith in the pluriverse to do this is a big ask in several registers. For one, we will have to contend with those who would demand we stay the course unless we say exactly what moving toward the pluriversal and the small entails. To these naysayers, I can only reply that demanding further details now to consider moving is tantamount to the frogs refusing to get out of the boiling water because we cannot say exactly how cold it is going to be outside. But there is something even more challenging than naysayers: putting our faith in the pluriverse to get traction toward uncommoning implies withdrawing it from the big, which is a jealous and demanding god. This is indeed a crucial test of viability for life projects.

We have seen in the ethnographic terrain that infrastructures of displacement manifest both as the abhorred and as the embraceable—that is, as the bulldozer that clears the forest in Paraguay but also as the human rights enabling the Yshiro to "defend" the yrmo, or as the mining development in Labrador but also as the regulations that protect a caribou herd in danger of being extirpated. Those infrastructures of displacement that bolster the universal effect but which we cherish are demanding entities that, like a coterie of major and minor gods, give us their protection but also place us under their obligation. This is why it is important to keep in sight that human rights and the bulldozer, protection of caribou and mining, go on constituting the universal effect together and that, as with a Janus-faced god, when paying heed to its benevolent face we keep nurturing its abhorred one as well. Keeping in sight this inherent connection makes it possible to (potentially) drive a wedge between what we are (including our obligations) and what we may become—a necessary step in conversion.

I concluded act 2 by suggesting that what might be demanded from those of us who are mainly with infrastructures of displacement is nothing short of the conversion that, without any guarantee that it was going to work, many emplaced collectives had to go through to remain viable in the face of colonially imposed infrastructures of displacement. Of course, conversion might be painful and sad, but above anything else, it is scary; powerful others do not take kindly to being forfeited, and consequences will ensue. "How can we turn our back on what caribou is telling us about what we need to do to save it as a species indicator?" my wildlife expert acquaintance might tell me. "If we do that, we will pay direly!" Someone might point out that it is easy for social scientists to offer conversion to natural scientists; the former are perhaps not as intensely obliged to the same gods as the latter. To balance the point, let's then imagine that conversion involves recanting human-centered universals, like the notion that human rights should apply equally everywhere. "How can I turn my back on the obligation to defend the dignity of the human above anything else, everywhere, and at all times?" many of my acquaintances in Humanitas might ask me. "If we do that, the world will fall into a chaos of amoral relativism and unrestrained abuse." These are not imagined dangers but rather potential risks of forfeiting the gods that help hold together the one-world world bequeathed by the infrastructures of displacement we are with.

As shown by the wildlife managers who were willing to seriously entertain our research team's proposals to stage "controlled equivocations" of atiku/caribou, conversion is not usually a path that anyone would "freely" choose but rather one that imposes itself because established ones become unviable for a variety of reasons. In these interlocutors' specific case, a loss of confidence regarding the infallibility of their own data and models, a subtle but generalized change in disposition with regards to running roughshod over those who do not accept their data and models, and, of course, a changing legal framework where all of the previous materialize as institutional and policy constraints add up to make established ways of enacting an orientation to the big if not unviable, at least more complicated. More generally, the various phenomena that one might lump under the banner of momentous challenges bring home for many an acute sense of the fragility of the infrastructures of displacement that sustain the universal effect and the big.[5] Of course this is not enough to push an all-out conversion of the displaced away from figures of the big, but it leaves many teetering on the brink of it. How to give them/us a little push over the edge?

A possible response to the question is, with violence. There are a few scholarly works, manifests, and works of fiction that present sabotage and ecoterrorism (understood as violent acts aimed at defending "the environment") almost as necessary to set "human civilization" back on track to a livable future, whatever that might be.[6] I am not sure sabotage and terrorism are necessary, but I do believe they are unavoidable. The kinds of situations these words designate (disruptions of livelihoods, more or less random violence, and so on) are what a growing set of modes of existence is already experiencing, and this will likely continue to expand and intensify. It is doubtful that this disruption and violence will not, at some point, turn directly and purposefully back onto the infrastructures that produce them. In any case, while I do lament the prospect, I neither condone nor condemn it anymore that I could do it with the outbreaks of zoonotic and vector-borne diseases that epidemiologists say follow deforestation.[7] However, as I see it, the disruptions that sabotage and so-called ecoterrorism are likely to produce are only going to add to the push to the brink of conversion without necessarily being definitory of it. The crucial push, I believe, must come from stories that are effective (in material-semiotic terms) not in convincing or alerting a public (which includes us) to the dangers it faces but rather in entrapping it into enacting infrastructures of emplacement that are viable in the specific conditions of heterogeneous here(s) and now(s).

The image of entrapping publics into enacting infrastructures of emplacement is inspired by Alberto Corsín Jiménez's depiction of the "trap" as an interface that imitates and redescribes its environment to generate variations of the latter as new possibilities.[8] The spiderweb imitates the medium in which the fly flies (and by extension, it also imitates the fly), but only enough to intersect it and turn the fly (redescribe it) into prey. The difference here is that what we want to trap (and redescribe) is ourselves, the displaced. In a sense the challenge is analogous to the one Peter Hershock says the Ch'an (or Zen) practitioner faces when she tries to make the Self reach no-Self by mobilizing the will of the Self. Interestingly, Hershock says that if the influence of the "Self" is to be sufficiently curbed it must be deceived into thinking that it is maintaining its central role as a free agent even as it goes on undermining the basis of its control: "In a very literal sense, [the Self] must be tricked into enlightenment [no-Self]."[9] In a similar way, most of us might need to be tricked or trapped into moving toward the small by being deceived/deceiving ourselves that we are still paying heed to the demands of the big as we go on eroding its infrastructures of displacement! But how? There are big enough stories that, being aware of their situatedness, could be helpful in this. I find a good example of this in the planetary social thought of Nigel Clark and Bronislaw Szerszynski that we encountered in act 2.

As you might recall, the general drift of this story is that the present state of the planet (the Anthropocene as a planetary dynamic) reflects a particular combination of two major forms of agential multiplicity: planetary multiplicity (nonhuman agencies) and earthly multitudes (human agencies). Thus, provided that we remain aware that this dynamic is a particular combination of agential multiplicities, speaking of the Anthropocene as a planetary geological dynamic does not mean that things have to be as they are now. In effect, the authors argue, other combinations of human and nonhuman potentialities are there, ready to be activated. Hence, "more than an issue of how to reduce our expenditure of energetic-material reserves . . . or a matter of lessening our dependence on fossil biomass or subterranean ores, it is a question of what planetary dynamics we might yet join or rejoin forces with."[10]

In this story, the agency of the "we" that might do something becomes redistributed so that the "thing" that acts will be a version of the planet itself, one that might impose itself over other, less life-enhancing, versions. In this way, the big narratives of geosciences can take events that beckon to the diminished viability of the one-world world and make them intelligible to a particular set of (modern) human agencies as a prodding in the direction of other versions of the planet. What makes the story compelling as a trap is that it imitates "the environment" of the displaced enough to make them go into it. In effect, it is a big planetary story, involving the big and authorized narratives of the geosciences, but it also redescribes "this environment" in such a way that brings its public all the way to an appreciation that it is the planet itself (with all the authority the displaced bestow to "nature," even if postnatural!) who foretells other pathways forward. Thus, the story leaves its public/prey primed to accept as plausible the idea that viruses, extreme weather, geopolitical turbulences, ecoterrorism, and other similar disruptions to infrastructures of displacement are the manifestation of a set of planetary (i.e., "natural") dynamics that point the direction in which we need to move—that is, toward uncommoning, emplacement, and the small.

Political ontology wants to pick up the displaced from where stories like planetary social thought leave them and trap them a little further into a sort of paradoxical move: bringing the human agencies for whom these kinds of stories are meaningful all the way to a standpoint from which it becomes evident, *in practice*, that what makes these big stories compelling, their very materiality, is part and parcel of the current predicaments they describe and, therefore, that at some point we will need to profoundly alter if not abandon them.

This *paradoxical move* includes political ontology itself. The point can be further expounded by addressing a poignant question many interlocutors have posed to me before: Isn't political ontology itself a big story? Yes, it is! This is the reason why, as you can see in my previous diagram, the icon that stands for political ontology is set close to the universal effect, to the pole of the big. As a practice of critical analysis, political ontology recognizes its grounding through infrastructures of displacement—just consider the (colonial) language in which it is written and the (university) audience to which is directed! But political ontology does not just inherit from modernization a deep entanglement with infrastructures of displacement; it also inherits from the life projects of emplaced collectives the possibility of conceiving an orientation toward the small and the pluriversal. Thus, its aim is to make it increasingly less possible, *in practice*, a story like political ontology that makes a "big call" for uncommoning. Indeed, the horizon that my political ontology chases has no colonial lingua franca, no scholarly canon, no conceptual toolboxes, and stories that could travel in the way the political ontology itself can travel here and now through the infrastructures of displacement it is partly grounded in.

At its core, a political ontology for emplacement is a big call to embrace uncommoning as a common challenge now so that the actual roads toward uncommoning become more uncommon tomorrow. In this sense, the paradoxical move I hope political ontology instigates is reminiscent of one of the "tricks" Hershock says the Ch'an tradition uses to trap the Self into no-Self—that is, indirection. Once the practitioners have set to reach no-Self they push themselves to relentlessly focus on the menial and repetitive tasks of monastic everyday life (cleaning, polishing, cooking, chanting, and so on) in order to attenuate the excitement, attention, discernment, and drive that continually give rise to the pursuing Self, even (and perhaps more so) in its pursuit of no-Self. In a similar way, once the pluriversal, emplacement, or the small have been spelled out as the horizon to pursue, we should carefully focus on the tasks of everyday life in the hope that if we orient them to nurture the specific multiplicity of the here and now in our grounding infrastructures, they will help loosen the hold that infrastructures of displacement have on us.

The Small Might Not Be Beautiful, and Yet . . .

Schumacher's epigraph at the beginning of this postlude, extracted from a text published in the early 1970s, is a testimony that a call to move toward the small is certainly not new. Indeed, the political ontology I have presented in the book does not purport to be inventing the wheel; the aim is more modest but not less ambitious, furnishing the "old wheel" with "tires" that might have a good grip on the terrain of an emerging postnatural formation of power that muddles in new ways any movement toward emplacement and the small. But, since the plead for this orientation is not new, there are conversations to be had with kindred projects generally leaning on that direction, particularly those that, while focusing on the "tasks of everyday life," are moved by a broadly defined concern with autonomy. Language revitalization, food and energy sovereignties, popular economies, feminist economies, transitions, degrowth, post-development, the ecosocial pact of the South, and designs otherwise are just a few labels for the kinds of agendas and projects I am aware of that, variably oriented to the specificity of various here(s) and now(s), might contribute to generating infrastructures of (or veering toward) emplacement, even if this is not their intended aim.[11] I see two general ways in which these agendas and projects can become fellow travelers for life projects. First, the general concern for autonomy in these projects may drive the public they attract to pay attention to uncommoning as a necessary component of (cosmo)politics. Second, their experiments with autonomous forms of undertaking the tasks of everyday life might generate concrete alternatives to increasingly unviable infrastructures of displacement and, hence, facilitate the conversion of which I spoke previously.

There is, however, a dissonance between a political ontology of life projects and some of these "progressive" agendas that must be tackled: if these agendas appear to me as the most obvious fellow travelers for political ontology it is because, to some extent, I share with them certain attachment to pluralism, equality, mutuality, democracy, and other similar values that, I contend, remit to a diffuse (perhaps even liberal) humanism. In fact, I was first attracted to the life projects I encountered in the yrmo because they resonated with this sensibility. However, as I became more familiar with these specific life projects, I began to realize two important points: first, that the resonance did not imply sameness with this sensibility—remember the a-humanness of emplaced collectives—and second, that these specific life projects expressed a particularly intense version of the principles of emplacement, an intensity whose degree would vary depending on the circumstances. In other words, I realized that the resonance I felt between those life projects and some elements of my diffuse humanist sensibility was circumstantial; not all life projects would resonate as well with them. In this respect, a political ontology that seeks to make room for emplacement must make a concerted effort not to allow this sensibility—which, let us not forget, arises out of the infrastructures of displacement that this political ontology seeks to forfeit—to prevent us from appreciating the potential for uncommoning in what does not resonate with it. I was alluding to this when I suggested in the interlude that the loss of authority of the Reason Police is an opportunity for unlikely synergies between "unreasonable claims."

As I pointed out, not all life projects will express principles of emplacement in a way that resonates with humanist/liberal sensibilities, not all life projects will express those principles with the intensity of those I have reported about in this book. Some might be generally oriented to the specificity of place and show no vocation for the big but still embrace steep hierarchies among their existents; others might be less hierarchical but assume that the order they envision should be "the order" and thus retain a vocation for the big on the back burner. What I have in mind are projects that might be oriented to the here and now of place but are pursued by, for example, groups partly composed of more or less retired Colombian paramilitaries, Pentecostals, or libertarians (all of them along with their nonhumans) and whose practices (at first sight, at least) appear too steeped in hierarchical, patriarchal, homophobic, racist, and/or speciesist strictures, not to mention their potential vocations to the big.[12] These are just a few of the possible shapes of collectives that some life projects might prefigure, which while veering toward a viable small in the here and now will not necessarily be "beautiful" to "our eyes." There is a whole research and action agenda to be developed around the ways in which diverging life projects engender different forms of emplacement and how to engage with those less palatable to our current sensibilities. The question is especially pertinent for two reasons. First, because there are versions of the small that a humanist/liberal-inflected sensibility would definitely not see as beautiful but are nevertheless gaining lots of traction, and, second, because I think it is precisely in relation to what we dislike or even detest that the possibility of making the pluriversal effect more effective depends. Let me tackle each point in turn.

The first point connects back with Latour's rejection of the small as a potential direction for the displaced. As I indicated, Latour refused the small as an option in part because he saw it associated with the emergence of right-wing populism in several places. He saw this development as one of the three responses, comprehensible but not effective, "to the powerful reaction of the Earth to what globalization has done to it."[13] These three responses included that of the 1 percent, who fantasize about saving themselves behind gated communities (or space colonization); the response of "the most wretched of all" who migrate to escape the consequences of globalization; and the right-wing response embraced by those who cling to secure borders to defend themselves from these "invaders." For Latour, all these responses were utterly ineffective because none of them addressed the underlying problem, that the globalization of (modern) practices that assume a transcendent common world leaves less and less livable ground for anyone to live on! Of course, if the alternatives are between the fantasy of escaping the planet, moving toward the xenophobic small (sheltered behind impossible secure borders), or composing a common world where a livable mode of existence may still be a possibility, the choice for the common world seems clear. However, if the problem is conceived as spanning from the imbalance between emplacement and displacement in grounding infrastructures, and we see a relation between this imbalance and the fact that, in dominant political imaginations there is too much commoning and too little uncommoning, the alternative is another. It is between insisting on commoning as the main thrust of (cosmo)politics or figuring out how to go on uncommoning, including in parallel with versions of the small that diverge from ours and that we may even find "ugly."[14]

The sensibility that informs those projects that I most easily see as fellow travelers for political ontology is less widely and deeply shared than many (including myself) would like it to be. There are other sensibilities for which the humanist/liberal one just sounds as more of the same, more expansion and imposition of modes of existence that are "not us, not from here." Let's not lose sight of the fact that not long ago many of the progressive projects I mentioned earlier were variously involved in what was then called the alter-globalization movement, which sought to articulate a variety of initiatives that, in contraposition to capitalist-driven globalization, shared the (democratic, egalitarian, pluralistic) values I have been describing as humanist. In this sense, and even if alter-globalization has been left aside as a general banner, many of these projects continue in the present moment, carrying with them a sort of inertia or inclination to displacement, which is expressed through their implicit demand for (sometimes legislated) guaranties that humanist values will prevail in the composition of small commons.[15] Of course, many of the most public agendas that seem to resonate better with those who would resist being legislated by what is "not us, not from here" are also largely derived from infrastructures of displacement. This is not surprising; given that infrastructures of emplacement have been severely weakened. Many of us (the displaced) do not know how to imagine the small other than as (common) units clearly delimited by borders, units that have enabled a play of scales that is central to the very assembling of the one-world world![16] Thus, the figures of "the common" that lean toward the small and that more easily take root among or give voice to the displaced, who now doubt the viability of the overstretched globalized infrastructures that they are with, are all very familiar: "our civilization," "our country," "our ethnos," or, at the breaking point of the concept, "our individuality." I surmise that the orientation to the small of these (largely modern-inflected) figurations of the common that are proposed as the antithesis of "the global" can be seen as one of the threads that connects so-called illiberal or postliberal trends in the international scene.[17] These are variously expressed in, among others, calls to challenge North Atlantic hegemony in favor of a multipolar geopolitical architecture (think Vladimir Putin and Xi Jinping, but also the BRICS+);[18] populists' calls for recanting the globalist dream in favor of regaining the greatness of the nation (think Donald Trump, Giorgia Meloni, Marine Le Pen, and Viktor Orban, among others); and the omnipresent calls to let the entrepreneurship of the individual flourish as the solution to top-down meddling of the state in social life (think Jair Bolsonaro and Javier Milei in Brazil and Argentina, respectively). There is a whole research agenda to be developed around how (and whether) these calls might be giving voice to and articulating a multiplicity of grassroots orientations to the small that exceed their explicit formulations. Might it be the case that these calls get traction because they resonate with a lack of fit that the displaced (human, nonhuman, and a-human) are experiencing (both in general and in highly specific ways) between themselves and the overextended collective or common they are with? If so, and to use Clark and Szerszynski's terms, these calls would be giving voice to a set of "planetary dynamics" edging toward a redrawing, if not a reduction, of the scale of this overextended collective/common.

In other words, even if not necessarily in the way one might prefer, they are giving uncommoning a voice with a potency that, in many settings, more progressive agendas have not been able to amass. What might be the cause of this differential potency? I can venture a couple of interrelated suggestions that might serve as potential foils for future inquiries about this.

The first is that some of the traction illiberal/postliberal calls garner may come from the fact that they openly tackle a question that progressive agendas seem ill-prepared or reluctant to address; namely, who is the "us" and the "here" of reference in calls to form smaller commons? Discussions around food and energy sovereignty, or around self-reliance and self-sufficiency, are indicative of this. In effect, sympathetic critics have pointed out that within progressive circles these discussions rarely define with clarity the scale of the sovereign/ self of reference, whether it is the farmer, the community, the nation-state, or a trans-scalar network.[19] This might reflect the pragmatics of scale-making where the self of reference is constantly being contested and negotiated, and thus it is advisable to keep it relatively open. Yet if this were the case, there is a point to be made about the importance of discussing more explicitly how these pragmatics play out in specific settings, how a certain common-in-the-making is shaping up in or as a "place," what is coming into it, what is not, and why.

The second suggestion centers on the dissonance between a humanist/ liberal sensibility and calls to uncommon. The tendency of progressive agendas to legislate guarantees might be perceived as contradictory with a call to focus on the specificity of "our place." In contrast, the stances advanced by some of the illiberal/postliberal trends I mentioned might appear more consistent. In effect, the motto many illiberals go by nowadays seems to be "We don't care how you want to live there; just don't tell us how to live here." Of course, the devil is in the detail of how the "us" and the "here" get scoped and scaled by negating the uncommon that exceeds the borders of their definitions. In this way, illiberal agendas mirror in reverse the aporias of progressive agendas oriented to the small: if the latter envisions an heterogeneity of smalls with unattainable guarantees for humanist values, the former envisions smalls with likewise unattainable guarantees of purity. Could the unattainability of a pure "we" and "here" be a handle around which to wrap our faith in the pluriverse? This is a faith we might need to push on with uncommoning in situations in which, to paraphrase poet Robert Frost, the only way out is through (rather than against) "ugly" figurations of the small. Could the impulse toward the uncommon that mobilizes these illiberal agendas be trapped so that instead of stopping at the familiar figurations of the small (veritable infrastructures of displacement), it continues to push against their limits leading to other versions of emplacement, perhaps more intense and thus perhaps more resonant with our present sensibilities? But are we willing to put these sensibilities at risk of being transformed in the process? These are the sort of experimental questions that we must ask ourselves, in relation to the various ways in which an orientation toward emplacement and the small might be insinuating itself around us from the entrails of displacement and in the specificity of our here and now.

Sorting out what is possible and/or acceptable implies inclusions and exclusions, and the most important hurdle in this context will be figuring out how to relate to what we exclude, to what we cannot live with. And here we come to the second reason why, as I argued prior, this question is crucial, and the possibility of making the pluriversal effect more effective depends on how we respond to it. Haraway's refrain of "staying with the trouble" is good to think through what this question entails: "Staying with the trouble requires making oddkin; that is, we require each other in unexpected collaborations and combinations, in hot compost piles. We become-with each other or not at all."[20]

Staying with the trouble and looking really hard into what it might require to uncommon with that which we dislike, detest, or fear is extremely important; after all, who can be our oddest kin, with whom can we have the most unexpected collaborations and combinations necessary for a project of uncommoning if not with those who confront us with existential challenges? We uncommon with each other (including some of our most intensely "Other" others) or not at all. This is why, with political ontology as analytics, for several years I have tended to focus on situations where the equivocations that might enable the uncommon to articulate as common become contentious and imply existential threats (even when one of the parties might not see it that way). It is not that I deny the existence of productive misunderstandings, pragmatic truths, and many other possible forms in which equivocations make possible the articulation between heterogeneous modes of existance, which, thus, might shape common collectives that remain nevertheless uncommon. Rather, the point has been to scrutinize those moments of potential existential threats because it is in them that the balance between the pluriversal and the universal effects seems to have been consistently tipped toward the latter, usually by the outright suppression of that which the one-world world cannot live with, which is anything that interrupts displacement and extension.[21] Thus, my first inspiration to imagine another way of relating to that which one cannot live with is the relation between yshiro and ylipiot, which I discussed earlier in the book. They don't like each other, they fear each other, and they avoid each other, for their direct encounter spells conflict, and likely death. This is not the agonism of adversaries; this is the antagonism of enemies. But their respective modes of existence make enough room for each other to exist, and they allow for buffering existents to take place in that room. The moral is that part of the trick of existing with that which is despised or threatens our existence is making room, reducing ourselves, and carefully letting be—that is, not letting anyone take all the room.

As I argued in the prelude, in emplaced collectives, the basis for making room and letting be is nothing like liberal tolerance but, rather, the pragmatics of carefulness. Tolerance understood in its liberal guise, as a self-satisfied dispensation given to others to have their "beliefs," is profoundly problematic.[22] But "liberal" is not the only mode of tolerance, and in the context of uncommoning, a pragmatics of carefulness might have something to gain from reclaiming the practice. Reclaiming tolerance for carefulness implies reconnecting the former term with its connotations of enduring, suffering, sustaining, supporting, and bearing. This is because at stake in uncommoning with carefulness is not the relation between a pretended sovereign in control of itself and its domains and a subordinated other whose otherness might be tolerated (always, up to a point) in the former's house. What is at stake in uncommoning with carefulness is the appropriate relation (including distance and enmity) that might be required between modes of existence that are divergent, perhaps mutually antagonistic, and yet (complexly, rhizomatically, or just mysteriously) also mutually dependent. Tolerance in this scenario connects with being faithful to the pluriverse as a pragmatic decision of expanded self-preservation. Tolerance enables us to let go of, endure, or even suffer through the dislike, revolt, and fear that our alters might instigate in us in order to sustain, support, and bear the pluriverse our existences depend upon. Tolerance in this sense is not meant to be blindly applied as a general rule; it must always remain connected to carefulness. In this way, tolerance is what might prevent battles (even bloody ones)—which at times will likely be necessary—from becoming wars of extermination. Tolerance also might apply a brake to the impulse to interfere and meddle with that which we do not know. In short, tolerance might make it possible to keep the pluriverse in sight as a cause that must not be abandoned, even (or especially) amid existential challenges.

In the Thick of the Story

Making the pluriversal a rallying cause brings to the fore what might appear to be its fundamental existential challenge, the one-world world and its universal effect. As Isabelle Stengers points out, the one-world world (she calls it the "global West") is "a world-destroying machine [that] cannot fit with other worlds."[23] However, while the universal and the pluriversal effects appear as the antithesis of each other, the tension has no resolution. As I pointed out before, the contrast between the universal—expressed as an ever-expanding one-world world—and the pluriversal—expressed as emplaced collectives that nowadays (r)exist in the crevices of the one-world world—was meant to identify and stage as a problem the imbalance between the infrastructures that ground each. However, this does not mean that the one-world world and emplaced collectives are the only, mutually exclusive alternatives. In fact, an important consequence of political ontology's bid to situate the pluriversal and the universal effects as symmetrical poles is that a variety of scales (and scopes) appropriate (or proportional) to various collectives become possible. In this regard, stories told by anthropology and history about scenarios before the one-world world became an overbearing presence offer glimpses of coetaneous and coexisting collectives with very different scales (and scopes). One only needs to read Eric Wolf's story about "the world in 1400" to get a sense of the possibilities.[24] In effect, if one reads "collectives" (with all that this concept carries) where Wolf writes "polities," the story insinuates the intense traffic and mutual inter- and intradependence between worldings that were strikingly divergent in scale and scope. In effect, in some senses (conventional and not), many of the collectives in Wolf's story can be deemed bigger than others; the grounding infrastructures of some of them might have extended geographically more than those of others; the relations between existents composing a collective might have been more hierarchical than those of another; some collective may have displayed an explicit and obvious expansive dynamic through time but others not so much.

There are two connected points about the "bigness" and/or "smallness" of these collectives that are worth some further thought. The first is simply that their ways of being big or small are not the same as those that we are used to in the context of the one-world world effect. For instance, I would venture that the words *Tawantinsuyu* (the four regions together), *Haudenosaunee* (the people of the long house) *confederacy*, or *galactic polity*, as either analytical or self-denominations, signal different ways of being big(ger), where commoning might have been expansive without quite turning into coloniality. This also implies that there may have been many ways of being small(er) while being entangled with these specific manifestations of the big—ways that were not reduced to existing as mere excess, to (r)existing under the constant pressure to become more and more aligned with a one-world world, or to cease to exist altogether. Attending to this, the possibility arises of imagining an ecology of collectives that, in their variable ways of being big(ger) and/or small(er), simultaneously provide articulations and buffering between modes of existence that cannot be adjacent to each other. The second point to be made is that the possibility of imagining this ecology depends on refusing the explicit or implicit teleology embedded in many of the stories that circulate about a "past" before the one-world world. The teleology that must be resisted is that once the movement toward the big starts, it is irreversible and will keep on going.

The teleology might arise from the presumption that every existent and collective is inherently oriented to expand. A presumption that in some narratives is given a "historical" inflection according to which one expression of the big somehow sowed the seeds for another big-ger (e.g., the chiefdom gave way to the state) which ineluctably ended up looking like the one we have now. The teleology might also be presented as a relation between the scale of collectives and their "technological capacity." Thus, the only thing that might have prevented Tawantinsuyu, Haudenosaunee, or galactic polities from becoming bigger was their limited technological capacity. Supposedly, if any of these collectives would have had the technological capacity, they would have expanded as much (and perhaps as destructively) as the modern has done it. Of course, what is missing from such techno-teleology is that the existents or infrastructures that constitute collectives scale more or less together, and this includes those "things" labeled "technology" as well as "visions of a good life." "Why is this technology better than this other one?" the naïve child would ask. "Because it is faster," the savvy adult would respond. "Why is it good that it is faster?" the child would pester, forcing the adult to dish out all the concealed presumptions that make up her world. In effect, if one keeps asking about the criteria being used to say that a given technology is better or more efficient than another, it quickly becomes apparent the entire assemblages of infrastructures that constitute the collective of reference, including those that I have called *visions of a good life*.[25] Another version of this teleology would adopt a Darwinian logic and say, "Fine, not all collectives are inherently oriented to expand, but once one does it, those which do not follow suit will end up being swallowed by those that do it." If we pay attention, it is possible to see the connection between this argument and Latour's argument that the scale of the mess generated by the expansion of modernity can only be responded to through the composition of a true common world. The subtext one could read in both arguments is that whether a big collective is composed well or not (i.e., it is something we want to live with or not), it cannot but swallow anything that does not match its scale. Hence, we can either make this big collective better or perish with it, but we cannot reduce its scale or unmake it.

Archaeologist Severin Fowles makes an argument that is apposite for neutralizing this kind of teleology.[26] In a nutshell, he argues that anthropologists (and archaeologists) have taken so-called simple societies (which, for the purpose of this argument, can be equated to my emplaced collectives) as the given, the starting point from which "complex societies" emerged. Given this assumption, the important question has always been how complex societies arose and sustained themselves: "No society, it was assumed, ever worked to reduce the scale of its settlements, to increase local autonomy, or to limit inequalities."[27] However, he argues, if one attends to the ebbs and flows between complexity and so-called simplicity without teleological preconceptions, it does appear that there have always been (what I would call *a-human*) agencies with intention at play, in both the emerging and the crumbling of so-called complex societies. Moreover, the agencies with an intention toward simplicity have at many points become stabilized, precisely as so-called simple societies. In other words, simplicity, which is anything but simple, is an achievement, and so too is the small.

I believe there is nothing that would authorize us to decree that the story of ebbs and flows between emplacement and displacement, between the small and the big, is finished. We are still in the thick of it, and stories like the one told in this book about life projects might be joining the agencies with intention that, along with viruses, ecoterrorists, bahluts, hackers, offended animal masters, and extreme weather events, tilt the flowing of the tide in the other direction. However, it is also very important not to introduce a reverse teleology under a normative guise, whereby all collectives should become emplaced ones. True, with their awesome "technologies" and infrastructures—that is, their politics of existence in divergence—emplaced collectives shine on the horizon that informs my political ontology for emplacement. But not every collective must reach that horizon for the imbalance between emplacement and displacement to cease being so lethal.

Intent-full forces toward uncommoning are already picking up steam, yet whether this will render worlds one will want to live in is uncertain. Moreover, it is uncertain whether narrating the momentous challenges we face as an imbalance between displacement and emplacement, between too much commoning and too little uncommoning, is a good description. At best we can say that if we live as if that were the case, and if we try enacting life projects, perhaps some of us will eventually find out that the proposition is worth being true because it has generated the appropriate infrastructures for being emplaced with others, in divergence.

ACKNOWLEDGMENTS

This book has been in the making for several years and came to fruition only because of the support given to me by an extended web of family, friends, and colleagues to whom I owe profound gratitude. I begin with Milan, Lorna, and Luna (in order of arrival to my life), who regardless of whether I am emplaced or displaced are always my grounding infrastructures; I am only with the three of you.

For over thirty years Modesto Martinez, Sonia Ozuna, Andres Ozuna, Perla Ortiz, Benito Romero, and all their children and grandchildren have made me part of their family every time I am in the Yshiro communities, and more recently they have also started to take in my partner and my children. I cannot put into words how much I appreciate and cherish your warmth and affection! I want to also thank Doña Rosa and Iyer Vera, Locoti, Betty Martinez, Don Celestino, Doña Ñeka, Don Ramon Zeballos Bibi, Cesar Barboza, Tani and Hadasa Baez, Lamberto Ferreira, Raquel Calonga, and Don Carlos Vera who, as always, remain generous and welcoming friends. A sign that time passes for all of us, many of the people whom I should thank for introducing me to the yrmo have now passed away: Don Veneto Vera, Don Tito Perez, Abuela Tama, Ama Ferreira, Yefe and Chiquilin Vera, Artigas and Gines Rizo, Ceferina Barra, Don Clemente Lopez, Don Serafin Escobar, and Gregorio Ozuna.

In Nitassinan/Labrador I must thank the generosity of Richard Nuna, Sebastian Piwas, Damien Benuen, Henen Andrew, Alex Andrew, the late Paul Pone, and Tony Jenkinson, all of whom guided me into the complexities of how their "emplaced collective" endures amid the relentless expansion of "Canada" into it. I am also grateful to Gerry Pasteen, Basile Penashue, and Jon Feldegajer for their invaluable assistance with our team's work. My colleague Scott Neilsen has always been ready to help and assist when I have been in

Labrador. I have a special debt of gratitude to my friends and colleagues Damian Castro and Carolina Tytelman who taught me the basics needed to start working with the Innu Nation and with whom I have continued to learn as we developed subsequent collaborative projects.

Marisol de la Cadena, Arturo Escobar, Harvey Feit, Eduardo Gudynas, and Cristina Rojas have been constant cothinkers, interlocutors, and sources of inspiration for the project of "political ontology," but many friends, colleagues, and a group of super talented students have enriched my thinking, either through comments on drafts of the book or more general discussions we have maintained since I embarked on this project. In alphabetical order, these are Maro Adjemian, Monica Amador, Penelope Anthias, Ricardo Aparicio, Cristobal Bonelli, Valentina Bonifacio, Anders Blok, Bruce Braun, Alec Brookes, Casper Bruun Jensen, Paola Canova, Ayelen Cavalli, Joel Correia, Alberto Corsín-Jimenéz, Lucas da Costa Maciel, Carol-Lynne D'Arcangelis, Maria Ehrnstrom-Fuentes, the late Gustavo Esteva, Jose Ferreira, Maria Firmino Castillo, Sandra Gomez, Lesley Green, Raquel Gutierrez Aguilar, Markus Kroger, Luciana Landgraf, Diego Landivar, John Law, Esben Leifsen, Josh Lepawsky, Marianne Lien, Pablo Mamani, Charles Mather, Atsuro Morita, Maria Guzman Gallegos, Keiichi Omura, Michal Osterweil, Sylvie Poirier, Nancy Postero, Pablo Mariman Quemenado, Lorna Quiroga, Dianne Rocheleau, Mariela Rodriguez, Guillermo Salas Carreño, Cecilia Salinas, Salvador Schavelzon, Astrid Stensrud, Juanita Sundberg, Maristella Svampa, Florencia Tola, Helen Verran, Rodrigo Villagra, and Eduardo Viveiros de Castro.

NOTES

1. Mind you, I am not speaking of that spectrum of displaced people for whom *not moving* is likely to result in the end of a livable life.

2. On polycrisis, see Tooze, "Welcome to the World of the Polycrisis"; Henig and Knight, "Polycrisis."

3. Wittgenstein, *Tractatus logico-philosophicus*, 90.

1. See Achtenberg and Currents, "Bolivia."

2. As is well known, the Washington consensus of the 1990s focused on financial valorization through policies of adjustment and privatization and redefined the state's role as being simply that of a regulatory scaffold for the market society. In contrast, fueled by the growing global demand for raw materials, the commodity consensus focused on the implementation of capital-intensive extractive projects where, in addition to transnational investors, the state could also play an active role. See Svampa, "Commodities Consensus."

3. Gudynas, "Diez Tesis Urgentes sobre el nuevo extractivismo." See also Gudynas, *Extractivisms*.

4. With different intensity, depending on the country, the neo-extractivist dispositive combined extractivism of raw materials for export with a new form of internal extractivism that siphoned state social expenditures through the expansion of microcredits and the general financialization of economic transactions. See Gago, *La razón neoliberal*.

5. This does not mean that communities themselves would not have become divided around these extractivist projects, but more often than not, those divisions have been purposely fueled by governments and corporations.

6. Zibechi, *Territories in Resistance*.

7. Chatterton, "Making Autonomous Geographies"; Collectivo Situaciones, *Bienvenidos a la selva*; Fernández, *Política y Subjetividad*; Uribe, "Emancipación social en un contexto de guerra prolongada."

8. In his recent book, Arturo Escobar counters the reduction of "the possible" precisely by questioning commonsensical understandings of "reality." See Escobar, *Pluriversal Politics*.

9. Cited in De la Cadena, *Earth Beings*, 169.

10. Blaser, *Governmentalities and Authorized Imaginations*; Blaser, "The Threat of the Yrmo"; Blaser, *Storytelling Globalization from the Chaco and Beyond*.

11. One of the first coordinated efforts we made with my colleagues to think through this situation with others was a workshop we hosted in Colombia titled "Política mas allá de la política / Politics Beyond Politics." That event put me initially in contact, mainly through the "node" that is Arturo Escobar himself, with the loose network of scholars, analysts, commentators, and activist/researchers who, as I mentioned in the preface, were trying to take the pulse of ongoing processes in Latin America and help give shape to political ontology. The ideas of these colleagues, not all cited in this book but included in the acknowledgments, have greatly informed my thinking, even if through our divergences.

12. Blaser, "Is Another Cosmopolitics Possible?"; Blaser, "Notes towards a Political Ontology."

13. My understanding of Science (with a capital *S*) draws on Isabelle Stengers's characterization of sciences other than the experimental ones (and particularly physics) as "satrapies laying claim by proxy to a force of which they are utterly devoid, and which they can only imitate." This force, argues Stengers, is the very exceptional achievement of the experimental sciences—namely, experimental objectivity or "proof," which is nothing more (or less) than using the setup of an experiment to give "reality the power to make a difference in the way it is interpreted." It was what she calls "propaganda" that presented this very exceptional achievement, specific to experimental setups, as a general method for obtaining "objective" (i.e., indubitable) knowledge. See Stengers, "The Challenge of Ontological Politics," 87–88. Let me stress then that the distinction between the sciences and Science seeks to signal a divergence between the specificity of the former, on the one hand, and the overblown claims to have the capacity to know reality as it is associated to the latter. Nevertheless, a thread connects what are otherwise very heterogeneous "modern knowledge practices": they all inherit from a method that regularly (but not always coherently) has enacted the modernist assumption of "one world out there" and multiple perspectives on it. On the way in which the tangle I call *Reason Police* becomes enshrined in the law, see Boulot and Sterlin, "Steps towards a Legal Ontological Turn."

14. I use the word *hegemony* in the Gramscian sense of a dominance that is *not mainly and/or explicitly* based on coercive imposition but rather involves a substantive component of persuasion.

15. Two good surveys of the connections and divergences between the ontological turn in anthropology and material-semiotics STS are Gad, Jensen, and Wintereik, "Practical Ontology" and Holbraad and Pedersen, *The Ontological Turn*.

16. For an overview of material semiotics, see Law, "Actor Network Theory and Material Semiotics."

17. See Blaser, *Storytelling Globalization from the Chaco and Beyond*.

18. Latour, *The Pasteurization of France*. See also Latour, "From Realpolitik to Dingpolitik or How to Make Things Public."

19. This trajectory is, of course, reversible, as a stabilized "fact" may again become "an issue," thus making visible the presence of the entire "assembly" that constitutes it: "Translation [or

articulation] is by definition always a misunderstanding, since common interests are in the long term necessarily divergent." Latour, *The Pasteurization of France*, 65.

20. Mol, *The Body Multiple*.

21. Latour, *Pandora's Hope*.

22. Latour, "Turning around Politics," 813.

23. Stengers, "The Cosmopolitical Proposal."

24. In Latour's case, cosmopolitics as the composition of the common world resembles the process through which matters of concern are slowly articulated into matters of fact, a resemblance that is fractally implicated in the constitution of everything, be it the microbe, the nation, or the common world. I will return to this point in the interlude.

25. On "intra-action," see Barad, *Meeting the Universe Halfway*.

26. I borrow the term *collective* from Latour, who has pointed out its contrasts with "society" in that the latter often refers to an association of humans while the former refers to the entire association of humans with their nonhumans (from animals to gods and so on). To some extent, following Descola, my slight modification to this is that rather than speaking of human and nonhumans (categories that are associated with a particular collective), I prefer to speak of collectives as associations of existents, adding the further point that those existents are themselves multiplicities. See Latour, *We Have Never Been Modern*; Descola, "Modes of Being and Forms of Predication."

27. For a recent rendering of such concerns, see Canessa, "Methods Really Do Matter"; Hornborg, "Mistranslating Relationism and Absolving the Market."

28. Here, the term *entanglement* picks up a degree of complexity that makes any pretense of purification utterly hopeless, as Dussart and Poirier have aptly argued. See Dussart and Poirier, "Knowing and Managing the Land."

29. Viveiros de Castro, "Perspectival Anthropology and the Method of Controlled Equivocation."

30. Viveiros de Castro has a beautiful analogy to get this idea across: thinking of translating with control—that is, with awareness of the equivocation—would be analogous to thinking of walking as controlled falling; we never have a final certitude that it works, only that it works so far as we have not fallen. See Viveiros de Castro, "Perspectival Anthropology and the Method of Controlled Equivocation," 5.

31. My notion of circulation as a sort of vital energy is inspired in Latour's "circulating reference." See Latour, *Pandora's Hope*.

32. Blaser and de la Cadena, "Introduction: Pluriverse Proposals for a World of Many Worlds," 6.

33. See Dos Santos and Tola, "¿Ontologías como modelo"; Eitel and Meurer, "Introduction: Exploring Multifarious Worlds"; Holbraad and Pedersen, *The Ontological Turn*; Ruiz Serna and Del Cairo, "Los debates del giro ontológico en torno al naturalismo moderno." Subsequently, unless explicitly indicated, when I use the term *political ontology* the reference is to this project.

34. See, for example, Biset, "Formas de lo común"; Biset, "¿Qué es una ontología política?"

35. Hetherington, "Introduction: Keywords of the Anthropocene," 6.

36. I am partially inspired by Doreen Massey's work for this relational conceptualization of place, although I also overlay upon it the kind of ontological multiplicity that I

have been illustrating with the bird/rabbit illusion. I do not think that in her own conceptualization of place as a meeting of trajectories Massey had in mind this kind of multiplicity, where more than one "place" can occur in the same location at the same time. In effect, Massey uses the notion of multiplicity to open up established notions of space and place as homogeneous categories (e.g., abstract space, self-identical, essentialized place) but stops at the "level" of phenomena/existents that are taken to constitute the actual multiplicity of those homogeneous categories. This stops short of conceiving of the kind of ontological multiplicity that I have been illustrating with the bird/rabbit image, which requires that the constitutive multiplicity of all phenomena/existents remain at the forefront regardless of level. Thus, political ontology does not stop operationalizing the notion of multiplicity at any level, for it takes multiplicity to be recursive and all-pervasive. As I said, collectives are multiplicities of existents that are themselves multiplicities that take place. And it is precisely by attending to the recursiveness and pervasiveness of multiplicity that it becomes possible to conceive of the bird/rabbit kind of multiplicity. It is, however, important to indicate that there is nothing inherent to Massey's notion of space and place that would prevent a more expansive operationalization of multiplicity in using them; she just does not do it. See Massey, *For Space*; Massey, *Space, Place, and Gender*; Massey, "A Counterhegemonic Relationality of Place"; Peck et al., "Symposium."

37. See Blaser, "Life Projects."

38. I emphasize the point to stave off a rather recurrent interpretive slippage in critical assessments of what is implied when an analysis proceeds by way of contrast. The slippage involves disregarding the careful work of staging a relational contrast, then quickly accusing the analysis of being binary when the binary is actually in the eyes of the beholder. For a recent iteration of the slippage, which in turn builds on various previous ones, see Nadasdy, "How Many Worlds Are There?"

39. Hetherington, "Introduction: Keywords of the Anthropocene," 6.

40. Of course, the underside of this transformation is the redistribution of these "disentangled tangles" as refuse, which my colleague Josh Lepawsky has forcefully brought into focus with his concept of "discard-scapes." See Lepawsky, *Reassembling Rubbish*. Markus Kröger speaks of "existential redistribution" to refer to these processes. See Kröger, *Extractivisms, Existences and Extinctions*.

41. This is a standard narrative, in actor-network theory, of how certain states of affairs gain stability and become the taken-for-granted terrain or hinterland in which subsequent action must operate. For a succinct rendering of the point, see Law, *After Methods*, 32–35.

42. Law, "What's Wrong with a One-World World?"

43. One could infer, via the example of Romani people, for instance, that some collectives might be more or less forcefully driven by their circumstances to take place through infrastructures of displacement, and yet in contrast to the modern collective, neither need nor seek to constantly expand them. See Toninato, "Romani Nomadism"; Sevillano, "Nomadism as Ancestral Homeland in the Romani Culture."

44. Latour, *We Have Never Been Modern*, 117–20.

45. Latour, *We Have Never Been Modern*, 119. Emphasis added.

46. The concept of coloniality is associated with a long-standing set of discussions about the relations between Latin American societies and modernity, particularly with

the shape these discussions adopted as modernity came to be conceived, in this milieu, as indissociable from justifications of internal colonialism. In North American academia, these discussions became known as the modernity/coloniality and decoloniality research program. This program built on and expanded Anibal Quijano's seminal concept of the coloniality of power. Succinctly, by modifying the noun *power*, the adjective *colonial* was intended to signal that the dominant pattern of global domination specific to the modern/capitalist world-system (based on racial, class, gender, and other classifications) originated at the turn of the sixteenth century with the conquest of what came to be called "the American continent." In other words, the term *colonial* was intended to modify a certain conception of "power" (mainly Marxist) that did not pay attention to the centrality of colonization in the process of modernization and its expansion. In this book, I am seeking to disentangle the concept of coloniality from its almost ordained association with modernity—not to "save" modernity from its inherent coloniality but so we can recognize the operations of coloniality even when they do not come in the guise of modernization. I will return to this point. For a succinct overview of the modernity/ coloniality research program, see Escobar, "Worlds and Knowledges Otherwise."

47. Even the examples that might clearly index an emplaced mode of being might be entangled with displacement in this way, as when relations with "local more-than-human-beings" such as spirit owners or ancestors require items obtained through commoditized circuits. See, for example, Carreño, "Places Are Kin" and Hirsch, "Investment's Rituals."

48. I take inspiration from Law and Joks for the notion of a "politics of how." See Law and Joks, "Indigeneity, Science, and Difference."

49. See Carneiro da Cunha, "Indigenous People"; Courtheyn, "Desindigenizados pero no vencidos"; Courtheyn, "Territories of Peace"; De la Cadena, *Earth Beings*; Escobar, *Sentipensar con la tierra*; Oslender, "Geographies of the Pluriverse"; Ruiz-Serna, *When Forests Run Amok*.

50. This preemptive deflection of an automatic association of my arguments with identity politics also informs two editorial decisions. One is the decision to not discuss sources from what could be labelled "Indigenous philosophies" in this introduction. Although these sources have been constantly central to my version of political ontology, I needed here to delay their discussion until after I made explicit my avoidance of a politics of who. The other is my decision to avoid the usual citational practice that prefixes the names of authors with the typical: "Indigenous [or specific ethnonym] scholar X argues that . . ." I understand the importance of doing this in many contexts, but there are also many problematic assumptions in this practice (about the automatic scope and author-ity—or lack thereof—that an identity label suggests), which rub against my intention to foreground a politics of how. Thus, I cite authors not because they represent this or that identity group but because the way in which they explain aspects of practices of emplace-ment have resonated the most with me.

51. Segato, "Patriarchy from Margin to Center."

52. The concept of minoritization also helps to describe a general mechanism that mo-bilizing the various categories of differentiation within the already universalized category of humans (e.g., gender, race, class, sexual orientation, and so on) at the same time ranks their relative importance and, according to their assignment to the relevant category,

grants them variable degrees of authority to present their "minor issues" in the public sphere of politics. We can see how, in this guise, minoritization is closely connected and entangled with the dynamics of ranking factualities, which I described under the rubric of reasonable politics. Indeed, in reasonable politics, disputes about factuality often also involve implicit or explicit disputes about the putative authority that differently "identified" human subjects have for establishing the relevant "facts" in a disagreement; this is why issues of authenticity become important in identity politics.

53. Of course, intensity is a perception relative to the standpoint of who perceives.

54. It is worth stressing that the need to be careful is not the same as being risk averse. In this regard, in their overview of ontological turns, Holbraad and Pedersen have me saying that adopting a position of open-endedness is risky and irresponsible when what I actually said was that each situation requires carefully weighing whether one must keep on or stop opening the black boxes that compose it, and that adopting the general rule that one must always either open or close them without attending to what the situation requires is simply reckless. For my original argument, see Blaser, "The Political Ontology of Doing Difference." For Holbraad and Pedersen's interpretation of my argument, see Holbraad and Pedersen, *The Ontological Turn*, 54.

PRELUDE

1. Barras, "Life Projects."

2. Escobar, *Encountering Development*; Rist, *The History of Development*.

3. It is worth clarifying that the word *life* in *life projects* does not gain meaning in relation to that of *death*. In this sense, life projects are not an expression of those salvific tropes that, riffing off concerns with finitude, are unavoidably connected with biopolitics. If anything, and equivocal as it might be, the term *life* here plays the role of an affirmation of a given mode of existence, which might have its own (other-than-biopolitical) categories of finitude, or even none.

4. Morris, "Emplacement."

5. I have chosen to base this discussion on written sources from across the continent rather than on my own ethnographic experience because I think it is important for readers to have direct access (through my citations) to the works of these intellectuals and the possibility of exploring further some topics I can only skim over in this chapter.

6. And it is precisely for this very same reason that discussions of ontology in material-semiotics enabled me to articulate in a language "hearable" within the academy what I encountered in my work with the Yshiro and exceeded the categories of analysis I was used to deploy. In other words, far from "discovering" anything new (which I doubt anyone has ever claimed), discussions of ontology have helped to open the categorical field for those of us strongly shaped by the universal effect of the modern collective, to better grasp something of what spokespersons from emplaced collectives have been saying all along. No surprise, then, that many of the principles I discuss here will resonate with my discussion in the introduction about the academic sources from which political ontology draws inspiration. And yet, the differences between sources of relationality are also very telling, as we will see soon.

7. Deloria, *The Metaphysics of Modern Existence*; Deloria, *Spirit and Reason*, 32–39.

8. Wildcat, "Indigenizing Politics and Ethics," 87–89.

9. As has been argued by Marshall Sahlins, what I call *symmetry of value* does not always imply the lack of hierarchies of other kinds between existents. Yet as Signe Howell suggests, conversely, not all hierarchical relations imply asymmetries of value. Here again applies my general point about thinking of these kinds of contrasts in terms of degrees rather than absolutes. See Howell, "Rules without Rulers?"; Sahlins, "In Anthropology"; Sahlins, "The Original Political Society."

10. Krenak, *Ideias para adiar o fim do mundo*, 21.

11. Viveiros de Castro discusses ethnonyms in similar terms to argue that rather than being nouns, they are pronouns—that is, indexes of the speaker's positionality in a system of relations. See Viveiros de Castro, "Cosmological Deixis and Amerindian Perspectivism."

12. For a similar point, see De La Cadena, "Runa."

13. Atleo, *Principles of Tsawalk*, 7.

14. Foucault, *The Order of Things*, xvi.

15. Atleo, *Principles of Tsawalk*, 1–2.

16. Cajete, *Native Science*; Cordova, *How It Is*; Burkhart, "What Coyote and Thales Can Teach Us"; Deloria, *The Metaphysics of Modern Existence*; Huanacuni, *Buen vivir*. My own conversations with Yshir intellectuals have rendered similar insights. See Blaser, *Storytelling Globalization from the Chaco and Beyond*.

17. This does not mean there are no connections between them. In fact, Scott Pratt has argued that the pragmatism I am presenting here is the one that originally inspired the strands better known in academia. See Pratt, *Native Pragmatism*.

18. And the same applies for the "subject," which cannot be claimed as the ultimate ground of "experience" without occluding the fact that such ground is itself the emergent effect of a weft of relations formed by other "subjects." See Burkhart, "What Coyote and Thales Can Teach Us."

19. Arola, "Native American Philosophy," 558.

20. Arola, "Native American Philosophy," 558.

21. McGregor, "Towards Coexistence," 76.

22. Deloria, *Spirit and Reason*, 46–47

23. Deloria, *Spirit and Reason*, 46.

24. Puig de la Bellacasa, *Matters of Care*.

25. Puig de la Bellacasa, *Matters of Care*, 11.

26. Deloria, *Spirit and Reason*, 40–60.

27. In its most restrictive meaning, topology refers to the study of how the properties of objects are maintained even as they are stretched and deformed but not broken. More generally, topology involves a conception of space and spatial relations primarily focused on the property of connections rather than on distance. For this brief characterization of topology, I follow Rose and Wylie, "Animating Landscape."

28. Here we come close to Viveiros de Castro's "Amerindian perspectivism," where standpoints do not refer to perspectives on a world but perspectives *from* a world. Viveiros de Castro, "Cosmological Deixis and Amerindian Perspectivism."

29. Viveiros de Castro would summarize the point thus: "The Other of the Other [is] not exactly the same as the Other of the Same." See Viveiros de Castro, "Perspectival Anthropology and the Method of Controlled Equivocation," 8.

30. Instead of the form *non-X*, which is patterned after "nonhuman" (which, incidentally, rehashes the centrality of the human even as it is mobilized by posthumanist tropes), I prefer to speak of *other-than* when referring to existents that obtain within a-human collectives. By this choice of words, I want to stress both the specificity of those existents and the uncertainty of the kind of relation they sustain with the existent of reference.

31. As it is obvious, both of them have their own accounts of themselves and their others. The reliability of my account thus must be measured by its practical consequences, which, in my case, and building on the performative pragmatism I infer from spokespersons of emplaced collectives, should be in terms of its contribution to performing a pluriverse—a point I will return to in the book's conclusion.

32. Cristobal Bonelli and Antonia Walford's very perceptive analysis clue me into this commonality across works variously using these buzzwords. See Bonelli and Walford, introduction to *Environmental Alterities*.

33. A similar point is brought home by Gad, Jensen, and Winthereik when they argue that "from the point of view of practical ontology it is more plausible to argue that Danish anthropologists share considerably more ontological baggage with one another than do an African witchdoctor with a Danish mailman. For the sake of argument we might assume that the Danish anthropologists (and the mailman) inhabit worlds consisting of things that include, for example, identity cards, publically funded infrastructure, functioning educational institutions, bicycle lanes, package tourism and pickled herring. And though each person may each conceptualize these 'shared' things differently, their orientations toward the world will have been shaped by these surrounding material-semiotic constellations." See Gad, Jensen, and Wintereik, "Practical Ontology."

34. This is so not only because there is no unmediated access to a standpoint, but also because being itself a constellation of standpoints, any standpoint is always equivocal, and, to use Atsuro Morita's beautiful formulation, "since equivocation happens recursively and at any scale, obscurity is always in the vicinity, or even within." Morita, "Afterword."

35. See Nahuelpan, "Desafíos de un diálogo epistémico intercultural"; Simpson, *As We Have Always Done*, 22–25.

36. Helen Verran has been crafting a powerful conceptual grammar to stage encounters between knowledge practices spanning from different metaphysical commitments that might result neither in subordination of one of the parties (as happens with reasonable politics) nor in the amalgamation/integration/synthesis of both. The aim is what she calls "doing difference together" or "going on together in difference." I prefer the term *divergence* for its inherent reference to a point of encounter (i.e., a category, an event, a limit, and so on) that makes it possible to render the contrast between entities as "difference." Verran, "Engagements between Disparate Knowledge Traditions"; Verran, "The Politics of Working Cosmologies Together While Keeping Them Separate"; Verran, "A Postcolonial Moment in Science Studies."

37. See Latour, "What If We Talked Politics a Little?"; Verran, "An Ontological Politics of Politics?"

38. Latour, "What If We Talked Politics a Little?," 149.

39. Simpson, *As We Have Always Done*, 61–62.

40. A way of figuring, from a "human" standpoint, what is involved in this kind of political practice is through the idea of coevolution within an ecological region, where diverging species adopt the shape and vital trajectories they do precisely through the various kinds of relations (cooperation, predation, reciprocity, and so on) they sustain with each other.

41. Eastman, *Soul of an Indian*, 70–71. Scott Pratt found an earlier published version of the story in Benjamin Franklin's writing. See Pratt, *Native Pragmatism*, 210–12.

42. See Law, *After Methods*, 32–35.

43. See Carr and Lempert, "Introduction: Pragmatics of Scale," 14. The notion of scale at play here builds on critical assessments of the concept that have stressed its dynamic character and thus attends to scale-making projects as opposed to taking scales as ontological givens.

44. Nurit Bird-David makes a similar argument, connecting "limits" to expansion with the demands of intimacy and closeness required by (more-than-human) kin relations. Bird-David, *Us, Relatives*.

45. Simpson, *As We Have Always Done*, 17. Emphasis added.

ACT I

1. Harry Truman, cited in Escobar, *Encountering Development*, 1.

2. Steffen et al., *Global Change and the Earth System*.

3. It is important to remember that speaking of "story" here involves, as Leroy Little Bear puts it, "not just the words and the listening but the actual living of the story." Thus, I refer to *the good life* and *the common good* indistinctly as visions, stories, and practices. Whether for ease of sentence flow I use one or another of these three terms, they are always synonymous. Little Bear, foreword to to *Native Science*.

4. See Escobar, *Pluriversal Politics*; Dussart and Poirier, *Entangled Territorialities*.

5. The literature from both the north and the south of the continent has accounted for the purchase that the concept of territory has gained in terms of a "turn," although analyses might emphasize different sources of the main impulse for the "territorial turn" (i.e., top-down, from state and agents of modernization versus bottom-up, from grassroots social movements). Svampa, *Neo-Extractivism in Latin America*; Bryan, "Rethinking Territory"; Haesbaert, *Território e descolonialidade*; Halvorsen, "Decolonising Territory."

6. The materials for this chapter come from my work with the Yshiro communities of Paraguay and their leadership. I have provided a detailed account of how I came to work with these communities in my book *Storytelling Globalization from the Chaco and Beyond*. Here it should suffice to indicate that our ongoing mutual collaboration goes back to 1991 and that, aside from shorter visits, I have lived in the communities for periods of time ranging from three months to eighteen months. Through periods of cohabitation and the years that have passed, I have developed very close relations of friendship, mutual care, and obligation with many Yshiro families. But given that communities are rarely as

harmonious as many would like to see them, the flipside of this closeness with some families has been distance with others, although the distance from and closeness with different families has changed through the years—a normal occurrence when one is involved as an active participant in matters that concern friends, acquaintances, and interlocutors in different ways. The point is important for underscoring that the story I present here about what happens in the yrmo would not necessarily resonate with all the Yshiro.

7. I have discussed at length the processes through which the Paraguayan state started to assert control over the area in Blaser, *Storytelling Globalization from the Chaco and Beyond*.

8. Coca and Reymondin, "Is the 'Paraguayan Gran Chaco' at Risk for Extreme Habitat Destruction?"; MacDonald, "Green Going Gone."

9. UCINY, Arcella, and Blaser, *Anuhu Yrmo*; UCINY, Arcella, and Blaser, "Biodiversity Conservation for Whom?" See also Ward, "The Bureaucracy of Nature."

10. In the inset map, it is possible to appreciate that Belaieff assumed a modern, state-like territoriality, with relatively clear borders for the Indigenous groups listed in it. However, there are strong indications that these groups had a more flexible understanding of their "territory." See Ferreira, "Societies 'against' and 'in' the State."

11. On "entrapment" as an alternative to the figure of "entanglement" that might be better suited to forms of predation, see Corsín Jiménez, "Anthropological Entrapments." On "piecemeal violence" in the Chacom, see Blaser, *Storytelling Globalization from the Chaco and Beyond*, 60–61.

12. Tobich designates what classical anthropology called "male societies," formed by a group of initiated males. It also designates the place where, in a given settlement, the group meets.

13. For the process of UCINY's creation, see Blaser, *Storytelling Globalization from the Chaco and Beyond*.

14. Hecht, "Interscalar Vehicles for an African Anthropocene."

15. As an advisor to UCINY, I have become involved with, and partake in, this network as well. Thus, in many senses, its members constitute important and valued interlocutors for the ideas presented in this book.

16. Ward, "The Bureaucracy of Nature."

17. See Guereña and Rojas, *Yvy Jára*, 72.

18. ISTHME—Estudio Meridional, "Elaboración coordinación y gestión del plan de ordenamiento urbano y territorial del municipio de Bahía Negra Producto 5," 8.

19. That the Secretariat was one of several within the Ministry of Agriculture and Livestock provides a hint about how the "environment" was valued within the governmental structure at the time. Since 2018, and still quite illustrative of the dominant logic, the Secretariat has been upgraded to the level of Ministry of the Environment . . . and Sustainable Development!

20. This original plan, in turn, spawned a series of activities (including subsequent participatory workshops) that continued over several years, some even morphing into new projects that are still underway.

21. Coordinadora de Derechos Humanos del Paraguay, *Situación de los derechos a la tierra y al territorio de los pueblos indígenas en el Paraguay*; Correia, "Indigenous Rights at a Crossroads."

22. On infrastructural violence in the Chaco, see Correia, "Life in the Gap."

23. I have known Calixto since 1991, and although we have different opinions on many issues, the good rapport we have enables us to be quite open about our disagreements, as his reference to "my" tobich oso signals.

24. Bonifacio, "Building Up the Collective"; Bonifacio and Villagra Carron, "Conexiones inestables."

25. Leaders became convinced that the characteristic instability of Yshiro leadership (including UCINY's) would conspire against any strategy that did not have wide support. In effect, through social pressure (gossip, stonewalling, ostracism), leaders are expelled from their position with relative ease and frequency. Although from the perspective of governmental and nongovernmental institutions that need stable interlocutors this is often seen as a problem, from the perspective of community members, it is not, for it forces the entire Yshiro leadership to be very mindful of their expectations. Thus, while leaders often initiate actions without much formal consultation, it is very difficult for them to sustain those actions without keeping enrolled a critical mass of community members. In other words, and paraphrasing Clastres, leaders remain leaders so long as they remain an instrument for realizing the visions of their followers, even if the latter might not yet know they had those visions! Clastres, *Society against the State*,

26. A much more detailed discussion of some aspects of the process through which UCINY came up with the strategy to recover the yrmo as a life project of the Yshiro is available in a report prepared for the International Development Research Centre of Canada, the agency that funded the final period of consultations in the communities. Blaser, "Co-management of Natural Resources across 'Radical Differences.'"

27. At the risk of restating the obvious, it is worth remarking how far this description of the Yshiro life project is from assuming homogeneity or propounding some essential defining trait—that is, the sin many critics attribute to any analysis they cast in that mixed bag called the "ontological turn in Anthropology." Far from emanating from a timeless essence, the specific "alterity" this life project emanates from is a constant and ongoing reweaving. Trajectory rather than self-same essence is what makes this life project unique and different.

28. Blaser, *Storytelling Globalization from the Chaco and Beyond*.

29. Rancière, *Disagreement*.

30. Rancière, *Disagreement*, 88.

31. Rancière, Panagia, and Bowlby, "Ten Theses on Politics."

32. I must note that Rancière discusses what I call *excess* under the rubric of "equality." I prefer *excess*, as it avoids the usual conflation of equality with sameness, although I am aware that Rancière's equality does not have that ring. For him, equality is a basic axiom of politics. As he puts it, "The presupposition of equality is a basis for the existence of politics in general." See Rancière et al., "Aesthetics and Politics Revisited," 296. In that sense, the order of the police is disrupted when this presupposition is put into practice, for "the essence of equality is not so much to unify as to declassify, to undo the supposed naturalness of orders and replace it with controversial figures of division." Rancière, *On the Shores of Politics*, 32–33. See also Rancière et al., "Jacques Rancière."

33. See Rancière, *On the Shores of Politics*, 50.

34. Rancière, *Disagreement*, 88. I draw on Peter Hallward for my discussion of Rancière's politics as theatrics. Hallward, "Staging Equality."

35. Swyngedouw, "Interrogating Post-democratization."

36. James Scott's concept of "public transcript" is apt to signal that there is a flipside to it, the "hidden transcript," although the very terms conjure up the need to specify the vantage point from which a transcript would appear as either public or hidden. Scott, *Domination and the Arts of Resistance*.

37. See Bonifacio and Villagra Carron, "Conexiones inestables"; Glauser, *Angaité's Responses to Deforestation*; Glauser, "Entendiendo las respuestas de un pueblo indígena del Chaco Paraguayo a la desposesión territorial."

38. Porto-Gonçalves, "Lucha por la tierra"; Porto-Gonçalves and Leff, "Political Ecology in Latin America." Although I cannot delve into it here, I want to signal that there are important resonances to be explored between Latin American (r)existencia and the term "survivance" used in Native (North) American circles. First introduced by Gerald Vizenor, "survivance is an active sense of presence, the continuance of native stories, not a mere reaction, or a survivable name. Native survivance stories are renunciations of dominance, tragedy and victimry." See Vizenor, *Manifest Manners*, vii.

39. See "Impacto ambiental es Abordado en Bahia Negra, Chaco," Diario Ultima Hora.

40. See Romero, "How Brazil's Fear of Losing the Amazon Guides Bolsonaro's Policies towards the Forest"; Watts, "Jair Bolsonaro Claims NGOs behind Amazon Forest Fire Surge."

41. Almiron, "Plan de ordenamiento territorial divide a pobladores de Bahia negra."

42. Weseluk, "Prospección de minerales metalicos y no metalicos."

1. Castree, "Changing the Anthropo(s)Cene."

2. There are various very insightful mapping exercises of the Anthropo(s)cene that accentuate other "cartographic criteria," so to speak. Bonneuil and Fressoz, *The Shock of the Anthropocene*; Castree, "The Anthropocene and Geography I"; Castree, "The Anthropocene and Geography II"; Castree, "The Anthropocene and Geography III"; Lorimer, "The Anthropo-Scene"; Lövbrand, Mobjörk, and Söder, "The Anthropocene and the Geo-political Imagination."

3. See "Anthropocene Timeline," Welcome to the Anthropocene (website), accessed December 8, 2023, https://www.anthropocene.info/anthropocene-timeline.php.

4. Steffen et al., "The Anthropocene."

5. Bulkeley and Newell, *Governing Climate Change*.

6. Biermann et al., "Earth System Governance," 15–16.

7. Bringel and Svampa, "Del consenso de los commodities al consenso de la descarbonización."

8. Early examples of such views range from programmatic proposals by the United Nations Environment Program to Mariana Mazzucato's neo-Keynesian proposals for a "green entrepreneurial state" to the exuberant Ecomodernist Manifesto of the Breakthrough Institute. See UNEP, "Towards a Green Economy"; Mazzucato, "The Entrepreneurial State" and *The Green Entrepreneurial State*; Asafu-Adjaye et al., *An Ecomodernist Manifesto*.

9. For an overview of this trajectory, see Meaney, "Fortunes of the New Green Deal."

10. On different forms of "green extractivism," see Voskoboynik and Andreucci, "Greening Extractivism"; Bruna, "A Climate-Smart World and the Rise of Green Extractivism"; Lang, Bringel, and Manahan, *Mas alla del colonialismo verde*.

11. See Malm and Hornborg, "The Geology of Mankind?"; Moore, "The Capitalocene."

12. See Malm and Hornborg, "The Geology of Mankind?"; Moore, *Capitalism in the Web of Life*.

13. Žižek, *Living in the End Times*, 333–34.

14. Swyngedouw, "Depoliticized Environments," 264.

15. Swyngedouw, "Depoliticized Environments," 270.

16. For a sample of these various positions and the debates among them, see Pollin, "De-growth vs. a Green New Deal"; Kallis, "A Green New Deal Must Not Be Tied to Economic Growth"; Ajl, *A People's Green New Deal*; Chomsky and Pollin, *Climate Crisis and the Global Green New Deal*; Malm, *How to Blow Up a Pipeline*; Chatterton, Featherstone, and Routledge, "Articulating Climate Justice in Copenhagen"; Sepúlveda Luque, "Swans, Ecological Struggles and Ontological Fractures."

17. Swyngedouw, "Depoliticized Environments."

18. For analysis of shifts in these movements, see Forchtner, *The Far Right and the Environment*; Moore and Roberts, *The Rise of Ecofascism*; Rohland, "COVID-19, Climate, and White Supremacy." French ideologue and politician Hervé Juvin offers a relatively coherent version of right populist thinking on the matter. In what amounts to a form of environmental determinism reminiscent of the German *Blut und Boden*, he proposes that solutions to the environmental crises are tied to the recognition that ethnocultural or civilizational diversity is indissoluble and emerges from specific environments. In its search for profits, the globalist neoliberal order has lifted all borders, thus unleashing mass migration that threatens the bond between people and place. See Juvin, *La grande séparation*. I cannot develop the point here, but it is important to recognize how, without being exactly the same, these kinds of arguments resonate with arguments being made in international politics, where China and Russia as well as a host of other emerging countries increasingly demand the recognition of a multipolar international order that, replacing the global liberal one, will respect "civilizational differences," including "illiberal" forms of governance.

19. Cited in Bivar, "The Patriot Ecology of the French Far Right." Le Pen was largely paraphrasing Juvin. But just in case someone might assume this is purely a European development, consider the following extracts from an opinion piece written by two US congressmen: "If we set aside the politically charged immigration debate for a moment, we can clearly see the negative environmental impacts these surges of illegal migrants create. The sheer quantity of illegal migrants results in destroyed vegetation, and desert areas become dumping grounds. . . . In their rush to politicize a crisis, we have yet to hear our Democratic colleagues on the Natural Resources Committee raise concerns regarding the long-term environmental harm illegal border crossings present." See Weterman and Gosar, "The Environmental Costs of the Border Crisis." On sprawling ecofascisms in the United States, see Rueda, "Neoecofascism."

20. Prasad, "Anti-science Misinformation and Conspiracies"; Liekefett, Bürner, and Becker, "Hippies Next to Right-Wing Extremists?"

21. Hamilton, "Human Destiny in the Anthropocene."

22. Hamilton, "Human Destiny in the Anthropocene," 42.

23. Hamilton, Bonneuil, and Gemenne, "Thinking the Anthropocene"; Latour, *We Have Never Been Modern.*

24. Metzger, "The Moose Are Protesting," and Sepúlveda Luque, "Swans, Ecological Struggles and Ontological Fractures."

25. See Barad, *Meeting the Universe Halfway*; Bennett, *Vibrant Matter*; Braun and Whatmore, *Political Matter*; Haraway, *When Species Meet.*

26. Bennett, *Vibrant Matter*, xi.

27. Cited in Haraway, *Staying with the Trouble*, 44.

28. Latour, "Waiting for Gaia," 27. On compositionism, see Latour, "An Attempt at a 'Compositionist Manifesto.'" On "compostisionism," see Haraway, *Staying with the Trouble.*

29. Latour, *Reassembling the Social.*

30. Latour, "Turning around Politics," 813.

31. See Fornillo, "El litio En Sudamérica."

32. Argento, "Entre el boom del litio y la defensa de la vida"; Grupo de Estudios en Geopolítica y Bienes Comunes, *Triangulo del litio.*

33. As Federici points out, although the discussion on the commons has a longer history, it became further enriched during the 1990s in the convergence between three developments: attempts to reimagine alternatives to capitalism after the demise of the statist model of revolution, the push back against the neoliberal attempt to subject every mode of existence into a resource (for the market economy), and the increasing visibility of environmental crises that would eventually be lumped under the label Anthropocene. See Federici, "Feminism and the Politics of the Commons."

34. For an overview of the approach, see Aligica et al., *Elinor Ostrom and the Bloomington School of Political Economy.*

35. Jiménez et al., *Lo común.*

36. Caffentziz and Federici, "Commons against and beyond Capitalism."

37. Linebaugh, *The Magna Carta Manifesto*, 279.

38. Hardt and Negri, *Commonwealth*, viii. Emphasis added. See also Bollier and Helfrich, *The Wealth of the Commons*; Bollier and Helfrich, *Patterns of Commoning*; Harvey, "The Future of the Commons."

39. Federici, *Re-enchanting the World*, 228–29.

40. Federici, *Re-enchanting the World*, 229. Emphasis added.

41. See Federici, *Revolution at Point Zero.*

42. Gutiérrez Aguilar and Salazar Lohman, "Reproducción comunitaria de la vida."

43. As Svampa has pointed out, these debates are themselves the latest iteration of long-standing debates in Latin American leftist circles about the political role (or lack thereof) that so-called marginal groups might play in the realization of a noncapitalist horizon. See Svampa, "Debates Latinoamericanos." But the discussions are of course also part of long-standing debates within the Marxist-inspired left about the relation between

constituent power (let's say *grassroots social mobilization*) and constituted power (institutions such as political parties and more general to the state).

44. A good example is how some years ago, but relatively contemporary to each other, left- and right-leaning governments were dismissing opposition to extractivism. For instance, Bolivian vice-president Alvaro Garcia Linera explained in an interview why its government was intent on disregarding local opposition to oil exploration in these terms: "Alongside the right to land of a people is the right of the state, of the state led by the Indigenous-popular and peasant movement, to superimpose the greater collective interest of all the people. And that is how we are going to proceed." See Svampa, "Entrevista a Alvaro García Linera." In turn, Peruvian president Alan Garcia dismissed opposition to extractivist plans in similar terms: "Enough is enough. These peoples are not monarchy, they are not *first-class citizens*. Who are 400,000 natives to tell 28 million Peruvians that you have no right to come here? This is a grave error, and whoever thinks this way wants to lead us to *irrationality and a retrograde primitivism*." See Paricahua, "The Aftermath of Bagua."

45. García Linera, *Geopolítica de la Amazonia*, 60–65.

46. García Linera, *Socialismo comunitario*, 17.

47. Cusicanqui, "Tipnis"; Gutiérrez Aguilar, "Prólogo"; Lohman, "'Se han adueñado del proceso de lucha'"; Machado and Zibechi, *Cambiar el mundo desde arriba*; Tapia Mealla, *El Estado de derecho como tiranía*; Rojas, "Pluriversalizar la sociedad para descolonizar el estado en Bolivia"; Schavelzon, *Plurinacionalidad y vivir bien*.

48. For the work of this collective, see the Horizontes Comunitarios website, accessed December 8, 2023, https://horizontescomunitarios.wordpress.com/.

49. Linsalata, "Repensar la transformación social desde las escalas espacio-temporales de la producción de lo común," 119.

50. Linsalata, "Repensar la transformación social desde las escalas espacio-temporales de la producción de lo común," 114.

51. Linsalata, "Repensar la transformación social desde las escalas espacio-temporales de la producción de lo común," 118.

52. Linsalata, "Repensar la transformación social desde las escalas espacio-temporales de la producción de lo común," 120.

53. Recall that pitino are not without their bahlut and the practices that the latter command from some yshiro like the tobich oso.

54. Anderson, *Imagined Communities*.

55. Although a growing body of literature attends to how nonhumans of all kinds participate in the composition of common "territories," the question of their role in scaling them remains largely unaddressed. See Ruiz-Serna, *When Forests Run Amok*; Di Giminiani, *Sentient Lands*; Escobar, "Sentipensar con la tierra"; Carman, Berros, and Medrano, "Presentación del dossier# 14 la irrupción política."

56. Fennell, "Ostrom's Law"; Marshall, "Nesting, Subsidiarity, and Community-Based Environmental Governance beyond the Local Level."

57. See Moore, *Capitalism in the Web of Life*; Navarro Trujillo and Linsalata, "Capitaloceno, luchas por lo común y disputas por otros términos de interdependencia en el tejido de la vida"; Juvin, *La grande séparation*.

58. "This is precisely the point where compositionism wishes to take over: *what is the successor of nature?* Of course, no human, no atom, no virus, no organism has ever resided 'in' nature understood as *res extensa*. They have all lived in the pluriverse, to use William James's expression—where else could they have found their abode?" Latour, "An Attempt at a 'Compositionist Manifesto,'" 477.

59. Latour, "An Attempt at a 'Compositionist Manifesto,'" 473–74. Emphasis added.

60. The scare quotes around the word "design" simply signal a recognition that for Latour, this is not simply a matter of "human" intent.

61. Most recently in his *Down to Earth*.

62. "Precisely because of the crimes [Europe/Modernity] has committed, smallness is not an option." Latour, *Down to Earth*, 102. The "small" to which Latour refers in this passage is associated with "the local"—that is, the flipside of "the global." Within this "modernist" contrast (which Latour refuses), the global is equated to the universal while the local is equated to the self-contained locality, and hence the "small" has, for Latour, the resonance of xenophobic nationalism. While I understand we are not talking of the same "small," I find it telling that Latour would not imagine the small as distinct from the local. I will return to this point in the postlude.

63. Latour, "Anthropology at the Time of the Anthropocene," 45.

64. Haraway, *Staying with the Trouble*, 43.

65. Puig de la Bellacasa, "Matters of Care."

66. Jensen and Blok see this "scientism" in several strands of new materialisms and find a paradigmatic example in Clark's *Inhuman Nature*. See Blok and Jensen, "The Anthropocene Event in Social Theory."

67. Puig de la Bellacasa, "Matters of Care."

68. At the center of the call is the feminist insight that the labor of care—broadly defined as "everything that we do to maintain, continue and repair 'our world' so that we can live in it as well as possible"—is rendered invisible by patriarchal thought and that countering this invisibilization requires the active work of critique.

69. Puig de la Bellacasa, "Matters of Care," 94. See also Sundberg, "Decolonizing Posthumanist Geographies."

70. Haraway, *Staying with the Trouble*, 101.

ACT II

1. Engels, "On Authority," 132.

2. On hybrid forums, see Callon, Lascoumes, and Barthe, *Acting in an Uncertain World*.

3. Callon, Lascoumes, and Barthe, *Acting in an Uncertain World*, 18. For a critical take on these kinds of promises, see Braun, "From Critique to Experiment?"

4. Blaser, "Is Another Cosmopolitics Possible?," 545–70; Blaser, "On the Properly Political (Disposition for the) Anthropocene."

5. My colleague Carolina Tytelman points out that Innu use both *nitassinan* and *nutshimit* to refer to what I call *emplaced collective*. She underscores, however, that "while values associated with Nitassinan are also associated with nutshimit, these terms express different dimensions of experience. Nitassinan is usually a political term associated with issues of identity and rights to access the territory, while nutshimit is most frequently

used to express personal connections and experiences in the territory, particularly when contrasted with the experience of life in permanent settlements." For simplicity, I generally use the word nitassinan (without capitalizing it) to refer to the emplaced collective, although when appropriate, I follow Innu usage of the word nutshimit where this makes sense. See Tytelman, "Place and Forest Co-management in Nitassinan/Labrador," 68. Again, recall my point about avoiding capitalization of ethnonyms to highlight their character as a specific kind of being in a specific emplaced collective.

6. In contrast to my experiences with the Yshiro communities, my relations with the Innu have been less intense and diverse. I lived with my family in the town of Happy Valley-Goose Bay neighboring the community of Sheshatshiu for four months in 2010 and made a few Innu friends and acquaintances at the time. My former students and now colleagues Carolina Tytelman and Damian Castro, who lived in nitassinan for two years with their children, were invaluable liaisons for this. Since then, I have visited both Innu communities (Sheshatshiu and Natuashish) a dozen times for various activities, and some of my acquaintances visit me in St. John's when they travel. But in general, the relations have been more work related and focused on planning and executing various research projects we developed together with the Innu Nation Environment Office.

7. Hummel et al., *Caribou and the North*.

8. Hummel et al., *Caribou and the North*, 29–30.

9. Hummel et al., *Caribou and the North*, 41.

10. Pratt, *Imperial Eyes*, 15.

11. Pratt, *Imperial Eyes*, 31.

12. The thirteenth edition of Linnaeus's *Systema Naturae*, edited by J. F. Gmelin in 1788, included caribou under the category "Cervus." Linnaeus, *Systema Naturae*, 175–78.

13. McGrath, "Wildlife Protection in Newfoundland, 1850–1929."

14. As several historians of wildlife conservation in Canada have pointed out, concerning a game animal, those early laws expressed governmental and elite anxieties about the touted wastefulness and profligacy of the popular classes in general and of Indigenous peoples in particular. Hence, until the 1920s and the emergence of professional wildlife management, governmental regulations were fundamentally geared to set limits for those who, unlike hunting sportsmen, were supposedly unable to do so themselves. These regulations typically imposed prohibitions or restrictions on selling meat, established the number of animals allowed to be hunted, defined hunting seasons, and delimited no-hunting areas. See Burnett, *A Passion for Wildlife*; Kulchyski and Tester, *Kiumajut (Talking Back)*; Sandlos, *Hunters at the Margin*; Usher, "Caribou Crisis or Administrative Crisis?"

15. "True North strong and free" is a phrase in Canada's national anthem. Caribou is described as a national icon on the web page of the Royal Canadian Mint, where the ubiquitous quarter dollar coin featuring the animal's head is produced. For the impact of early explorers and naturalists on the imagination of a Canadian wilderness, see Sandlos, *Hunters at the Margin*.

16. I take the quip from Johnathan Luedee's groundbreaking thesis on the environmental history of the Porcupine caribou herd, from which (along with the work of my

colleague John Sandlos) I also draw substantially in my subsequent tracing of the trajectory of caribou as technoscientific artifact. See Luedee, "Science, Borders, and Boundaries in the Western Arctic."

17. Of course, responding to emerging environmental legislation was not the only reason corporations promoted Northern science; overcoming other "natural" obstacles to their extractive designs was also quite central.

18. Science sponsored by corporations whose "vested interests" are other than caribou or their habitats has been constantly under scrutiny by parties such as wildlife and environmental protection interest groups (and their backers in government), for whom caribou and their habitats constitute their "vested interests." Yet the circulation of "experts" through the academy, the government, private firms, and nonprofits has increasingly rendered difficult the outright disqualification of any expert's authority solely based on their "workplace."

19. For a brief overview of the context in which this recognition began to take shape, see chapters 13 and 14 of Miller, *Skyscrapers Hide the Heavens*.

20. Hegel and Schimiegelow, "NACW at Thirty," 6.

21. Hummel et al., *Caribou and the North*, 189.

22. "Un *atenogen*, nous disait un conteur de La Romaine, 'c'est ce qu'on doit transmettre afin que les générations futures sachent ce qu'il convient de savoir.'" (An atenogen, said a storyteller from La Romaine, is what must be passed on so that future generations know what they need to know.) Savard, *Le rire précolombien dans le Québec d'aujourd'hui*, 63–67.

23. See Armitage, "Religious Ideology among the Innu of Eastern Quebec and Labrador"; Castro and Andrew, *Atiku Napeu*; Henriksen, *Hunters in the Barrens*.

24. Rockwood, *Memorandum on General Policy in Respect to the Indians and Eskimos of Northern Labrador*, 9; Tanner, *Outlines of the Geography, Life and Customs of Newfoundland-Labrador*.

25. See McGee, *Cultural Stability and Change among the Montagnais Indians of the Lake Melville Region of Labrador*, 31. In a 1988 entry in her published diaries, elder Tshaukuesh Elizabeth Penashue expresses how the Innu interpreted what drove the government to settle them: "Pien Penashue [a highly respected elder] said that they want to control us, to keep us from hunting—that's why they give us pensions, so they can have our land." Penashue and Yeoman, *Nitinikiau Innusi*, 10.

26. Andrew and Sarsfield, "Innu Health."

27. Castro, "Meating the Social"; Natcher, Castro, and Felt, "Hunter Support Programs and the Northern Social Economy"; Tytelman, "Place and Forest Co-management in Nitassinan/Labrador."

28. Wallich, *North-Atlantic Sea-Bed*, 46.

29. In a revealing passage of the published work-related anecdotes of a former wildlife officer, the author criticizes the "irrationality" of the Innu vis-à-vis the government in an altercation that occurred in 1976, by depicting the former's position as claiming "their god-given right to take from the land what they wanted and when they wanted it, *biology and herd management be damned*." Payne, *Wildlife Delights and Dilemmas*, 56.

30. Innu hunting and burial grounds were also submerged without warning. See Loring et al., "The Archaeology and Ethnohistory of a Drowned Land." In 2020, Innu Nation

began court procedures against Hydro-Québec to pay, as coresponsible, $4 billion in compensation. See, e.g., "Hydro-Québec: Your Bill Is 50 Years Past Due," Past Due (website), accessed February 14, 2024, https://50yearspastdue.ca/.

31. In Canada, "comprehensive land claims" are geared to trade diffuse Aboriginal "title" over a territory for clearly defined rights and privileges over more circumscribed areas and resources. Diffuse Aboriginal title over large territories does not deter provincial governments from granting corporations permits to exploit their natural resources. Thus, although carrying the price of "extinguishing" any right to their entire territory, a land claim settlement implies legal certainty and substantial (albeit short-lived) flows of money and jobs from resource development to the communities. Given the trade-offs, comprehensive land claims often produce divisions within communities; the Labrador Innu land claim is not different in this regard. See Samson and Cassell, "The Long Reach of Frontier Justice."

32. See Armitage and Kennedy, "Redbaiting and Racism on Our Frontier"; Barron, "In the Name of Solidarity"; Wadden, *Nitassinan*.

33. "All the animals are scared of the jets, from all the noise made by them. The caribou, the caribou that roams around in heavily wooded areas, it also gets scared. The beaver just stays put in his lodge; he can't go out and fix his lodge, he just stays put and eventually loses weight. All the animals lose weight—they don't eat." Antane and Kanikuen, "The Innut and Their Struggle against Assimilation," 28.

34. The resources brought by the operations were important for many people. In effect, a federal defense minister of the time claimed that the operations brought over $100 million per year just to the local economy of Goose Bay. Thus, while the general public and civil organizations outside Labrador were sympathetic to the Innu, most of the non-Indigenous public—in addition to the federal, provincial, and municipal governments—were not. In turn, although the Inuit represented by the Labrador Inuit Association generally opposed low-level flying, they were pliable to negotiation. See Armitage and Kennedy, "Redbaiting and Racism on Our Frontier." Finally, the other Indigenous organization, the Labrador Métis Nation, which would later rename itself Knunatukavut (representing Inuit of Southern Labrador), emerged during the conflict, and many of its members were in favor of low-level flights. See Hallett, "Against Prevailing Currents," 170n66.

35. Detractors argued that the Innu justification to refuse participating in monitoring was bogus. According to them, the Innu alleged that the low-level flying interfered with a so-called traditional way of life, which was anything but, as shown by the fact that Innu families were being flown to their hunting camps with taxpayers' money. According to their detractors, the real motive of the Innu opposition was to get the upper hand in negotiations over rights to land to which other Labradorians had a right as well. Armitage and Kennedy, "Redbaiting and Racism on Our Frontier."

36. Mol, *The Body Multiple*.

37. This, she argued, is accomplished through a series of operations by which different performances either are made to hold together as a single entity or are kept apart to avoid mutual interference.

38. Blaser, "Doing and Undoing Caribou/Atiku."

39. Thus, wildlife managers, environmental NGOs, corporate representatives, outfitters, and Indigenous groups might dispute certain interventions to manage specific herds, but they will all refer back to the technoscientific version—for instance, by contesting the methodologies used to establish "significant units" for management, finding fault with specific techniques used to generate data, or even raising the specter of uncertainty and perfectibility inherent to scientific knowledge—in order to refuse a course of action that jeopardizes their own versions. This latter response is typical when it comes to clashes between corporations' and scientists' versions in the context of development projects, often resulting in the corporate sponsorship of further research that frequently, and despite lip service to the "precautionary principle," is undertaken while projects proceed. The shifting outcomes as well as the relative regularities that can be observed in these contexts speak to the relative weight that Capitalism, Science, and the State have vis-à-vis each other in shaping the "behavior" of the Reason Police in specific circumstances.

40. Griffiths et al., *Voisey's Bay Mine and Mill Environmental Assessment Panel Report*, 203.

41. Far from being a sleight of hand to discard them, the distinction between different aspects within (or categories of) Traditional Knowledge has been touted by Usher as a necessity. He argues that in a context where its mandated inclusion, while well intended, has not paid enough attention to the determination of exactly "how TEK and science can be presented and judged in comparable terms in the public arenas of environmental assessment and management," such partitioning is unavoidable. See Usher, "Traditional Ecological Knowledge in Environmental Assessment and Management," 185. See also Houde, "Six Faces of Traditional Ecological Knowledge."

42. For Voisey's Bay mine, see Griffiths et al., *Voisey's Bay Mine and Mill Environmental Assessment Panel Report*. For the Lower Churchill hydrodevelopment, see *Lower Churchill Hydroelectric Generation Project Joint Review Panel Report*.

43. Innu Nation Task Force on Mining Activities, *Ntesinan Nteshiniminan Nteniunan*; *Lower Churchill Hydroelectric Generation Project Joint Review Panel*, vol. 17, 71–72.

44. Innu Nation Task Force on Mining Activities, *Ntesinan Nteshiniminan Nteniunan*.

45. Newfoundland and Labrador Government, "Focusing Our Energy."

46. The impact assessment process included the inhabitants of several towns downstream and around Lake Melville (into which the river drains), and several other aboriginal organizations (two Inuit from Labrador and a few Innu from the Québec side of the border). Innu Nation was, however, the major interlocutor. Given that Innu Nation's claim for rights in the area to be affected were the most substantive, even without a finalized land claim agreement, it was the actor with the most capacity to complicate the smooth advance of the project. Thus, important enticements to get Innu Nation on board were offered by the province in the form of a recognition of damages and a promise of compensation for the first (Upper) Churchill hydroelectric project, an agreement in principle that would finally lead to a land claim settlement, and an impact and benefits agreement for the present project that promised substantial financial benefits for the Innu communities. All three aspects of this enticement were included in the Tshash Petapen (New Dawn) Agreement, which was set for ratification by the Innu communities after the impact assessment discussions but informed them throughout.

47. The situation of the herd was not fully considered in the impact assessment studies presented by the hydroelectric provincial corporation, allegedly because the project would affect only a marginal portion of the herd's migratory range. Although in public hearings, both governmental and nongovernmental experts pointed out this "gap" as significant, the review panel ended up assuming that direct effects from the project would "not likely be significant" and instead recommended that a management program be implemented for the herd. The lack of attention to this issue was one of the reasons the Sierra Club of Canada filed a court petition to stop the project. There were also controversies about financial aspects of the project and the lack of consideration given to less grandiose alternatives. For these points, see *Lower Churchill Hydroelectric Generation Project Joint Review Panel Report*, 114–17, 184.

48. McLoughlin et al., "Declines in Populations of Woodland Caribou"; Vors and Boyce, "Global Declines of Caribou and Reindeer."

49. Each of these categories within the larger one of "species-at-risk" are intended to match a level of risk and an adequate degree of managerial intervention.

50. Innu Nation had accepted participating in a government-created recovery team alongside biologists and wildlife managers, but it soon withdrew, as Innu hunters found the creation of no-hunting zones based on the delimitation of herds irrelevant to the problematic as their own experts understood it. More on this soon.

51. See CBC, "Innu May Hunt"; CBC, "Labrador Hunters." Our team produced a documentary of the hunt. See Castro and Andrew, *Atiku Napeu*.

52. Stengers, "The Challenge of Ontological Politics," 102–3.

53. Latour, *Politics of Nature*, 124.

54. In a province with a small population, I have had opportunities for informal but very open conversations with many people (friends, acquaintances, and circumstantial interlocutors) who work or have worked in federal or provincial agencies in charge of researching, monitoring, and managing wildlife (e.g., Canadian Wildlife Service, and Newfoundland Wildlife Division) as well as aquatic ecosystems (Department of Fisheries and Oceans). While I draw on those conversations for the subsequent discussion, I also attend to the fact that, as jobs and working relations are on the line, my interlocutors are very reluctant to engage on this topic openly; thus, I have taken care to disguise who they are.

55. Recognizing the alterity of "other things" (than ourselves)—that is, that they are also something else than what we say they are—certainly generates an unknown. But then the question is, Under what conditions does that unknown call for more knowledge? For what purpose, with what means, and despite what? Curiosity is too general an answer to these questions; in each instantiation, it needs to be examined so we can inquire into the kinds of worlds that our curiosity-driven knowing practices are producing.

56. Tsing, "A Multispecies Ontological Turn?," 239.

57. Tsing, "A Multispecies Ontological Turn?," 244.

58. Tsing, Mathews, and Bubandt, "Patchy Anthropocene."

59. Recall that when not obvious, divergent multiplicity will not necessarily be visible without an interruption; equivocations can sometimes be productive misunderstandings that live on without ever making themselves evident.

60. Stengers, "The Challenge of Ontological Politics," 95.

61. Clark and Szerszynski, *Planetary Social Thought*.

62. Clark and Szerszynski, *Planetary Social Thought*, 35.

63. Clark and Szerszynski, *Planetary Social Thought*, 178. On carbon democracy, see Mitchell, "Carbon Democracy."

64. Clark and Szerszynski, *Planetary Social Thought*, 167.

65. Clark and Szerszynski, *Planetary Social Thought*, 167.

66. Povinelli, *Geontologies*.

67. Povinelli makes explicit that this subtending formation of power has "long operated openly in settler late liberalism"; thus, the change is that it has now become visible everywhere. Povinelli, *Geontologies*, 5.

68. In fact, I would risk asserting that the centrality of the natural sciences in geontopower is even more intense than in biopower: not only does social engineering become at best a subset of geoengineering in dreams (and nightmares) of governance, but also the relations between continuities and discontinuities (between humans and nonhumans, and between life and nonlife) narrated by, for example, chemistry, physics, geology, and biology become more compelling even to social scientists than those narrated by their own "classical" human-centered disciplines.

69. With the "right circumstances," I want to flag that under contemporary conditions, being careful with atiku is also entangled with infrastructures of displacement.

70. Povinelli, *Geontologies*, 29.

71. The whole agenda of "reconciliation" has been further boosted with the finding since 2021 of hundreds of unmarked graves of Indigenous children that were taken into residential schools since the late 1870s to the 1980s.

72. Although before the ban was passed, the government warned that "environmental concerns" necessarily override "Aboriginal rights to hunt" in the ongoing court proceedings (in which one of our team members, Damian Castro, has been called as an expert witness), the provincial government is not making a case about environmental concerns but rather is contesting that the Innu have aboriginal rights to hunt atiku at all. In effect, they have been questioning whether the practices associated with hunting atiku have continued since before the European arrival. Even for nonlegal experts such as my CWS interlocutor, the tack adopted to date seems quite preposterous.

73. Kunuk and Cohn, *The Journals of Knud Rasmussen*.

74. The film suggests that Avva's daughter interacting with the spirit of her deceased husband might have something to do with the duress the group has to endure.

75. A "cynical" version of a "one-reality" conversion would see it simply as opportunistic theatrics, therefore meaning that the "new truth" is not taken to be real, and conversion has no real effects beyond a facade.

POSTLUDE

1. Hay, "Political Ontology."

2. Latour, *Down to Earth*, 102.

3. See Latour, *Facing Gaia: Six Lectures*, 128.

4. This critique was what clued me into the need to carefully look into how the pragmatics of scale play out in political imagination. See Viveiros de Castro and Danowski,

"Humans and Terrans in the Gaia War," 185. It is important to recognize that in the published book based on the Gifford lectures, Latour does not make the argument about other modes of existence being able or not able to scale up to the problem of the Anthropocene, although I am not aware that he directly responded to his colleagues' friendly critique. See Latour, *Facing Gaia: Eight Lectures*.

5. Events like the COVID-19 pandemic and the war in Ukraine have been key to bring home for many an acute sense of the fragility of the infrastructures of displacement that subtend the big. But a string of more regular phenomena that disrupt "services" because infrastructures have not been designed to withstand the extreme weather events we are currently seeing, or because they are hacked for criminal, geopolitical, or so-called ideological purposes, also contribute to make the frailty of the big a rather close and personal experience. Two telling "anecdotes" from the place I live are illustrative. One is the unprecedented increase in home gardening in the wake of the pandemic (see CBC, "Seedlings for Sale"). From what I gleaned in a Backyard Farming Facebook group, where I am a member, much of what drives this spike are concerns about the reliability of global food supply chains. The other is a cyberattack that paralyzed the province's health-care system in 2021 (from blood work to cancer care) when its network was "kidnapped" for ransom. Then we learned how common this has become and how often the institutions attacked try to hide it for a variety of reasons, from escaping liability to keeping the public's trust. For the increasing role of hacking in both the functioning and disruption of infrastructures, see Burkart and McCourt, *Why Hackers Win*.

6. See Invisible Committee, *The Coming Insurrection*; Invisible Committee, *To Our Friends*; Invisible Committee, *Now*; Malm, *How to Blow Up a Pipeline*; Robinson, *The Ministry for the Future*.

7. See Morand and Lajaunie, "Outbreaks of Vector-Borne and Zoonotic Diseases Are Associated with Changes in Forest Cover and Oil Palm Expansion at Global Scale."

8. Corsín Jiménez, "Spiderweb Anthropologies" and "'Anthropological Entrapments.'"

9. Hershock, *Liberating Intimacy*.

10. Clark and Szerszynski, *Planetary Social Thought*, 75.

11. On language revitalization, see Rosborough and Rorick, "Following in the Footsteps of the Wolf." On food sovereignty, see Pimbert, "Constructing Knowledge for Food Sovereignty, Agroecology and Biocultural Diversity." On energy sovereignty, see Powell and Long, "Landscapes of Power." On popular economy, see Gago, Cielo, and Gachet, "Presentación del dossier." On feminist economy, see Rodríguez Enríquez, "Economía feminista y economía del cuidado." For transitions, degrowth, and post-development, see Escobar, "Degrowth, Postdevelopment, and Transitions," and Kallis, *Degrowth*. On ecosocial pacts, see Svampa, "La pandemia desde América Latina." On designs otherwise, see Gutiérrez Borrero, "Resurgimientos"; Escobar, *Designs for the Pluriverse*.

12. See Amador Jimenez, "Making Ciénaga"; Simbsler, "Trusting the Lord, Conquering the Land"; Sarrazin and Redondo, "Indigenas evangélicos y diversidad cultural."

13. Latour, *Down to Earth*, 21.

14. Susan Harding is a good example of how to critically engage the "ugly" without being drawn by our own established sensibilities. See Harding, "Getting Things Back to Normal."

15. In literature associated with these agendas, the implicit demand I refer to appears primarily through "absences." In effect, this literature tends report how the communities, groups, or initiatives they focus on reflect the values being promoted and seldom how they might run counter to them. While often remaining implicit, I think this operates as a sort of guarantee that the politics being reported about is on the "good side," the one that appeals to those that share "our" (the reporters') sensibility. A more explicit expression of this tendency to demand guarantees is well reflected in the attempts to legislate them through concepts such as the Rights of Nature, despite all the impasses inherent in enrolling "the law" in the maintenance of the pluriversal. See Tănăsescu, "Rights of Nature, Legal Personality, and Indigenous Philosophies"; Rawson and Mansfield, "Producing Juridical Knowledge."

16. It is in this spirit that I read Kim TallBear's proposal, addressed primarily to her Indigenous peers, to seriously consider "making kin" as a creative alternative diplomatic strategy "to nationalist assertions of inherent sovereignty." To me, this sounds like a call for an effort to escape the pull of infrastructures of displacement. TallBear, "Caretaking Relations, Not American Dreaming," 37–38.

17. Kauth and King, "Illiberalism"; Öniş and Kutlay, "The New Age of Hybridity and Clash of Norms."

18. BRICS+ stands for the nascent coalition formed by Brazil, Russia, India, China, and South Africa, plus a plethora of new emerging economies that have recently been accepted into it.

19. Edelman et al., "Introduction: Critical Perspectives on Food Sovereignty"; MacRae, "Food Sovereignty and the Anthropology of Food"; Iles and Montenegro de Wit, "Sovereignty at What Scale?"

20. Haraway, *Staying with the Trouble*, 4.

21. On pragmatic truths, see Almeida, "Anarquismo ontológico e verdade no antropoceno." See also my discussion with Casper Bruun Jensen in Blaser and Jensen, "Political Ontology and Practical Ontology."

22. See Povinelli, *The Cunning of Recognition*; Stengers, "The Curse of Tolerance."

23. Stengers, "The Challenge of Ontological Politics," 86.

24. Wolf, *Europe and the People without History*.

25. Philosopher of science Yuk Hui captures this "wholeness" to some extent with his concept of "cosmotechnics"—namely, the "unification between the cosmic order and the moral order through technical activities." Hui, *The Question concerning Technology in China*, 19–20.

26. See Fowles, "The Evolution of Simple Society."

27. See Fowles, "The Evolution of Simple Society," 23.

BIBLIOGRAPHY

Achtenberg, Emily, and Rebel Currents. "Bolivia: TIPNIS Marchers Face Accusations and Negotiations." North American Congress on Latin America, August 26, 2011. https://nacla.org/blog/2011/8/26/Bolivia-tipnis-marchers-face-accusations-and-negotiations.

Ajl, Max. *A People's Green New Deal*. London: Pluto, 2021

Aligica, Paul Dragos, Elinor Ostrom, Vincent Ostrom, Charles M. Tiebout, and Robert Warren. *Elinor Ostrom and the Bloomington School of Political Economy: Polycentricity in Public Administration and Political Science*. Vol. 1. Minneapolis: Lexington, 2014.

Almeida, Mauro. "Anarquismo ontológico e verdade no antropoceno." *Ilha, Florianópolis* 23, no. 1 (2021): 10–29. https://doi.org/10.5007/2175-8034.2021.e78405.

Almiron, Carlos. "Plan de ordenamiento territorial divide a pobladores de Bahia negra." ABC Digital, 13 June, 2022. https://www.abc.com.py/nacionales/chaco/2022/06/13/plan-de-ordenamiento-territorial-divide-a-pobladores-de-bahia-negra/. Accessed 12 December 2023.

Amador Jimenez, Monica. "Making Ciénaga: Amphibious Entanglements in a Body of Water in Colombia." PhD diss., University of Oslo, 2021.

Anderson, Benedict. *Imagined Communities: Reflections on the Origin and Spread of Nationalism*. New York: Verso, 2006.

Andrew, Ben, and Peter Sarsfield. "Innu Health: The Role of Self-determination." Circumpolar Health, 1984. Proceedings of the 6th International Congress on Circumpolar Health." *Nutrition Today* 20, no. 2 (1985): 428–30.

Antane, Shinipest, and Pien Kanikuen. "The Innut and Their Struggle against Assimilation." *Native Issues* 4, no. 2 (1984): 25–33.

Argento, Melisa. "Entre el boom del litio y la defensa de la vida: Salares, Agua, Territorios y comunidades en la región Atacameña." In *Litio En Sudamérica: Geopolítica, energía y territorios*, edited by Bruno Fornillo, 173–220. Buenos Aires: CLACSO, 2019.

Armitage, Peter. "Religious Ideology among the Innu of Eastern Quebec and Labrador: Traditions Amérindiennes." *Religiologiques (Montréal)* 6 (1992): 63–110.

Armitage, Peter, and John C. Kennedy. "Redbaiting and Racism on Our Frontier: Military Expansion in Labrador and Quebec." *Canadian Review of Sociology and Anthropology* 26, no. 5 (1989): 798–817.

Arola, Adam. "Native American Philosophy." In *Oxford Handbook of World Philosophies*, edited by William Edelglass and Jay L. Garfield, 554–65. Oxford: Oxford University Press, 2011.

Asafu-Adjaye, John, Linus Blomqvist, Stewart Brand, Barry Brook, Ruth de Fries, Erle Ellis, Christopher Foreman, David Keith, Martin Lewis, Mark Lynas, Ted Nordhaus, Roger Pielke Jr., Rachel Pritzker, Joyashree Roy, Mark Sagoff, Michael Shellenberger, Robert Stone, and Peter Teague. *An Ecomodernist Manifesto*. Accessed October 19, 2021. http://www.ecomodernism.org/manifesto.

Atleo, Richard (Umeek). *Principles of Tsawalk: An Indigenous Approach to Global Crisis*. Vancouver: University of British Columbia Press, 2011.

Barad, Karen. *Meeting the Universe Halfway: Quantum Physics and the Entanglement of Matter and Meaning*. Durham, NC: Duke University Press, 2007.

Barras, Bruno. "Life Projects: Development Our Way." In *In the Way of Development: Indigenous Peoples, Life Projects and Globalization*, edited by Mario Blaser, Harvey A. Feit, and Glenn McRae, 47–51. London: Zed, 2004.

Barron, Jennifer. "In the Name of Solidarity: The Politics of Representation and Articulation in Support of the Labrador Innu." *Capitalism, Nature, Socialism* 11, no. 3 (2000): 87–112.

Bennett, Jane. *Vibrant Matter*. Durham, NC: Duke University Press, 2010.

Biermann, Frank, Michelle Betsill, Joyeeta Gupta, Norichika Kani, Louis Lebel, Diana Liverman, Heike Schroeder, and Bernd Siebenhüner. "Earth System Governance: People, Places and the Planet. Science and Implementation Plan of the Earth System Governance Project." Earth System Governance Project, 2009. https://www.earthsystemgovernance .org/publication/earth-system-governance-people-places-and-the-planet-science-and -implementation-plan-of-the-earth-system-governance-project/.

Bird-David, N. *Us, Relatives: Scaling and Plural Life in a Forager World*. Vol. 12. Berkeley: University of California Press, 2017.

Biset, Emmanuel. "Formas de lo común." *Revista caja muda* 8 (2016): 16–28.

Biset, Emmanuel. "¿Qué es una ontología política?" *Revista internacional de pensamiento político* 15 (2021): 323–46. https://doi.org/10.46661/revintpensampolit.5613.

Bivar, Venus. "The Patriot Ecology of the French Far Right." *Environmental History* 27, no. 4 (2022): 618–24.

Blaser, Mario. "Co-management of Natural Resources across 'Radical Differences': Case Study of the Yshiro in Paraguay." St. John's, Newfoundland: Memorial University of Newfoundland, 2013. https://idl-bnc-idrc.dspacedirect.org/bitstream/handle /10625/51496/IDL-51496.pdf.

Blaser, Mario. "Doing and Undoing Caribou/Atiku: Diffractive and Divergent Multiplicities and Their Cosmopolitical Orientations." *Tapuya: Latin American Science, Technology and Society* 1, no. 1 (2018): 47–64.

Blaser, Mario. "Governmentalities and Authorized Imaginations: A (Non-Modern) Story about Indians, Nature, and Development." PhD diss., McMaster University, 2003.

Blaser, Mario. "Is Another Cosmopolitics Possible?" *Cultural Anthropology* 31, no. 4 (2016): 545–70.

Blaser, Mario. "Life Projects: Indigenous Peoples' Agency and Development." In *In the Way of Development: Indigenous Peoples, Life Projects and Globalization*, edited by Mario Blaser, Harvey A. Feit, and Glenn McRae, 26–44. London: International Development Research Centre, 2004.

Blaser, Mario. "Notes towards a Political Ontology of 'Environmental' Conflicts." In *Contested Ecologies: Dialogues in the South on Nature and Knowledge*, edited by Lesley Green, 13–27. Cape Town, South Africa: HSRC Press, 2013.

Blaser, Mario. "On the Properly Political (Disposition for the) Anthropocene." *Anthropological Theory* 19, no. 1 (March 2019): 74–94.

Blaser, Mario. "The Political Ontology of Doing Difference . . . and Sameness." *Theorizing the Contemporary: Fieldsights*. Last modified January 13, 2014. https://culanth.org /fieldsights/the-political-ontology-of-doing-difference-and-sameness.

Blaser, Mario. *Storytelling Globalization from the Chaco and Beyond*. Durham, NC: Duke University Press, 2010.

Blaser, Mario. "The Threat of the Yrmo: The Political Ontology of a Sustainable Hunting Program." *American Anthropologist* 111, no. 1 (2009): 10–20.

Blaser, Mario, and Marisol de la Cadena. "Introduction: Pluriverse Proposals for a World of Many Worlds." In *A World of Many Worlds*, edited by Marisol de la Cadena and Mario Blaser, 1–22. Durham, NC: Duke University Press, 2018.

Blaser, Mario, and C. B. Jensen. "Political Ontology and Practical Ontology: Continuing of a Debate." Supplement, *Berliner Blätter* 84 (2023): S1–S18.

Blok, Anders, and Casper Bruun Jensen. "The Anthropocene Event in Social Theory: On Ways of Problematizing Nonhuman Materiality Differently." *Sociological Review* 67 (2019): 1195–211.

Bollier, David, and Silke Helfrich. *Patterns of Commoning*. Amherst, MA: Commons Strategy Group and Off the Common, 2015.

Bollier, David, and Silke Helfrich, eds. *The Wealth of the Commons: A World Beyond Market and State*. Amherst, MA: Levellers, 2014.

Bonelli, Cristobal, and Antonia Walford. Introduction to *Environmental Alterities*, edited by Cristobal Bonelli and Antonia Walford, 13–42. Manchester: Mattering, 2021.

Bonifacio, Valentina. "Building Up the Collective: A Critical Assessment of the Relationship between Indigenous Organisations and International Cooperation in the Paraguayan Chaco." *Social Anthropology* 21, no. 4 (2013): 510–22.

Bonifacio, Valentina, and Rodrigo Villagra Carron. "Conexiones inestables, imprevistas y pérdidas: Expandiendo la arena política en la cooperación para el desarrollo y comunidades indígenas en el Chaco Paraguayo." *Revista de antropologia* 59, no. 3 (2016): 90–114.

Bonneuil, Christophe, and Jean-Baptiste Fressoz. *The Shock of the Anthropocene: The Earth, History, and Us*. New York: Verso, 2016.

Boulot, Emille, and Joshua Sterlin. "Steps towards a Legal Ontological Turn: Proposals for Law's Place beyond the Human." *Transnational Environmental Law* 11, no. 1 (2022): 13–38.

Braun, Bruce. "From Critique to Experiment? Rethinking Political Ecology for the Anthropocene." In *The Routledge Handbook of Political Ecology*, edited by Tom Perreault, Gavin Bridge, and James McCarthy, 124–36. Oxfordshire: Routledge, 2015.

Braun, Bruce, and Sarah J. Whatmore, eds. *Political Matter: Technoscience, Democracy, and Public Life*. Minneapolis: University of Minnesota Press, 2010.

Bringel, B., and M. Svampa. "Del consenso de los commodities al consenso de la descarbonización." *Nueva sociedad*, no. 306 (2023): 51–70.

Bruna, Natacha. "A Climate-Smart World and the Rise of Green Extractivism." *Journal of Peasant Studies* 49, no. 4 (2022): 839–64.

Bryan, Joe. "Rethinking Territory: Social Justice and Neoliberalism in Latin America's Territorial Turn." *Geography Compass* 6, no. 4 (2012): 215–26.

Bulkeley, Harriet, and Peter Newell. *Governing Climate Change*. 2nd ed. Oxfordshire: Routledge, 2015.

Burkhart, Brian Yazzie. "What Coyote and Thales Can Teach Us: An Outline of American Indian Epistemology." In *American Indian Thought: Philosophical Essays*, edited by Anne Waters, 15–26. Oxford: Blackwell, 2004.

Burkart, Patrick, and Tom McCourt. *Why Hackers Win: Power and Disruption in the Network Society*. Berkeley: University of California Press, 2019.

Burnett, J. Alexander. *A Passion for Wildlife: The History of the Canadian Wildlife Service*. Vancouver: University of British Columbia Press, 2000.

Caffentzis, George, and Silvia Federici. "Commons against and Beyond Capitalism." Supplement, *Community Development Journal* 49, no. S1 (2014): 92–105.

Cajete, Gregory. *Native Science: Natural Laws of Interdependence*. Santa Fe: Clear Light, 2000.

Callon, Michel, Pierre Lascoumes, and Yannick Barthe. *Acting in an Uncertain World: An Essay on Technical Democracy*. Cambridge, MA: MIT Press, 2009.

Canessa, Andrew. "Methods Really Do Matter: A Response to Marisol de la Cadena." *HAU Journal of Ethnographic Theory* 7, no. 2 (2017): 15–17.

Carman, María, María Valeria Berros, and Celeste Medrano. "Presentación del dossier # 14 la irrupción política, ontológica y jurídica de los no-humanos en los mundos antropocénicos." *Quid 16: Revista del área de estudios urbanos* 14 (2020): 1–14.

Carneiro da Cunha, Manuela, and Mauro W. B. De Almeida. "Indigenous People, Traditional People, and Conservation in the Amazon." *Daedalus* 129, no. 2 (2000): 315–38.

Carr, E. Summerson, and Michael Lempert. "Introduction: Pragmatics of Scale." In *Scale: Discourse and Dimensions of Social Life*, edited by E. Summerson Carr and Michael Lempert, 1–22. Berkeley: University of California Press, 2016.

Carreño, Guillermo Salas. "Places Are Kin: Food, Cohabitation, and Sociality in the Southern Peruvian Andes." *Anthropological Quarterly* 89, no. 3 (2016): 813–40.

Castree, Noel. "The Anthropocene and Geography I: The Back Story." *Geography Compass* 8, no. 7 (2014): 436–49.

Castree, Noel. "The Anthropocene and Geography II: Current Contributions." *Geography Compass* 8, no. 7 (2014): 450–63.

Castree, Noel. "The Anthropocene and Geography III: Future Directions." *Geography Compass* 8, no. 7 (2014): 464–76.

Castree, Noel. "Changing the Anthropo(s)Cene: Geographers, Global Environmental Change and the Politics of Knowledge." *Dialogues in Human Geography* 5, no. 3 (November 2015): 301–16.

Castro, Damian. "Meating the Social: Sharing Atiku-euiash in Sheshatshiu, Labrador." PhD diss., Memorial University of Newfoundland, 2015.

Castro, Damian, and Alex (Nikashant) Andrew, dir. *Atiku Napeu*. Montreal: Life Projects Network, 2016.

CBC. "Innu May Hunt Caribou Despite Ban." CBC News, January 29, 2013. http://www.cbc.ca/news/canada/newfoundland-labrador/story/2013/01/29/nl-innu-caribou-hunt-129.html.

CBC. "Labrador Hunters, Airline Charged in Illegal Caribou Hunt." CBC News, January 22, 2014. https://www.cbc.ca/news/canada/newfoundland-labrador/labrador-hunters-airline-charged-in-illegal-caribou-hunt-1.2506763.

CBC. "Seedlings for Sale: How Home Gardening Has Sparked a Boom for These Farms." CBC News, June 3, 2020. https://www.cbc.ca/news/canada/newfoundland-labrador/-gardening-interest-1.5592853.

Chatterton, Paul. "Making Autonomous Geographies: Argentina's Popular Uprising and the 'Movimiento de Trabajadores Desocupados' (Unemployed Workers Movement)." *Geoforum* 36 (2005): 545–61.

Chatterton, Paul, D. Featherstone, and P. Routledge. "Articulating Climate Justice in Copenhagen: Antagonism, the Commons, and Solidarity." *Antipode* 45 (2013): 602–20. https://doi.org/10.1111/j.1467-8330.2012.01025.x.

Chomsky, Noam, and Robert Pollin. *Climate Crisis and the Global Green New Deal: The Political Economy of Saving the Planet*. New York: Verso, 2020.

Clark, Nigel. *Inhuman Nature: Sociable Life on a Dynamic Planet*. London: SAGE, 2011. http://dx.doi.org/10.4135/9781446250334.

Clark, Nigel, and Bronislaw Szerszynski. *Planetary Social Thought: The Anthropocene Challenge to the Social Sciences*. Newark, NJ: Polity, 2020.

Clastres, Pierre. *Society against the State: Essays in Political Anthropology*. Translated by R. Hurley. New York: Zone, 1989.

Coca, Alejandro, and Louis Reymondin. "Is the 'Paraguayan Gran Chaco' at Risk for Extreme Habitat Destruction?" Terr-i, August 27, 2012. http://www.terra-i.org/news/news/Is-the-Paraguayan-Gran-Chaco-at-risk-for-extreme-habitat-destruction-.html.

Collectivo Situaciones. *Bienvenidos a la selva: Diálogos a Partir de la sexta declaración del EZLN*. Buenos Aires: Tinta Limón Ediciones, Universidad Internacional de Andalucía, 2005.

Coordinadora de Derechos Humanos del Paraguay. *Situación de los derechos a la tierra y al territorio de los pueblos indígenas en el Paraguay*. Asunción, Paraguay: Tierra Viva, 2013.

Cordova, Viola F. *How It Is: The Native American Philosophy of V. F. Cordova*. Edited by Kathleen Dean Moore, Kurt Peters, Ted Jojola, and Amber Lacy. Tucson: University of Arizona Press, 2007.

Correia, Joel Edward. "Indigenous Rights at a Crossroads: Territorial Struggles, the Inter-American Court of Human Rights, and Legal Geographies of Liminality." *Geoforum* 97 (2018): 73–83.

Correia, Joel Edward. "Life in the Gap: Indigeneity, Dispossession, and Land Rights in the Paraguayan Chaco." PhD diss., University of Colorado, 2017.

Corsín-Jiménez, Alberto. "'Anthropological Entrapments': Ethnographic Analysis before and after Relations and Comparisons." *Social Analysis: The International Journal of Anthropology* 65, no. 3 (2021): 110–30.

Corsín-Jiménez, Alberto. "Spiderweb Anthropologies." In *A World of Many Worlds*, edited by Marisol de la Cadena and Mario Blaser, 53–82. Durham, NC: Duke University Press, 2018.

Courtheyn, Christopher. "Desindigenizados pero no vencidos: Raza y resistencia en la comunidad de paz y la Universidad Campesina en Colombia." *Revista colombiana de antropologica* 56, no. 1 (2020): 146–65.

Courtheyn, Christopher. "Territories of Peace: Alter-Territorialities in Colombia's San José de Apartadó Peace Community." *Journal of Peasant Studies* 45, no. 7 (2018): 1432–59.

Cusicanqui, Silvia Rivera. "Tipnis: La larga marcha por nuestra dignidad." In *Piel blanca, máscaras negras: Crítica de la razón decolonial*, edited by Gaya Makaran and Pierre Gaussens, 315–41. Mexico City: National Autonomous University Press, 2020.

De la Cadena, Marisol. *Earth Beings: Ecologies of Practice across Andean Worlds*. Durham, NC: Duke University Press, 2015.

De la Cadena, Marisol. "Runa: Human but Not Only." HAU: *Journal of Ethnographic Theory* 4, no. 2 (September 2014): 253–59. https://doi.org/10.14318/hau4.2.013.

Deloria, Vine, Jr. *The Metaphysics of Modern Existence*. Golden, CO: Fulcrum, 2012.

Deloria, Vine, Jr. *Spirit and Reason: The Vine Deloria Jr. Reader*. Golden, CO: Fulcrum, 1999.

Descola, Philippe. "Modes of Being and Forms of Predication." HAU *Journal of Ethnographic Theory* 4, no. 1 (2014): 271–80.

Di Giminiani, Piergiorgio. *Sentient Lands: Indigeneity, Property, and Political Imagination in Neoliberal Chile*. Tucson: University of Arizona Press, 2018.

Dos Santos, Antonela, and Florencia Tola. "¿Ontologías como modelo, método o política? Debates contemporáneos en antropología." *Avá: Revista de antropología* 29 (2016): 71–98.

Dussart, Françoise, and Sylvie Poirier, eds. *Entangled Territorialities: Negotiating Indigenous Lands in Australia and Canada*. Toronto: University of Toronto Press, 2017.

Dussart, Françoise, and Sylvie Poirier. "Knowing and Managing the Land: The Conundrum of Coexistence and Entanglement." In *Entangled Territorialities*, edited by Françoise Dussart and Sylvie Poirer, 1–24. Toronto: University of Toronto Press, 2021.

Eastman, Charles A. *Soul of an Indian: And Other Writings from Ohiyesa*. Novato, CA: New World Library, 2001.

Edelman, M., T. Weis, A. Baviskar, S. M. Borras Jr., E. Holt-Giménez, D. Kandiyoti, and W. Wolford. "Introduction: Critical Perspectives on Food Sovereignty." *Journal of Peasant Studies* 41, no. 6 (2014): 911–31.

Eitel, Kathrin, and Michaela Meurer. "Introduction: Exploring Multifarious Worlds and the Political within the Ontological Turn(s)." *Berliner Blätter* 84 (2021): 3–19.

Engels, Frederick. "On Authority." In *The Marx-Engels Reader*, edited by Robert C. Tucker, 730–33. New York: W. W. Norton, 1978. First published 1972.

Escobar, Arturo. "Degrowth, Postdevelopment, and Transitions: A Preliminary Conversation." *Sustainability Science* 10, no. 3 (2015): 451–62.

Escobar, Arturo. *Designs for the Pluriverse*. Durham, NC: Duke University Press, 2018.

Escobar, Arturo. *Encountering Development: The Making and Unmaking of the Third World*. Princeton, NJ: Princeton University Press, 1995.

Escobar, Arturo. *Pluriversal Politics*. Translated by David Frye. Durham, NC: Duke University Press, 2020.

Escobar, Arturo. "Sentipensar con la tierra: Las luchas territoriales y la dimensión ontológica de las epistemologías del sur." *AIBR: Revista de Antropología Iberoamericana* 11, no. 1 (2016): 11–32.

Escobar, Arturo. *Sentipensar con la tierra: Nuevas lecturas sobre desarrollo, territorio y diferencia*. Medellín: Universidad Autónoma Latinoamericana UNAULA, 2014.

Escobar, Arturo. "Worlds and Knowledges Otherwise: The Latin American Modernity/ Coloniality Research Program." *Cultural Studies* 21, no. 2–3 (2007): 179–210.

Fernández, Ana María. *Política y subjetividad: Asambleas barriales y fábricas recuperadas*. Buenos Aires: Tinta Limón Ediciones, 2006.

Federici, Silvia. "Feminism and the Politics of the Commons." In *Former West: Art and the Contemporary after 1989*, edited by Maria Hlalvajova and Simon Sheikh, 379–90. Cambridge, MA: MIT Press, 2017.

Federici, Silvia. *Re-enchanting the World: Feminism and the Politics of the Commons*. Oakland, CA: PM, 2018.

Federici, Silvia. *Revolution at Point Zero: Housework, Reproduction, and Feminist Struggle*. Oakland, CA: PM, 2012.

Fennell, Lee. "Ostrom's Law: Property Rights in the Commons." *International Journal of the Commons* 5, no. 1 (2011): 9–27.

Ferreira, Andrey Cordeiro. "Societies 'against' and 'in' the State—from Exiwa to the Retakings: Territory, Autonomy and Hierarchy in the History of the Indigenous Peoples of Chaco-Pantanal." *Vibrant: Virtual Brazilian Anthropology* 15, no. 2 (2018): 1–27.

Forchtner, Bernhard, ed. *The Far Right and the Environment: Politics, Discourse and Communication*. New York: Routledge, 2019.

Fornillo, Bruno. "El litio en Sudamérica: Geopolítica, energía y territorios." *Ciencia, docencia y tecnología* 32, no. 62 (2021).

Foucault, Michel. *The Order of Things*. Oxfordshire: Routledge, 2005. First published 1970.

Fowles, Severin. "The Evolution of Simple Society." *Asian Archaeology* 2, no. 1 (2018): 19–32.

Gad, Christopher, Casper Bruun Jensen, and Brit Ross Winthereik. "Practical Ontology: Worlds in STS and Anthropology." *Nature Culture* 3 (2015): 67–86.

Gago, Verónica. *La razón neoliberal: Economías barrocas y pragmática popular*. Buenos Aires: Tinta Limón, 2014.

Gago, Verónica, Cristina Cielo, and Francisco Gachet. "Presentación del dossier: Economía popular: Entre la informalidad y la reproducción ampliada." *Íconos: Revista de ciencias sociales* 62 (2018): 11–20.

García Linera, Álvaro. *Geopolítica de la Amazonia: Poder hacendal-patrimonial y acumulación capitalista*. La Paz: Vicepresidencia del Estado Plurinacional de Bolivia, 2012.

García Linera, Álvaro. *Socialismo comunitario: Un horizonte de época*. La Paz: Ediciones de Vicepresidencia, 2015.

Glauser, Marcos. *Angaité's Responses to Deforestation: Political Ecology of the Livelihood and Land Use Strategies of an Indigenous Community from the Paraguayan Chaco.* Vol. 30. Münster: LIT Verlag, 2019.

Glauser, Marcos. "Entendiendo las respuestas de un pueblo indígena del chaco Paraguayo a la desposesión territorial." Supplement, *Gestión y Ambiente* 21, no. S2 (2018): 86–94.

Griffiths, Lesley, Samuel Metcalfe, Lorraine Michael, Charles Pelley, and Peter Usher. *Voisey's Bay Mine and Mill Environmental Assessment Panel Report.* Ottawa: Minister of Public Works and Government Services, 1999.

Grupo de Estudios en Geopolítica y Bienes Comunes. *Triangulo del litio: Un area de disputa estratégica entre potencias globales en nombre de la transició energética.* Buenos Aires: Rosa Luxemburg Foundation, 2020.

Gudynas, Eduardo. "Diez tesis urgentes sobre el nuevo extractivismo." In *Extractivismo, politica y sociedad,* edited by J. Schuldt, Alberto Acosta, and Alberto Barandiarán, 187–225. Quito, Ecuador: CAAP, CLAES, 2009.

Gudynas, Eduardo. *Extractivisms: Politics, Economy, and Ecology.* Halifax: Fernwood, 2021.

Guereña, Arantxa, and Luis Rojas. *Yvy Jára: Los dueños de la tierra en Paraguay.* Asunción, Paraguay: OXFAM, 2016.

Gutiérrez Aguilar, Raquel. "Prólogo." In *Se han adueñado del proceso de lucha,* edited by Huáscar Salazar Lohman, 11–15. Cochabamba, Bolivia: SOCEE/Autodeterminación, 2015.

Gutiérrez Aguilar, Raquel, and Huáscar Salazar Lohman. "Reproducción comunitaria de la vida: Pensando la transformación social en el presente." *El Apantle, revista de estudios comunitarios* 1 (2015): 15–50.

Gutiérrez Borrero, Alfredo. "Resurgimientos: Sures como diseños y diseños otros." *Nómadas* 43 (2015): 113–29.

Haesbaert, Rogério. *Território e descolonialidade: Sobre o giro (Multi) territorial/de (s) colonial na "América Latina."* Buenos Aires: CLACSO, 2021.

Hallett, Vicki S. "Against Prevailing Currents: The History of *Them Days* Magazine in Labrador." *Acadiensis: Journal of the History of the Atlantic Region / Acadiensis: Revue d'histoire de la région Atlantique* 48, no. 2 (2019): 146–76.

Hallward, Peter. "Staging Equality: Rancière's Theatrocracy." *New Left Review* 37 (2006): 109–29.

Halvorsen, Sam. "Decolonising Territory: Dialogues with Latin American Knowledges and Grassroots Strategies." *Progress in Human Geography* 43, no. 5 (2019): 790–814.

Hamilton, Clive. "Human Destiny in the Anthropocene." In *The Anthropocene and the Global Environmental Crisis,* edited by Clive Hamilton, Christophe Bonneuil, and François Gemenne, 32–43. London: Routledge, 2015.

Hamilton, Clive, Christophe Bonneuil, and François Gemenne. "Thinking the Anthropocene." In *The Anthropocene and the Global Environmental Crisis,* edited by Clive Hamilton, Christophe Bonneuil, and François Gemenne, 1–14. London: Routledge, 2015.

Haraway, Donna. *Staying with the Trouble: Making Kin in the Chthulucene.* Durham, NC: Duke University Press, 2016. Kindle ed.

Haraway, Donna J. *When Species Meet.* Minneapolis: University of Minnesota Press, 2008.

Harding, Susan. "Getting Things Back to Normal: Populism, Fundamentalism and Liberal Desire." *Social Anthropology/Anthropologie sociale* 29, no. 2 (2021): 310–15.

Hardt, Michael, and Antonio Negri. *Commonwealth*. Cambridge, MA: Harvard University Press, 2009.

Harvey, David. "The Future of the Commons." *Radical History Review* 109 (2011): 101–7.

Hay, C. "Political Ontology." In *The Oxford Handbook of Contextual Political Analysis*, edited by Robert E. Goodin and Charles Tilly, 78–96. New York: Oxford University Press, 2006.

Hecht, Gabrielle. "Interscalar Vehicles for an African Anthropocene: On Waste, Temporality, and Violence." *Cultural Anthropology* 33, no. 1 (2018): 109–41.

Hegel, Troy, and Fiona Schimiegelow. "NACW at Thirty: A Work in Progress." Special Issue, *Rangifer* 35, no. 23 (2015): 6–7.

Henig, David, and Daniel M. Knight. "Polycrisis: Prompt for an Emerging Worldview." *Anthropology Today* 39, no. 4 (2023): 3–6.

Henriksen, George. *Hunters in the Barrens: The Naskapi on the Edge of the White Man's World*. St. John's: Institute of Social and Economic Research, Memorial University of Newfoundland, 1973.

Hershock, Peter D. *Liberating Intimacy: Enlightenment and Social Virtuosity in Ch'an Buddhism*. Albany: State University of New York Press, 1996.

Hetherington, Kregg. "Introduction: Keywords of the Anthropocene." In *Infrastructure, Environment, and Life in the Anthropocene*, edited by Kregg Hetherington, 1–14. Durham, NC: Duke University Press, 2019.

Hirsch, Eric. "Investment's Rituals: 'Grassroots' Extractivism and the Making of an Indigenous Gold Mine in the Peruvian Andes." *Geoforum* 82 (2017): 259–67.

Holbraad, Martin, and Morten Axel Pedersen. *The Ontological Turn: An Anthropological Exposition*. Cambridge: Cambridge University Press, 2017.

Hornborg, Alf. "Mistranslating Relationism and Absolving the Market: A Response to Marisol de la Cadena." *HAU Journal of Ethnographic Theory* 7, no. 2 (2017): 19–21.

Houde, Nicolas. "The Six Faces of Traditional Ecological Knowledge: Challenges and Opportunities for Canadian Co-management Arrangements." *Ecology and Society* 12, no. 2 (2007): 34–51.

Howell, Signe. "Rules without Rulers?" *HAU: Journal of Ethnographic Theory* 7, no. 2 (2017): 143–47.

Huanacuni, Fernando. *Buen vivir / Vivir bien: Filosofía, políticas, estrategias y experiencias regionales Andinas*. Cusco, Perú: CAOI, 2010.

Hui, Yuk. *The Question concerning Technology in China: An Essay in Cosmotechnics*. Vol. 3. Cambridge, MA: MIT Press, 2019.

Hummel, Monte, Justina C. Ray, Robert Redford, Stephen Kakfwi, and Robert Bateman. *Caribou and the North: A Shared Future*. Toronto: Dundurn Press, 2008.

Iles, A., and M. Montenegro de Wit. "Sovereignty at What Scale? An Inquiry into Multiple Dimensions of Food Sovereignty." *Globalizations* 12, no. 4 (2015): 481–97.

"Impacto ambiental es Abordado en Bahia Negra, Chaco." *Diario Ultima Hora*, May 14, 2022. https://www.ultimahora.com/impacto-ambiental-es-abordado-bahia-negra-chaco-n3001709.html.

Innu Nation Task Force on Mining Activities. *Ntesinan Nteshiniminan Nteniunan: Between a Rock and a Hard Place*. Sheshatshiu, Canada: Innu Nation Office, 1996. http://www.ryakuga.com/best/innureport.html.

Invisible Committee. *The Coming Insurrection*. Semiotext(e), 2009.

Invisible Committee. *Now*. Semiotext(e), 2017.

Invisible Committee. *To Our Friends*. Semiotext(e), 2015.

ISTHME—Estudio Meridional. "Elaboración, coordinación y gestión del plan de ordenamiento urbano y territorial del municipio de Bahía Negra Producto 5: Anteproyecto detallado escala distrital." Translated by Mario Blaser. Asunción, Paraguay: WWF Paraguay, 2019.

Jiménez Martín, Carolina, José Francisco Puello-Socarrás, Alejandro Robayo Corredor, and Mario Rodríguez Ibáñez. *Lo común: Alternativas Políticas desde la diversidad*. Bogotá, Colombia: Planeta Paz, 2017.

Juvin, Hervé. *La grande séparation: Pour une écologie des civilisations*. Paris: Editions Gallimard, 2013.

Kallis, Giorgos. *Degrowth*. Newcastle upon Tyne: Agenda, 2018.

Kallis, Giorgos. "A Green New Deal Must Not Be Tied to Economic Growth." *Truthout*, 2019. https://truthout.org/articles/a-green-new-deal-must-not-be-tied-to-economic -growth/.

Kauth, Jasper, and Desmond King. "Illiberalism." *European Journal of Sociology / Archives Européennes de sociologie 61*, no. 3 (2020): 365–405.

Krenak, Ailton. *Ideias para adiar o fim do mundo*. Rio de Janeiro: Companhia das Letras, 2019.

Kröger, Markus. *Extractivisims, Existences and Extinctions: Monoculture Plantations and Amazon Deforestation*. New York: Routledge, 2022.

Kulchyski, Peter, and Frank Tester. *Kiumajut (Talking Back): Game Management and Inuit Rights, 1900–70*. Vancouver: University of British Columbia Press, 2007.

Kunuk, Zacharias, and Norman Cohn, dir. *The Journals of Knud Rasmussen*. Canada, Denmark, and Greenland: Igloolik Isuma Productions and Barok Films, A/S, 2006.

Lang, Miriam, Breno Bringel, and Mary Ann Manahan, eds. *Mas allá del colonialismo verde: Justicia global y geopolítica de las transiciones ecosociales*. Buenos Aires: CLACSO, 2023.

Latour, Bruno. "Anthropology at the Time of the Anthropocene: A Personal View of What Is to Be Studied." In *The Anthropology of Sustainability*, edited by Marc Brightman and Jerome Lewis, 35–49. New York: Palgrave Macmillan, 2017.

Latour, Bruno. "An Attempt at a 'Compositionist Manifesto.'" *New Literary History* 41, no. 3 (2010): 471–90.

Latour, Bruno. *Down to Earth: Politics in the New Climatic Regime*. Cambridge: Polity, 2018. Kindle ed.

Latour, Bruno. *Facing Gaia: Eight Lectures on the New Climatic Regime*. Cambridge: Polity, 2017.

Latour, Bruno. *Facing Gaia: Six Lectures on the Political Theology of Nature*. Edinburgh: Being the Gifford Lectures on Natural Religion, 2013. http://www.earthboundpeople .com/wp-content/uploads/2015/02/Bruno-Latour-Gifford-Lectures-Facing-Gaia-in -the-Anthropocene-2013.pdf.

Latour, Bruno. "From Realpolitik to Dingpolitik or How to Make Things Public." In *Making Things Public: Atmospheres of Democracy*, edited by Latour and Peter Weibel, 14–41. Cambridge, MA: MIT Press, 2005.

Latour, Bruno. *Pandora's Hope: Essays on the Reality of Science Studies.* Cambridge, MA: Harvard University Press, 1999.

Latour, Bruno. *The Pasteurization of France.* Cambridge, MA: Harvard University Press, 1993.

Latour, Bruno. *Politics of Nature: How to Bring the Sciences into Democracy.* Cambridge, MA: Harvard University Press, 2004.

Latour, Bruno. *Reassembling the Social: An Introduction to Actor-Network-Theory.* Oxford: Oxford University Press, 2005.

Latour, Bruno. "Turning around Politics: A Note on Gerard de Vries' Paper." *Social Studies of Science* 37, no. 5 (2007): 811–20. https://doi.org/10.1177/0306312707081222.

Latour, Bruno. "Waiting for Gaia: Composing the Common World through Arts and Politics." In *What Is Cosmopolitical Design? Design, Nature and the Built Environment*, edited by Albena Yaneva and Alejandro Zaera-Polo, 21–32. Farnham: Ashgate, 2015.

Latour, Bruno. *We Have Never Been Modern.* Cambridge, MA: Harvard University Press, 1993.

Latour, Bruno. "What If We Talked Politics a Little?" *Contemporary Political Theory* 2, no. 2 (2003): 143–64.

Law, John. "Actor Network Theory and Material Semiotics." *New Blackwell Companion to Social Theory* 3 (2009): 141–58.

Law. John. *After Methods: Mess in Social Science Research.* New York: Routledge, 2004.

Law, John. "What's Wrong with a One-World World?" *Distinktion: Scandinavian Journal of Social Theory* 16, no. 1 (2015): 126–39.

Law, John, and Solveig Joks. "Indigeneity, Science, and Difference: Notes on the Politics of How." *Science, Technology, & Human Values* 44, no. 3 (2019): 424–47.

Law, John, and Vicky Singleton. "Object Lessons." *Organization* 12, no. 3 (2005): 331–55.

Lepawsky, Josh. *Reassembling Rubbish: Worlding Electronic Waste.* Cambridge, MA: MIT Press, 2018.

Liekefett, Luisa, Ann-Kathrin Bürner, and Julia C. Becker. "Hippies Next to Right-Wing Extremists? Identifying Subgroups of Antilockdown Protesters in Germany Using Latent Profile Analysis." *Social Psychology* 54, no. 3 (2023): 123–35.

Linebaugh, Peter. *The Magna Carta Manifesto.* Berkeley: University of California Press, 2008.

Linnaeus, Carl (Caroli a Linné). *Systema naturae per regna tria naturae: secundum classes, ordines, genera, species, cum characteribus, differentiis, synonymis, locis.* Edited by J. F. Gmelin. 1788. Available at the Biodiversity Heritage Library. Accessed April 5, 2024. https://www.biodiversitylibrary.org/item/83109#page/193/mode/1up.

Linsalata, Lucia. "Repensar la transformación social desde las escalas espacio-temporales de la producción de lo común." In *Revista de estudios comunitarios: Producir lo común, entramados comunitarios y luchas por la vida*, edited by El Apantle, 111–20. Madrid: Traficantes de Sueños, 2019.

Little Bear, Leroy. Foreword to *Native Science: Natural Laws of Interdependence*, by Gregory Cajete, xii. Santa Fe: Clear Light, 2000.

Lohman, Huascar Freddy Salazar. "'Se han adueñado del proceso de lucha': Horizontes comunitario-populares en tensión y la reconstitución de la dominación en la Bolivia del MAS." PhD diss., Benemérita Universidad Autónoma de Puebla, 2015.

Lorimer, Jamie. "The Anthropo-Scene: A Guide for the Perplexed." *Social Studies of Science* 47, no. 1 (February 2017): 117–42.

Loring, Stephen, Moira T. McCaffrey, Peter Armitage, and Daniel Ashini. "The Archaeology and Ethnohistory of a Drowned Land: Innu Nation Research along the Former Michikamats Lake Shore in Nitassinan (Interior Labrador)." *Archaeology of Eastern North America* 31 (2003): 45–72.

Lövbrand, Eva, Malin Mobjörk, and Rickard Söder. "The Anthropocene and the Geopolitical Imagination: Re-writing Earth as Political Space." *Earth System Governance* 4 (2020): 1–8.

Lower Churchill Hydroelectric Generation Project Joint Review Panel. Hearing held at Sheshatshiu Innu School. Vol. 17. Ottawa: Canadian Environmental Assessment Agency, March 22, 2011. Archived December 22, 2022, at the Internet Archive. https://web.archive.org/web/20221222092842/https://www.ceaa.gc.ca/050/documents/48945/48945F.pdf.

Lower Churchill Hydroelectric Generation Project Joint Review Panel Report. Ottawa: Canadian Environmental Assessment Agency, August 2011. Archived September 13, 2015, at the Internet Archive. https://web.archive.org/web/20150913093540/http://www.env.gov.nl.ca/env/env_assessment/projects/Y2010/1305/lower_churchill_panel_report.pdf.

Luedee, Jonathan. "Science, Borders, and Boundaries in the Western Arctic: Environmental Histories of the Porcupine Caribou Herd." PhD diss., University of British Columbia, 2018.

MacDonald, Christine. "Green Going Gone: The Tragic Deforestation of the Chaco." *Rolling Stone*, July 28, 2014. https://www.rollingstone.com/culture/culture-news/green-going-gone-the-tragic-deforestation-of-the-chaco-116951/.

Machado, Decio, and Raúl Zibechi. *Cambiar el mundo desde arriba: Los límites del progresismo.* La Paz, Bolivia: Centro de Estudios para el Desarrollo Laboral Agrario, 2016.

MacRae, Graeme. "Food Sovereignty and the Anthropology of Food: Ethnographic Approaches to Policy and Practice." *Anthropological Forum* 26, no. 3 (2016): 227–32.

Malm, Andreas. *How to Blow Up a Pipeline.* New York: Verso, 2021.

Malm, Andreas, and Alf Hornborg. "The Geology of Mankind? A Critique of the Anthropocene Narrative." *Anthropocene Review* 1, no. 1 (January 2014): 62–69. https://doi.org/10.1177/2053019613516291.

Marshall, Graham R. "Nesting, Subsidiarity, and Community-Based Environmental Governance beyond the Local Level." *International Journal of the Commons* 2, no. 1 (2008): 75–97.

Massey, Doreen. "A Counterhegemonic Relationality of Place." In *Mobile Urbanism: Cities and Policymaking in the Global Age*, vol. 17, edited by Eugene McCann and Keven Ward, 1–14. Minneapolis: University of Minnesota Press, 2011.

Massey, Doreen B. *For Space.* London: SAGE, 2005.

Massey, Doreen B. *Space, Place, and Gender.* Minneapolis: University of Minnesota Press, 1994.

Mazzucato, Mariana. "The Entrepreneurial State." *Soundings* 49, no. 49 (2011): 131–42.

Mazzucato, Mariana. *The Green Entrepreneurial State*. London: Routledge, 2015.

McGee, John T. *Cultural Stability and Change among the Montagnais Indians of the Lake Melville Region of Labrador*. Washington, DC: Catholic University of America Press, 1961.

McGrath, Darrin. "Wildlife Protection in Newfoundland, 1850–1929." *Newfoundland Quarterly* 90 (Winter 1997): 25–30.

McGregor, Deborah. "Towards Coexistence." In *In the Way of Development: Indigenous Peoples, Life Projects, and Globalization*, edited by Mario Blaser, Harvey A. Feit, and Glenn McRae, 72–91. London: Zed, 2004.

McLoughlin, Philip D., Elston Dzus, B. O. B. Wynes, and Stan Boutin. "Declines in Populations of Woodland Caribou." *Journal of Wildlife Management* (2003): 755–61.

Meaney, Thomas. "Fortunes of the New Green Deal." *New Left Review* 138 (November–December 2022): 79–102.

Metzger, Jonathan. "The Moose Are Protesting: The More-than-Human Politics of Transport Infrastructure Development." In *Planning Against the Political*, edited by Jonathan Metzger, Philip Allmendinger, and Stijn Oosterlynck, 192–214. New York: Routledge, 2014.

Miller, James. *Skyscrapers Hide the Heavens: A History of Native-Newcomer Relations in Canada*. 4th ed. Toronto: University of Toronto Press, 2018.

Minister of Environment. *Joint Review Panel Report, Lower Churchill Hydroelectric Generation Project, Nalcor Energy, Newfoundland and Labrador*. Ottawa: Minister of Environment, 2011.

Mitchell, Timothy. "Carbon Democracy." *Economy and Society* 38, no. 3 (2009), 399–432.

Mol, Annemarie. *The Body Multiple: Ontology in Medical Practice*. Durham, NC: Duke University Press, 2003.

Moore, Jason W. *Capitalism in the Web of Life: Ecology and the Accumulation of Capital*, 1st ed. New York: Verso, 2015.

Moore, Justin W. "The Capitalocene, Part I: On the Nature and Origins of Our Ecological Crisis." *Journal of Peasant Studies* 44, no. 3 (2017): 594–630.

Moore, Sam, and Alex Roberts. *The Rise of Ecofascism: Climate Change and the Far Right*. New York: John Wiley, 2022.

Morand, Serge, and Claire Lajaunie. "Outbreaks of Vector-Borne and Zoonotic Diseases Are Associated with Changes in Forest Cover and Oil Palm Expansion at Global Scale." *Frontiers in Veterinary Science* 8 (2021). https://doi.org/10.3389/fvets.2021.661063.

Morita, Atsuro. "Afterword." In *The World Multiple: The Quotidian Politics of Knowing and Generating Entangled Worlds*, edited by K. Omura, G. Otsuki, S. Satsuka, and A. Morita, 248–55. London: Routledge, 2019.

Morris, Christopher G. "Emplacement." *Academic Press Dictionary of Science and Technology*, 4th ed. Amsterdam: Elsevier Science and Technology, 1992.

Nadasdy, Paul. "How Many Worlds Are There? Ontology, Practice, and Indeterminacy." *American Ethnologist* 48, no. 4 (2021): 357–69. https://doi.org/10.1111/amet.13046.

Nahuelpan, Hector. "Los desafíos de un diálogo epistémico intercultural: Pueblo mapu-che, conocimientos y universidad." In *Conocimientos y prácticas políticas: Reflexiones desde nuestras prácticas de conocimiento situado*, edited by Arturo Escobar, 315–46. Chiapas: CIESAS, UNICACH, PDTG-UNMSM, 2011.

Natcher, David, Damian Castro, and Lawrence Felt. "Hunter Support Programs and the Northern Social Economy." In *Northern Communities Working Together*, edited by Chris Southcott, 183–97. Toronto: University of Toronto Press, 2018.

Navarro Trujillo, Mina, and Lucia Linsalata. "Capitaloceno, luchas por lo común y dis-putas por otros términos de interdependencia en el tejido de la vida: Reflexiones desde América Latina." *Relaciones internacionales* 46 (2021): 81–98. https://doi.org/10.15366/relacionesinter nacionales2021.46.005.

Newfoundland and Labrador Government. "Focusing Our Energy: An Energy Plan for Newfoundland and Labrador," 2007.

Öniş, Ziya, and Mustafa Kutlay. "The New Age of Hybridity and Clash of Norms: China, BRICS, and Challenges of Global Governance in a Postliberal International Order." *Alternatives* 45, no. 3 (2020): 123–42.

Oslender, Ulrich. "Geographies of the Pluriverse: Decolonial Thinking and Ontological Conflict on Colombia's Pacific Coast." *Annals of the American Association of Geogra-phers* 109, no. 6 (2019): 1691–1705.

Paricahua, Felix. "The Aftermath of Bagua: Lessons for Democracy in Peru." Andean Democracy Research Network, 2009. https://democracy.network.arts.ubc.ca/2009/09/assault-on-democracy-in-the-peruvian-amazon/.

Payne, Neil F. *Wildlife Delights and Dilemmas: Newfoundland and Labrador*. St. John's: DRC, 2011.

Peck, Jamie, Doreen Massey, Katherine Gibson, and Victoria Lawson. "Symposium: The Kilburn Manifesto: After Neoliberalism?" *Environment and Planning A* 46, no. 9 (2014): 2033–49. https://doi.org/10.1068/akilburn.

Penashue, Tshaukuesh Elizabeth, and Elizabeth Yeoman. *Nitinikiau Innusi: I Keep the Land Alive*. Winnipeg: University of Manitoba Press, 2019.

Pimbert, Michel P. "Constructing Knowledge for Food Sovereignty, Agroecology and Biocultural Diversity: An Overview." In *Food Sovereignty, Agroecology and Biocultural Diversity*, edited by Pimbert, 1–56. London: Routledge, 2017.

Pollin, Robert. "De-growth vs. a Green New Deal." *New Left Review* 112 (2018): 5–25.

Porto-Gonçalves, Carlos Walter. "Lucha por la tierra: Ruptura metabólica y reapro-piación social de la naturaleza." *Polis: Revista Latinoamericana* 15, no. 45 (2016): 291–316.

Porto-Gonçalves, Carlos Walter, and Enrique Leff. "Political Ecology in Latin Amer-ica: The Social Re-appropriation of Nature, the Reinvention of Territories and the Construction of an Environmental Rationality." *Desenvolvimento e meio ambiente* 35, no. 1 (2015): 65–88.

Povinelli, Elizabeth A. *The Cunning of Recognition*. Durham, NC: Duke University Press, 2002.

Povinelli, Elizabeth A. *Geontologies: A Requiem to Late Liberalism*. Durham, NC: Duke University Press, 2016.

Powell, Dana E., and Dáilan J. Long. "Landscapes of Power: Renewable Energy Activism in Diné Bikéyah." In *Indians and Energy: Exploitation and Opportunity in the American Southwest*, edited by Sherry L. Smith and Brian Frehner, 231–62. Santa Fe: School for Advanced Research Press, 2010.

Prasad, A. "Anti-science Misinformation and Conspiracies: COVID-19, Post-Truth, and Science & Technology Studies (STS)." *Science, Technology and Society* 27, no. 1 (2022): 88–112.

Pratt, Mary Louise. *Imperial Eyes: Travel Writing and Transculturation*. 2nd ed. London: Routledge, 2008.

Pratt, Scott L. *Native Pragmatism: Rethinking the Roots of American Philosophy*. Bloomington: Indiana University Press, 2002.

Puig de la Bellacasa, María. "Matters of Care in Technoscience: Assembling Neglected Things." *Social Studies of Science* 41, no. 1 (2011): 85–106.

Puig de la Bellacasa, María. *Matters of Care: Speculative Ethics in More Than Human Worlds*. Minneapolis: University of Minnesota Press, 2017.

Rancière, Jacques. *Disagreement: Politics and Philosophy*. Minneapolis: University of Minnesota Press, 1999.

Rancière, Jacques. *On the Shores of Politics*. London: Verso, 1995.

Rancière, Jacques, Davide Panagia, and Rachel Bowlby. "Ten Theses on Politics." *Theory & Event* 5, no. 3 (2001). https://doi.org/10.1353/tae.2001.0028.

Rancière, Jacques, Gavin Arnall, Laura Gandolfi, and Enea Zaramella. "Aesthetics and Politics Revisited: An Interview with Jacques Rancière." *Critical Inquiry* 38, no. 2 (2012): 289–97.

Rancière, Jacques, Solange Guénoun, James H. Kavanagh, and Roxanne Lapidus. "Jacques Rancière: Literature, Politics, Aesthetics: Approaches to Democratic Disagreement." *SubStance* 29, no. 2 (2000): 3–24.

Rawson, Ariel, and Becky Mansfield. "Producing Juridical Knowledge: 'Rights of Nature' or the Naturalization of Rights?" *Environment and Planning E: Nature and Space* 1, no. 1–2 (2018): 99–119.

Rist, Gilbert, *The History of Development: From Western Origins to Global Faith*. London: Zed, 1997.

Robinson, Kim Stanley. *The Ministry for the Future*. London: Hachette, 2020.

Rockwood, Walter. *Memorandum on General Policy in Respect to the Indians and Eskimos of Northern Labrador*. St. John's: Provincial Archives of Newfoundland and Labrador, 1955.

Rodríguez Enríquez, Corina María. "Economía feminista y economía del cuidado: Aportes conceptuales para el estudio de la desigualdad." *Caracas* 256 (March/April 2015): 30–44.

Rohland, Eleonora. "COVID-19, Climate, and White Supremacy: Multiple Crises or One?" *Journal for the History of Environment and Society* 5 (2020): 23–32.

Rojas, Cristina. "Pluriversalizar la sociedad para descolonizar el estado en Bolivia." In *Nuevos enfoques para el estudio de los estados Latinoamericanos*, edited by Pablo Andrade, 191–221. Quito, Ecuador: Universidad Andina Simón Bolívar / Corporación Editora Nacional, 2020.

Romero, Luiz. "How Brazil's Fear of Losing the Amazon Guides Bolsonaro's Policies towards the Forest." CNN, June 22, 2021. https://www.cnn.com/2021/06/22/americas /brazil-amazon-fear-meme-bolsonaro-intl/index.html. Accessed December 12, 2023.

Rosborough, T'łat'łaḵuł Patricia, and čuucqa Layla Rorick. "Following in the Footsteps of the Wolf: Connecting Scholarly Minds to Ancestors in Indigenous Language Revitalization." *AlterNative: An International Journal of Indigenous Peoples* 13, no. 1 (2017): 11–17.

Rose, Mitch, and John Wylie. "Animating Landscape." *Environment and Planning D: Society and Space* 24, no. 4 (2006): 475–79. https://doi.org/10.1068/d2404ed.

Rueda, Daniel. "Neoecofascism: The Example of the United States." *Journal for the Study of Radicalism* 14, no. 2 (2020): 95–125.

Ruiz-Serna, Daniel. *When Forests Run Amok: War and Its Afterlives in Indigenous and Afro-Colombian Territories.* Durham, NC: Duke University Press, 2023.

Ruiz-Serna, Daniel, and Carlos Del Cairo. "Los debates del giro ontológico en torno al naturalismo moderno." *Revista de estudios sociales* 55 (2016): 193–204.

Sahlins, Marshall. "In Anthropology, It's Emic All the Way Down." *HAU: Journal of Ethnographic Theory* 7, no. 2 (2017): 157–63.

Sahlins, Marshall. "The Original Political Society." *HAU: Journal of Ethnographic Theory* 7, no. 2 (2017): 91–128.

Samson, Colin, and Elizabeth Cassell. "The Long Reach of Frontier Justice: Canadian Land Claims 'Negotiation' Strategies as Human Rights Violations." *International Journal of Human Rights* 17, no. 1 (2013): 35–55.

Sandlos, John. *Hunters at the Margin: Native People and Wildlife Conservation in the Northwest Territories.* Vancouver: University of British Columbia Press, 2011.

Sarrazin, Jean Paul, and Saira Pilar Redondo. "Indígenas evangélicos y diversidad cultural: Análisis de una problemática multiculturalista." *Revista de derecho* 49 (2018): 203–28.

Savard, Rémi. *Le rire précolombien dans le Québec d'aujourd'hui.* Montreal: L'Hexagone / Parti pris, 1977.

Schavelzon, Salvador. *Plurinacionalidad y vivir bien/buen vivir: Dos conceptos leídos desde Bolivia y Ecuador post-constituyentes.* Quito, Equador: Abya Yala, 2015.

Schumacher, Ernest Friederich. "Small Is Beautiful." *Radical Humanist* 37, no. 5 (August 1973): 18–22.

Scott, James C. *Domination and the Arts of Resistance: Hidden Transcripts.* New Haven, CT: Yale University Press, 1990.

Segato, Rita Laura. "Patriarchy from Margin to Center: Discipline, Territoriality, and Cruelty in the Apocalyptic Phase of Capital." *South Atlantic Quarterly* 115, no. 3 (2016): 615–24.

Sepúlveda Luque, Claudia. "Swans, Ecological Struggles and Ontological Fractures: A Posthumanist Account of the Río Cruces Disaster in Valdivia, Chile." PhD diss., University of British Columbia, 2016.

Sevillano, Ana Belén Martín. "Nomadism as Ancestral Homeland in the Romani Culture." *Discrimination* 5, no. 1 (2023): 1.

Simbsler, David. "'Trusting the Lord, Conquering the Land': Pentecostals, Landless Movement and Grassroots Politics from Dilma Rousseff to Jair Bolsonaro." *Bulletin of Latin American Research* (2021). https://doi.org/10.1111/blar.13167.

Simpson, Leanne Betasamosake. *As We Have Always Done: Indigenous Freedom through Radical Resistance*. Minneapolis: University of Minnesota Press, 2017.

Steffen, Will, Jacques Grinevald, Paul Crutzen, and John McNeill. "The Anthropocene: Conceptual and Historical Perspectives." *Philosophical Transactions, Series A, Mathematical, Physical, and Engineering Sciences* 369, no. 1938 (2011): 842–67.

Steffen, Will, A. Sanderson, P. D. Tyson, J. Jäger, P. A. Matson, B. Moore III, F. Oldfield, K. Richardson, H. J. Schellnhuber, B. L. Turner II, and R. J. Wasson. *Global Change and the Earth System: A Planet Under Pressure*. Global Change—the IGBP Series. Berlin: Springer, 2004.

Stengers, Isabelle. "The Challenge of Ontological Politics." In *A World of Many Worlds*, edited by Marisol de la Cadena and Mario Blaser, 83–111. Durham, NC: Duke University Press, 2018.

Stengers, Isabelle. "The Cosmopolitical Proposal." In *Making Things Public*, edited by Bruno Latour and Peter Weibel, 994–1003. Cambridge, MA: MIT Press, 2005.

Stengers, Isabelle. "The Curse of Tolerance." *Cosmopolitics II* (2011): 303–11.

Sundberg, Juanita. "Decolonizing Posthumanist Geographies." *Cultural Geographies* 21, no. 1 (2014): 33–47.

Svampa, Maristella. "Commodities Consensus: Neoextractivism and Enclosure of the Commons in Latin America." *South Atlantic Quarterly* 114, no. 1 (2015): 65–82. https://doi.org/10.1215/00382876-2831290.

Svampa, Maristella. "Debates Latinoamericanos." *Indianismo, desarrollo, dependencia y populismo. Buenos Aires: Edhasa* 23 (2016): 430–36.

Svampa, Maristella. "Entrevista a Alvaro García Linera." *Le monde diplomatique*, September 11, 2009. https://maristellasvampa.net/antisemitismo-olvidos-y-manipulaciones -por-ezequiel-adamovsky-maristella-svampa-y-horacio-tarcus-en-pagina-12–230709/.

Svampa, Maristella. "La pandemia desde América Latina: Nueve tesis para un balance provisorio." *Nueva sociedad* 291 (2021): 80–100.

Svampa, Maristella. *Neo-Extractivism in Latin America: Socio-Environmental Conflicts, the Territorial Turn, and New Political Narratives*. Cambridge: Cambridge University Press, 2019.

Swyngedouw, Erik. "Depoliticized Environments: The End of Nature, Climate Change and the Post-Political Condition." *Royal Institute of Philosophy Supplement* 69 (2011): 256.

Swyngedouw, Erik. "Interrogating Post-democratization: Reclaiming Egalitarian Political Spaces." *Political Geography* 30, no. 7 (2011): 370–80.

TallBear, Kim. "Caretaking Relations, Not American Dreaming." *Kalfou* 6, no. 1 (2019): 24–41.

Tănăsescu, Mihnea. "Rights of Nature, Legal Personality, and Indigenous Philosophies." *Transnational Environmental Law* 9, no. 3 (2020): 429–53.

Tanner, Väinö. *Outlines of the Geography, Life and Customs of Newfoundland-Labrador (the Eastern Part of the Labrador Peninsula: Based upon Observations Made During the Finland-Labrador Expedition in 1937, and the Tanner Labrador Expedition in 1939, and Upon Information Available in the Literature and Cartography*. Helsinki-Helsingfors, Finland: Tilgmann, 1944.

Tapia Mealla, Luis. *El estado de derecho como tiranía*. La Paz, Bolivia: CIDES-UMSA, 2011.

Toninato, Paola. "Romani Nomadism: From Hetero-Images to Self-Representations." *Nomadic Peoples* 22, no. 1 (2018): 143–61.

Tooze, Adam. "Welcome to the World of the Polycrisis." *Financial Times*, October 28, 2022. https://www.ft.com/content/498398e7-11b1-494b-9cd3-6d669dc3de33.

Tsing, Anna. "A Multispecies Ontological Turn?" In *The World Multiple: The Quotidian Politics of Knowing and Generating Entangled Worlds*, edited by K. Omura, G. Otsuki, S. Satsuka, and A. Morita, 233–47. London: Routledge, 2019.

Tsing, Anna, Andrew S. Mathews, and Nils Bubandt. "Patchy Anthropocene: Landscape Structure, Multispecies History, and the Retooling of Anthropology: An Introduction to Supplement 20." Supplement, *Current Anthropology* 60, no. S20 (2019): S186–97.

Tytelman, Carolina. "Place and Forest Co-management in Nitassinan/Labrador." PhD diss., Memorial University of Newfoundland, 2016.

UCINY, Dario Arcella, and Mario Blaser, dirs. *Anuhu Yrmo*. Mexico: Grupo Documenta, 2016.

UCINY, Dario Arcella, and Mario Blaser. "Biodiversity Conservation for Whom?" Life Projects Network, 2013. https://cicada.world/partners/indigenous-groups/yshir/.

United Nations. "Report of the Conference of the Parties on its 21st Session, Held in Paris from 30 November to 13 December 2015: Addendum." United Nations Digital Library, accessed October 27, 2021. https://digitallibrary.un.org/record/831052.

United Nations Environment Programme (UNEP). "Towards a Green Economy. Pathways to Sustainable Development and Poverty Eradication. A Synthesis for Policy Makers." Nairobi: United Nation Environment Programme, 2011.

Uribe, María Teresa. "Emancipación social en un contexto de guerra prolongada: El caso de la comunidad de paz de San José de Apartadó." In *Emancipación social y violencia en Colombia*, edited by Boaventura de Sousa Santos and Maurico García Villegas, 186–215. Bogotá, Colombia: Grupo Editorial Norma, 2004.

Usher, Peter. "Caribou Crisis or Administrative Crisis? Wildlife and Aboriginal Policies on the Barren Grounds, 1947–60." In *Cultivating Arctic Landscapes: Knowing and Managing Animals in the Circumpolar North*, edited by David G. Anderson and Mark Nuttall, 172–99. New York: Berghahn, 2004.

Usher, Peter. "Traditional Ecological Knowledge in Environmental Assessment and Management." *ARCTIC* 53, no. 2 (2000): 183–93.

Verran, Helen. "Engagements between Disparate Knowledge Traditions: Toward Doing Difference Generatively and in Good Faith." In *Contested Ecologies: Dialogues in the South on Nature and Knowledge*, edited by Lesley Green, 141–61. Cape Town: HSRC Press, 2013.

Verran, Helen. "An Ontological Politics of Politics?" *Current Anthropology* 54, no. 5 (2013): 564–65. https://doi.org/10.1086/672270.

Verran, Helen. "The Politics of Working Cosmologies Together While Keeping Them Separate." In *A World of Many Worlds*, edited by Marisol de la Cadena and Mario Blaser, 112–30. Durham, NC: Duke University Press, 2018.

Verran, Helen. "A Postcolonial Moment in Science Studies: Alternative Firing Regimes of Environmental Scientists and Aboriginal Landowners." *Social Studies of Science* 32, no. 5–6 (2002): 729–62.

Viveiros de Castro, Eduardo. "Cosmological Deixis and Amerindian Perspectivism." *Journal of the Royal Anthropological Institute* 4, no. 3 (1998): 469–88.

Viveiros de Castro, Eduardo. "Perspectival Anthropology and the Method of Controlled Equivocation." *Tipití: Journal of the Society for the Anthropology of Lowland South America* 2, no. 1 (2004): 3–22.

Viveiros de Castro, Eduardo, and Déborah Danowski. "Humans and Terrans in the Gaia War." In *A World of Many Worlds,* edited by Marisol de la Cadena and Mario Blaser, 172–204. Durham, NC: Duke University Press, 2018.

Vizenor, Gerald. *Manifest Manners: Narratives on Postindian Survivance.* Lincoln, NE: Bison, 1999.

Vors, Liv, and Mark Boyce. "Global Declines of Caribou and Reindeer." *Global Change Biology,* no. 11 (2009): 2626–33.

Voskoboynik, Daniel Macmillen, and Diego Andreucci. "Greening Extractivism: Environmental Discourses and Resource Governance in the 'Lithium Triangle.'" *Environment and Planning E: Nature and Space* 5, no. 2 (2022): 787–809.

Wadden, Marie. *Nitassinan: The Innu Struggle to Reclaim Their Homeland.* Madeira Park: Douglas & McIntyre, 1991.

Wallich, George Charles. *The North-Atlantic Sea-Bed: Comprising a Diary of the Voyage on Board H. M. S. Bulldog, in 1860; and Observations on the Presence of Animal Life, and Great Depths in the Ocean.* London: Forgotten Books, 2018.

Ward, Lucas. "The Bureaucracy of Nature: How Integrated Resource Management Excludes the Poor." PhD diss., University of Colorado, 2010.

Watts, Jonathan. "Jair Bolsonaro Claims NGOs behind Amazon Forest Fire Surge—but Provides No Evidence." *Guardian,* August 2019. https://www.theguardian.com/world /2019/aug/21/jair-bolsonaro-accuses-ngos-setting-fire-amazon-rainforest.

Weseluk, Juan Carlos. "Prospección de minerales metalicos y no metalicos." Proponente Valquiria Explorations S.A. Registro MADES CTCA: I 804. Agosto 2022.

Weterman, Bruce, and Paul Gosar. "The Environmental Costs of the Border Crisis." *Washington Examiner,* March 22, 2021. https://www.washingtonexaminer.com /opinion/op-eds/the-environmental-cost-of-the-border-crisis.

Wildcat, Daniel R. "Indigenizing Politics and Ethics: A Realist Theory." In *Power and Place: Indian Education in America,* edited by Vine Deloria and Wildcat, 87–101. Golden, CO: Fulcrum, 2001.

Wittgenstein, Ludwig. *Tractatus logico-philosophicus.* Translated by Charles K. Ogden and Frank P. Ramsey. London: Kegan Paul, Trench, Trubner, 2021. https://www .gutenberg.org/files/5740/5740-pdf.

Wolf, Eric R. *Europe and the People without History.* Berkeley: University of California Press, 1982.

Zibechi, Raúl. "Bolivia-Ecuador: el estado contra los pueblos indios." *Lutas sociais* 24, (2010): 132–39.

Zibechi, Raúl. *Territories in Resistance: A Cartography of Latin American Social Movements.* Translated by Ramor Ryan. Oakland, CA: AK, 2012.

Žižek, Slavoj. *Living in the End Times.* New York: Verso, 2011.

INDEX

Martinez, Doña Anita, 45–46
Massey, Doreen, 189n36
materiality, 15, 19
material-semiotics, 7–9, 12, 21, 50, 56, 107, 173,
    188n15, 192n6, 194n33
McGregor, Deborah, 41
mediation, 51, 69, 114, 139, 194n34
Meloni, Giorgia, 178
Memorial University, Newfoundland, 126
Michel, Ben, 142
Michi Saagiig Nishnaabeg, 54
Mi'kmaq language, 127
Milei, Javier, 178
mining, 2, 4, 7, 35, 133–34, 138, 140–42,
    171
minoritization, 28–30, 111–12, 191n52
missionaries, 55–58, 67–68, 87
modern collective, the, 58, 92, 133, 162,
    190n43, 192n6; and big stories, 96–98,
    121–22; and caribou, 127, 133; introduction
    to, 13, 20–26, 30–32; and life projects,
    33–38; and the yrmo, 66, 70, 77, 87–88
modernity, 5, 13, 46–48, 83, 91, 183, 190n46,
    191n46, 202n62; and atiku (caribou), 105,
    117, 121, 136, 139
modernization, 22, 39, 71, 92, 95, 167–68,
    191n46; and the Anthropocene, 96–97,
    99, 101, 106, 115, 118–20; and caribou,
    126–32, 138; and the good life, 33–35,
    58–59, 70, 79, 93, 159; and the Yshiro,
    64–68, 87
modernization fixed, 60, 97, 120
modes of existence, 9, 39, 44, 61, 91–93, 112,
    116, 159, 164, 172, 177, 181–82, 209n4
Mol, Annemarie, 8, 138, 149
momentous challenges, 22–24, 27, 30–34,
    94–95, 158–68, 172, 184; and the Anthro-
    pocene, 97, 116, 119–20, 125; and climate
    change, 59–61
monte (bush), 77–79
Morales, Evo, 1
morality, 42, 67, 70, 146, 167–68, 172
more-than-humans, 6–7, 38, 149, 191n47; and
    caribou, 131, 147; and the common, 110,
    121; and yshiro, 47, 49, 64, 67–68, 114.
    See also nonhumans
multiculturalism, 5, 56, 82–83, 87–88,
    147

multiplicities, 11–12, 53, 69, 77, 125–26, 157,
    189n36; and atiku (caribou), 138–42,
    144–45; diffractive, 139–40, 144, 148;
    divergent, 126, 138, 140–41, 144–53, 156,
    207n60; of place, 15–18, 22, 35, 57–58, 161;
    planetary, 150–51, 173
multispecies, 50, 106, 121, 129, 131, 147

Nahuelpan, Hector, 52
naming, 82
narrative clusters, 98–109, 115–23, 139, 153,
    159–63, 166, 170, 202n58
national common, 108, 111, 113, 116
nationalism, 104, 128, 178, 202n62
NATO, 133–34, 137–40, 205nn34–35
Natuashish, 126, 203n6
Natura, 69–86, 93–95, 103
naturalists, 127, 130, 203n15
natural resources, 6, 13, 92, 109, 114, 140,
    205n31
natural sciences, 101, 119–21, 147, 208n69
nature, 5, 23, 33, 49, 110, 124–25, 174, 202n58;
    and atiku (caribou), 127, 131, 137; and the
    common, 116–18; vs. culture, 19, 56, 105,
    121–22
Navarro, Mina, 112
negative proxies, 61, 71, 95
Neihard, John, 44
neo-extractivism, 2, 187n4
neoliberalism, 1–3, 72, 91, 108
Newfoundland, Canada, 126–27, 133, 136,
    142
NGOs, 3, 5, 79–81, 83, 104, 206n39. See also
    Humanitas; Natura
nishnaabeg peoples, 54
Nishnaabewin, 52
nitassinan, 126, 132–44, 151, 164–65, 185,
    202n5, 203n6
noise, 80, 89–90, 92, 137, 142, 205n33
nonhumans, 23, 38–39, 48–51, 105–7,
    114–16, 119–22, 150, 173, 189n26, 194n30;
    knowledge of, 129, 146–48, 160. See also
    more-than-humans
non-Indigenous peoples, 29, 81, 155
North American Caribou Workshop,
    131
North West River, Labrador, 136
Nunatsiavut Government, 143

NunatuKavut Council, 143
Nuu-chah-nulth peoples, 39–40

obedience, 53–56, 90, 117
Oglala Sioux peoples, 44
Ojaiesa (Charles Eastman), 55, 57–58
ologolak (capivara), 38–39, 47
one-world world, 20–21, 55–57, 88, 93–95,
    115–16, 119–22, 150, 157–59, 167, 172–74,
    178–83
ontological turn, 7, 9, 14, 37, 188n15, 191n54,
    192n54, 197n27
ontologies, 147, 149, 189n36, 194n33, 195n43;
    and material semiotics, 8, 12, 192n6; and
    reasonable politics, 6, 14
Orban, Viktor, 178
Ortiz, Andres Ozuma, 85
Ostrom, Elinor, 109

Pachamama, 168
Pacto Ecosocial del Sur, 103
Paraguay, 2–4, 64–65, 71–75, 95, 103,
    120, 171, 195n6–195n7. *See also* Yshiro
    communities
Paraguay River, 63
Parks, Rosa, 90
participatory planning processes, 100
Pasteur, Louis, 8
peace movements, 137
peasants, 3, 28, 71, 111, 120, 201n44
pedagogical and piecemeal violence, 67
peikara (maracas), 38–39
perceptibilities/imperceptibilities, 24
personhood, 38
perspectives, 193n28; and Nuu-chah-nulth
    peoples, 39–40; and reality, 20, 105,
    159–60; and reasonable politics, 5–7, 9,
    146–48
persuasion, 56, 120, 188n14
Peru, 4
planetary social thought, 150, 173–74
pluriverse, the, 9–16, 22, 27, 44, 53, 77, 88,
    161–63, 202n58; faithfulness to, 89–95, 171,
    174–75, 177, 180–82; and life projects, 62,
    166; and modernity, 117–19, 160, 168
policing, 5, 30, 56, 89–90, 92, 101, 142
political autonomy, 3
political ecology, 7

political economy, 7, 75
political imaginations, 15, 24–28, 31, 35, 61,
    90, 96–98, 122, 158–69, 177, 208n4
political ontology, 188n11, 189n33, 190n36,
    191n50, 192n6; of emplacement, 158–66,
    174–77, 180–84; introduction to, 1–3, 12–
    14, 24–32; and science-plus, 145, 149–50;
    and small stories, 40, 44, 49, 166
politics, understandings of, 3, 9, 14, 40, 47, 52,
    89–93, 160; and the Anthropocene, 101,
    105–8; and emplaced collectives, 52–58
politics as usual, 5
populism, right-wing, 94–95, 103–4, 108,
    177–78, 199n18
postdevelopment, 103, 175
posthumanism, 50, 106, 121
postnatural, the, 120–23, 125, 127, 145, 149,
    174–75; and atiku (caribou), 131, 137–38,
    148, 150, 153, 156
postpolitical, the, 101–3, 109
Povinelli, Elizabeth, 152–53, 208n68
power, 32, 89, 122, 125, 149, 171, 175, 191n46,
    208n68
pragmatics, 14, 26–27, 40–44, 55, 91, 180–81,
    193n17, 194n31, 208n4; of scale, 58, 163,
    179, 208n4
Pratt, Marie Louise, 127
Pratt, Scott, 193n17
primitivists, 3–4
principle of symmetry of value, 38–41,
    193n9
progressive governments, 2–3, 7, 112, 179
properly communal common, the, 112–13
protests, 1–2, 136–38
Puerto Leda ranch, 46
Puig de la Bellacasa, María, 43, 119, 122
Putin, Vladimir, 178

Québec, Canada, 133, 136
Quijano, Anibal, 191n46

railways, 17–18, 21–22, 70, 88, 124, 133
ranching: cattle, 64, 67–69, 73–75, 78, 94;
    reindeer and caribou, 128–29
Rancière, Jacques, 89, 91–92, 101, 106, 142,
    197n32
rationality, 33–34, 60, 105, 144, 152, 159, 176,
    203n29

www.ingramcontent.com/pod-product-compliance
Lightning Source LLC
Chambersburg PA
CBHW030823290525
27270CB00016B/172